Beyond Goodbye

An extraordinary true story of a shared death experience

Annie Cap

To my mother,
whose efforts to contact me,
before and after she died, changed my life forever.
I'll always be grateful to her.
And to my husband,
who I will always love and cherish,
as much as I do my mom.

*In memory of my mother, Betty Cap
(30 years old in this picture)*

Contents

*Annie and her mother, Betty
(Circa 1990)*

Acknowledgements

I wish to thank everyone who knowingly or unknowingly contributed to my personal growth, especially those who helped me process and understand what happened between my mother and I, and those who came to my aid when I was frightened and dealing with the confusion created by my expanded senses. It would take too many pages to list everyone who has helped me, but if you know you have and you don't find your name here, please accept my heartfelt appreciation.

I wish to mention some of you who have been exceptionally helpful or who are extremely special to me, these include: my husband, my parents and immediate family, my good friend from Seattle who I called Katrina in this book, Diana Brito-Kelly and her husband Sean Kelly, and Kelly Jayne Roper who volunteered her precious time to read my manuscript when I needed to know if it would captivate or bore the reader. Kelly read it completely in a little over a day and after giving me "a thumbs up" surprised me with a list of corrections! Kelly ended up helping me proof and edit *Beyond Goodbye* and I'm so grateful to her.

Also I want to thank Doreen Virtue, Gordon Smith, Mia Dolan, Kira Raa, Joseph Smith, Sally Macgregor and Janis Perry for passing on their wisdom and experience.

I'm very grateful to all the researchers attempting to help us understand what may happen when we die by investigating near-death experiences and other end of life phenomena. I particularly wish to mention those who gave so generously of their precious time and knowledge, those special people who allowed me to interview them and then helped me so greatly by refining my attempt to explain briefly what they have studied for decades. I feel indebted to these lovely people around the world. Listed in alphabetical order they are: P.M.H. Atwater, Elizabeth Fenwick, Dr. Peter Fenwick, David Lorimer, Dr. Pim van Lommel, Dr. Penny Sartori, Yolaine Stout and Barbara Harris Whitfield. Additionally, although we only communicated via email, I'm grateful to Dr. Bruce Greyson for his kindness and assistance.

There are two more people whom I interviewed during my investigation that deserve mention - thanks go to Daniel Hill and Tami Close, who shared their near-death experiences and personal transformations with me. Lastly, I wish to thank all of you who encouraged me via your comments on Facebook – you know who you are!

Blessings to all of you,
Annie

"No one comes alone.
No one leaves alone.
No one is ever actually alone."

Foreword

In this book, breakthrough coach and author Annie Cap describes her deeply personal journey of trying to make sense of and understand an experience that coincided with the time of the death of her mother 5000 miles away in Oregon, USA.

Although not a new phenomenon, empathic or shared death experiences are now becoming more widely discussed and reported. An empathic or shared death experience is an experience in which a person connected to a dying person or present at the death bed also shares in part of the dying person's journey into death.

The impact of the empathic experience was so overwhelming that Annie was driven to gain a greater understanding. She shares her wonderfully personal journey of a spiritual transformation which culminated in the writing of this book. The sincerity with which this book is written will be of great help to others who may have gone through similar experiences or those faced with the uncertainty of their own impending death or those coming to terms with the loss of a loved one.

Beginning with a brief history of her family background Annie goes on to describe the series of events that led her to her investigations. There are many important issues raised that may one day affect us all including the great angst felt when a loved one lives in another country and is separated by physical distance. She also highlights important dilemmas faced by family members around the issue of 'do not resuscitate' orders. This is such a pertinent point which many people have difficulty understanding and accepting. Each situation is unique to each person and their family and such choices are difficult to make for all concerned especially in light of the technology available to further our life span.

It also shows how much control people have over the timing of their death. Her mum knew she was dying the night before but made a decision to wait until morning so that more of her children could be there. Included are nice examples of death bed coincidences that occurred at the time of her mother's death. Annie also describes with the bewilderment that is so common, the after-death communications she received following her mother's death.

Throughout Annie's seven year quest for a greater understanding of her empathic experience, many opportunities arose in which she was able to explore spiritual aspects of life and she describes the paths that she chose to pursue in depth.

The whole process led her to write about her experience and seek explanations from those already engaged in the field of near-death research. The ease with which she communicated with the researchers in this field and how everything flowed is testimony to Annie's spiritual path.

Very interestingly, the changes instigated in Annie's life after her mother's death were consistent with the findings of near-death experiencers found by researchers. In fact it is apparent that Annie now exhibits the same characteristic changes that some NDErs do post NDE such as heightened intuition, healing, electrical sensitivity and more love and tolerance for others to name but a few.

In this book Annie opens herself up totally, describing her personal, spiritual exploration exposing all of her feelings and experiences. This is a most brave thing to do as many people who experience this hide it or don't talk about it, certainly not publicly, and most block it and never explore it.

Not only has Annie revealed a fertile area for research into the after effects of empathic death experiences but she has also laid the platform for others to also come forward and talk about their experiences too. I'm sure many people will be comforted and will benefit greatly from reading this book.

Dr. Penny Sartori, PhD, RGN, lecturer and author of *The Near-Death Experiences of Hospitalized Intensive Care Patients: A Five Year Clinical Study*

Introduction

Although I experienced something out-of-the-ordinary and other-worldly when my mother died, even more surprising for me was what happened after her death and from then on.

It's taken me a few years, seven actually as you'll find out soon enough, to feel willing to discuss what *really* took place back then and in the weeks, months and years that followed. It was all so wonderful, yet so shocking and frightening at times, that I didn't speak about it openly until now.

Although my life and perceptions were strangely and dramatically disrupted by my mom's death, now that the dust has settled I've recognized how it expanded and improved everything – over time.

To reach this point of wanting to share my story, I had a lot of help from my mom – oddly enough from beyond the grave and from my husband, Matthew, who is very much alive and thankfully never doubted me. In the last few months, I have received generous support from some of the world's top researchers studying the phenomena surrounding death and dying.

While my one-to-one interviews with these experts helped me enormously to personally understand my own experiences as well as the subsequent *unwanted* after-effects, they also made me realize that these *exceptional events* are actually normal and relatively common.

In societies that embrace death as an integral part of life, my experiences are considered desirable, celebrated and even anticipated rather than feared and denied. However, here in the west, and in some other societies and religions, we are forced to hide these wonderful and very spiritual experiences – especially any involving after-death contact. To avoid ridicule, being thought crazy, or even punished there is little talk of "after-death communications" (ADC).

The death and dying or end of life phenomena I investigated included: "near-death experiences" (NDEs), a life-changing spiritual event frequently occurring when someone has died but is brought back to life, "shared" and "empathic death experiences" or "shared near-death experiences" (SDEs), when someone participates in another's death or near-death experience, and what are referred to as "deathbed coincidences" and "deathbed visions" which were first documented by the Swiss psychiatrist Elisabeth Kübler-Ross and include contact, appearances and messages from deceased individuals and other timely occurrences which happen when someone dies.

Also, I've learned that there are many situations that can cause someone to unexpectedly shift into extreme states of consciousness or heavenly and other-worldly realities. Besides near-death experiences and *real* death, there are any number of additional valid experiences that fall under the umbrella heading of "Spiritually Transformative Experiences" (STE). All of these occurrences *regularly* cause the experiencers' lives to never be the same.

In this book, I'll share my rather naive and honest story just as it occurred. Many of my experiences are written from indelible memories or directly transcribed from my diaries for accuracy. You should get a sense of watching someone who doesn't yet understand what's happening to her. When I was going through my experiences, I wasn't aware that researchers consider them to be *normal*. None of it felt *normal* to me. It was confusing and seemed chaotic, including what immediately followed my mom's death and my after-death experiences of her.

It would have been nice to have read someone else's similar account and benefitted from their first-hand knowledge, but for reasons I'll never comprehend, I had to *feel* my way through this *unassisted*. While I have learned now that there are regular and almost predictable repercussions to these profound experiences, I remind myself of my personal beliefs that everything happens for a reason and in the right time. Clearly, I must have been meant to find my way through my maze of transitions seemingly alone, but never really alone. I must have needed to work out what it all meant *to me,* for myself, to gain the most insight.

My intention with this book is to help those who may have lost their own mother, or perhaps their father, their child or someone else whom they have loved very deeply. I have chosen to candidly share my story revealing how I really felt throughout my process of change. Death, as I discovered, has a way of affecting everyone it touches, leaving an impacting wake. I decided to trust that my honesty, something I've always valued, will provide the greatest support possible for those who are afraid of death, have experienced something they haven't yet been able to put into words or those who are attempting to come to terms with an approaching death in their own family.

I read once that in order to really heal or process any significant personal experience, it must be shared entirely with at least one other living being. I thank you for being that person who hears my story.

Part One

My story. What really happened…

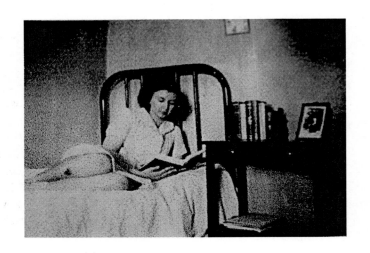

Annie's mother, Betty reading
(Mid-late 1940's, age unknown)

Chapter One

The seventh child, seven years after

Why did I wait seven years to make sense of what happened to me when my mom died? This is the question that has popped into my head, over and over, these past few months.

Maybe I waited this long because I was unprepared for her death? Or maybe it was because losing her was probably my greatest personal loss, until only recently? It's worth considering though, that it had less to do with the loss of my mother and more to do with all the crazy things that happened alongside of her death and ever since. Perhaps I just needed time to process and accept the personal changes I experienced.

Once in a while I catch myself using my fingers, like a child, to count up the years since she died, regretfully without me by her side. Whether it's been seven years or seventy, I know I'll never forget that day.

Somehow from almost five thousand miles away, my mom managed to connect with me from her deathbed! Her spirit, or what some would call her soul or consciousness, bridged time and space when she reached out to me just before and as she died. Surprisingly and uncomfortably, I experienced her last breaths. I felt them as if they were mine. We shared something extraordinary during her final minutes and again after, experiences that have ultimately changed the course of my life and my beliefs forever.

The number seven seems to permeate my existence and perhaps everyone else's too. Patterns or cycles of seven show up all over the place, in nature, science and even religion. This number, or sequences of it, appear to carry some kind of influence and magnitude all of their own. In Eastern philosophies and religions like Buddhism, seven appears to have a sort of mystical, transcendental or even magical meaning and significance. Maybe I'll find out that there is a very good reason why I waited that exact amount of time before sharing my experience.

I was born the seventh child of a large family and in today's terms, a quite dysfunctional one. My mother was called Betty, although her real name was Bertoline. She'd been named after her Swiss great-grandmother whom she'd never known. Somewhat understandably my mom only became aware of her true birthname when she was berated by her school teacher for lying. She'd written "Betty" on the top of her paper instead of "Bertoline". It was a mouthful, to say the least, and a very different name, possibly never heard before in the United States. My mom definitely preferred "Betty" and even had trouble spelling her real first name once she knew about it.

Like my father, Betty lived as a child in Minnesota. My mom was born the eldest daughter into a Baptist family, while my father's family were Catholic. I hadn't realized that my parents' religious differences had been so troublesome for them, until this year when I started talking to my mother's remaining siblings about her childhood.

Raised as a strict Baptist, my mom hadn't been allowed to wear make-up, dance, listen to music or go to the movies. But that hadn't stopped her from drawing attention from others. She was a very classically pretty woman with tons of interests and was blessed with the hour-glass figure so popular of the time. Mom boasted a twenty-inch waistline, a body many would envy, along with her wholesome Andrews Sisters looks. Although good Baptist girls weren't supposed to think lustfully about boys, I'm sure like every other red-blooded, American girl-next-door, my mom must have. She'd been brought up to believe that dressing provocatively was a sin, as was, of course, making love for any reason other than procreation. Drinking alcohol was another sinful act my mom wasn't to engage in, while living at home anyway.

My mom's mother (Grandma Elaine Valentine – born on Valentine's Day) never told my mother anything about sex or being a woman. Her periods or how children were conceived were never discussed. Instead her mother had left this important education to others and simply instructed Betty to always hold a penny between her knees whenever she was alone with a man. That was Grandma Elaine's idea of contraception.

I suppose as an outsider looking back, my father Tom might have appeared as an unlikely match for my mother. That is if religion, family background, temperament and assets were the only things you considered. But observing my parents, in the good times and in the bad, I can honestly say that there was something very special about them. When they were together there was an almost perceptible, tangible, slight tingle in the air. I remember a kind of mesmerizing feeling around them and I'm not referring to the many times they argued or fought. It occurred when they were happy with each other or life in general. I realize now that it might have been coming from my mom. I remember feeling it most strongly when I was alone with her as a child.

We all used to say (my brothers, sisters and I) that my mom and dad's relationship was like oil and water, they didn't mix, but in fact I think they were more like star-crossed lovers. I've suspected for a long time that their volatile outbursts and emotional personalities were fueled, like Romeo's and Juliet's, by the drama of their own parents. Their families' dividing choices of religion, and the extreme, and constant challenges they faced (mostly because of us kids) were major contributors to their high levels of stress. Putting stress aside, passion was perhaps the most obvious character trait which defined both of their lives.

My father's upbringing and family's lifestyle were very different than that of my mother's. First of all, and perhaps most importantly, he was a Catholic. Catholics could do tons of things that strict Baptists couldn't do or were not supposed to do. Most Catholics I've ever known, including my father and his priests, certainly liked to drink.

Dad was also an excellent dancer, as secretly was my mom. I remember watching them as a young child. They were two of the most amazing and charismatic jitterbug and swing dance partners I had ever seen. Not allowed to dance openly as a Baptist, my mother confessed that she'd taught her younger sister to dance as well without their mother Elaine ever finding out. As soon as my mom had heard that her baby sister, Laura, was to be crowned Homecoming Queen she knew that she'd have to teach her how to dance. Homecoming Queens, after all, were expected to dance with their Homecoming King in front of the entire school. I think my mom was a bit of a rebel actually, and so much stronger back then, than the person she became later in life after being worn down by too many years of fighting with my dad.

As I was growing up, my experiences highlighted that adult male Catholics could do pretty much whatever they liked, regardless of what it said in the Bible and in the Ten Commandments. They could swear, make love outside of wedlock, have affairs and even hurt their *loved ones* without any lasting penalty because their religion offered a way to gain quick forgiveness. I observed quite early on that any sinful act or downright nasty bad behavior could be cleared by simply confessing to a priest.

It didn't seem to matter what it was, the priest could clear your conscience if you only confessed. This never sat well with me and was the main reason I detoured away from religion at a very early age. I couldn't fathom the ease at which abusive or neglectful partners and parents could be freed of their sins every Sunday or even midweek if they popped in to talk to a priest.

One moment you're a sinner, doomed to rot in Hell or Purgatory, that half-way house for mild sinners, and the next moment you are as innocent as a newborn. But better, because you've already been baptized! All that was required to cleanse your soul as I recall (which really ticked me off by the way) was to go to "Confession". You'd enter a little booth which was like crawling into a tiny dark closet but without the hangers or shoes, something I've never been too keen on anyway, and you'd kneel down before talking to the hidden priest waiting silently on the other side, only separated from you by a thin partitioning wall. There was no light inside the booth after the two separate entrance doors were shut and only enough space for one person on either side. The booth is called a "Confessional". Usually there were two or three Confessionals at the back or side of the Catholic churches we attended.

Once you'd entered the Confessional, you'd kneel down in the dark and tell your sins to the, mostly silent, priest who sat behind a curtain or a mesh screen. Then after you had admitted all your errors, listing every sin, "unclean thought" or blasphemy that you could remember since the last time you'd confessed, the priest would add them up quietly to determine the severity of your actions. Then regardless of what you'd done, he'd ask you to go back to your pew and recite some prayers in compensation! I thought this punishment was too effortless. You were freed just like that. There weren't any other consequences of your actions and sinful ways. A few "Hail Mary's" or "Our Father's" later and your slate was clean again. I used to call Catholicism, "the stand up, sit down, fight, fight, fight religion," mimicking a cheerleader's chant because that's what we did. At church we'd stand up, sit down, or kneel, whatever and whenever the priest told us to. After confession we'd recite some more and at home my parents would just fight, fight, fight, unpredictably whenever they were together.

If you had done something really bad when you confessed your sins to the priest, you might be asked to say the Rosary. I don't recall ever completing the Rosary litany myself, but I'm sure I must have been taught how to do it, although I promptly forgot how. From the start, when the nuns and priest first introduced the confession concept to me, I knew I would never need to say the Rosary. I was purposefully well behaved and put the Rosary completely and immediately out of my head for good. Like so many things I was taught or witnessed, I discarded this form of apology as craziness. I fully rejected the practice of confession, even as a child, after the initial time I was made to do it. I thought it was ridiculous. I still do, unless you're truly sorry for your behavior.

Regardless of my lack of interest and lack of need for performing the Rosary, I remember it involved reciting particular prayers on each and every bead along the chain and longer prayers on the metal medallion before the bit that led to the crucifix itself. It took forever to recite and I'd always wondered what all the old ladies and nuns in the back pews of our church could have possibly done so wrong. It seemed they were continually seen kneeling, head down in prayer, busy whispering the Rosary over and over! Now that I'm older and wiser, I've realized this *probably* had nothing to do with sinning. Saying the Rosary repeatedly was intended to bring them closer to their God. But when I was in grade school, me and my brother Tim, who's closest to my age and my mom's sixth born, always had a good chuckle whenever we saw them with their lips moving silently and their fingers quickly holding each bead.

More differences

Like their parents' religious beliefs, their families' financial situations were also extremely different. Dad's parents were quite well off, while my mother's parents were very poor and struggled due to my mom's father's health complications.

My dad's father had come to America from a small town outside of Prague, in what used to be called Bohemia and he spoke five languages fluently. He had a very good job and was well connected in the community. As well as having a lovely home, my dad's family could afford a lake-front summer cabin. We often spent our summer holidays swimming there avoiding the many snapping turtles.

In stark contrast, as a child my mother had to sell handmade goods door to door. When she was old enough, she worked for pennies an hour at The Dime Store to help her mother pay the bills. When things became really difficult for them, my mom was sent away to live with her deaf-mute grandparents. At one time, she even lived with one of her high school teachers and his wife and worked as their nanny.

My father, on the other hand, as his family were well-off, learned to play the piano and to play golf. He had a summer job as a caddy at the local golf course and earned large tips from the wealthy doing something he greatly enjoyed.

My mother had been very athletic, outgoing and even played the drums when she was young. She and my father were only one year apart in high school and both played in the marching band. She had tons of commonsense and was very smart as well. Betty was fun and full of exuberance even though her home life was difficult to say the least.

My father was, and still is, a very handsome and intelligent man. He's wonderfully creative, yet practical, business-minded and hardworking. However, he's also a strict disciplinarian and perfectionist, just like his father had been. This meant he was not an easy man to live with, not as a child, or as his wife.

Regardless of the many differences in their upbringings, my parents would eventually end up together. Even though their backgrounds, demeanors and religions were like polar opposites. It seemed they were drawn together and destined to collide like two great magnets.

My mom's dad

My mom's father, my Grandpa Benedict, had contracted encephalitis (inflammation of the brain) during World War I, after being bitten by a mosquito. My Aunt Laura told me that his brain had swelled so much that he had slept for thirty days and thirty nights. Once Grandpa had recovered, the doctors only said that he had "sleeping sickness" now. They didn't tell anyone about the other possible consequences.

When Grandpa Benedict returned from the war to his fiancée, my Grandmother Elaine, he was a very different man. He was no longer the person that he had been. But no one, even he, was fully aware of just how different he would become because of the illness. His *sickness* caused him to fall asleep driving a car and he was also prone to losing his awareness and concentration at any moment.

My mom told me that Grandma Elaine married him anyway – because that's what people did in those days. However, I've also heard recently from my mom's sister that no one really knew he'd actually suffered brain damage from the extreme inflammation he'd experienced, until much later.

My grandmother kept her commitment to my grandfather. Maybe she knew that her life might be a bit more challenging but I'm sure she had no way of knowing just how much. Only as the years passed, did it become clear that Benedict's mental capabilities and even his personality had been severely altered. Still today, all I've really been openly told is that he became unpredictable, but I think I can read between the lines.

His illness had irreversibly changed him and ultimately altered all my mom's immediate family's lives as well, in more ways than they could ever have anticipated. Each of them was affected by his experience and behavior. Although he was a very generous, kind and loving father, he struggled to hold down a job from the very start of his marriage. He grew vegetables on an acre of land and sold them locally to the grocery stores and markets. However, he never had permanent, consistent employment.

Due to the brain damage Grandpa had suffered, he experienced difficulties with normal levels of self-control. He became grossly overweight and it was later discovered that he'd been frequently hallucinating.

Unfortunately, it's been rumored, that Grandpa Benedict also developed a taste for gambling which must have been a nightmare for my Grandma Elaine. She'd been forced to be the major breadwinner all along and the added surprise of gambling must have presented a further terrible challenge. Grandma had four children to support (my mom being the second child and the eldest girl) and a very large and impulsive husband, during the time of the Great Depression when so many people were out of work. My mother had no option but to help her family. Along with her brothers and sisters, she played an important role in the finances of their household.

It was only very recently that I learned that Grandpa Benedict had actually become mentally ill from the encephalitis. My mother's younger sister, my Aunt Laura, who's in her eighties now told me that although it had never been discussed in those terms and that her mother had never mentioned to them that there was ever anything wrong with their father, she realized later as an adult that he'd been mentally ill. As they were growing up, no one ever admitted this. What was going on with Grandpa was never talked about. As kids, they just thought their dad had a form of sleeping sickness that made it difficult for him to work. I've also discovered that as time passed, Grandpa's illness progressed and he started to go missing. While some of his absences could be explained by looking for work in other states like California, others were not.

My mom, her mother, and all of her siblings worked very hard to survive the Depression years. These were very trying times for everyone in the United States but probably more so if the male head of the family wasn't able to work regularly or gambled away his small earnings.

Aunt Laura admitted to me that they must have been very poor. Although she never felt they were. When I asked her about her life growing up with my mother, she told me that one Christmas a couple of men from the fire department knocked on their door. They had gifts or rather donations for them. She remembered, like it was yesterday, her father telling the firemen to give the gifts to those that were really needy. Aunt Laura told me that they always had food and were clean and presentable. That said, she also recalled having to stay home from school because her only pair of shoes were being repaired. My cousin (her daughter) tells me that Aunt Laura is a little like Imelda Marcos now and has hundreds of shoes.

Aunt Laura described the time she and my mom went to the large department store in town with their mother and how she'd bought them their first real coats. Before that time, they had been handmade. Aunt Laura said they both felt beautiful in them. It's all beginning to make sense now why my mother always had to have a wonderful winter coat when she was alive. It was very important to her. She had been fifteen or sixteen years old when her mother was finally able to afford store-bought coats for her and her sister.

It's been truly amazing to find out these things about my mother's history now only after she has died. She never complained about her childhood. I knew she'd sold things door to door as a little girl to make money during the Depression years but I hadn't heard much else.

My parents get together

After my parents finished high school, I'm told that my father went off to fight in the war (World War II) and my mother went to Washington DC after passing an exam to work as a secretary in the Pentagon. When the war ended, my mother and my father (then both single) came back to their hometown in Minnesota. They fell in love, much to the dismay of my mother's parents who hated that my dad was a Catholic!

When my parents married, my Grandma Elaine and her husband Grandpa Benedict were so outraged that my mom was marrying a Catholic that they refused to attend their eldest daughter's wedding. Religion prejudiced their respect for their daughter, my mother, and it wrongly clouded their love for her. My Aunt Laura told me that part of the reason they were so against the marriage was because as Baptists they were discriminated against. The Catholic employers, in their town, would not employ a Baptist apparently. This had made her father's chances of finding work even worse. I wonder if maybe prejudice bosses were a way for her mother to explain Grandpa's employment problems rather than admitting he was mentally challenged since the war. Both could well be true of course.

During my mother's and father's marriage they were what are called "practicing Catholics". This meant many things. It meant going to church every Sunday and raising their children to be Catholics but it also meant that they weren't allowed to use any form of birth control, with the exception of what is called "the Rhythm Method".

The main principle in using the Rhythm Method is to only make love during predictably "safe" times in a woman's menstrual cycle or finding alternatives to *regular* intercourse. I suppose the Rhythm Method might work pretty well, or let's be honest it might work sometimes, for some people, but it hardly worked at all for my parents. My father was a traveling sales manager and his schedule often meant that he was home for only a day or two, usually during the "unsafe" times of my mom's cycle. But I shouldn't complain because that's why I'm alive. After all I'm the last of seven.

Mom had nine pregnancies that she knew of, or was able to count anyway. She had miscarried two babies in between the seven of us and if you look at the number of years between each of our ages it's very easy to figure out when these occurred. Mom really didn't know how many miscarriages she'd had in total. She said that sometimes it was hard to tell because, "You can miscarry so early in a pregnancy." Also, it was different when she was young and having kids. She told me people didn't make such a big deal about having a miscarriage then.

After one particular miscarriage her doctor had casually told her, "just put it in a Mason jar and bring it in tomorrow," if she wanted him to look at it to check it out. This sort of death was just part of normal life. It was expected and no one seemed to grieve much over it, not like we do today, unless it was a late third trimester miscarriage or a full-term still-birth. Women then seemed to see miscarriages as the body's natural way of sorting out when the baby wasn't developing properly. They accepted them, when they happened, as okay and even right.

Regardless of how many times my mother actually conceived I had the great honor of being number seven. Shortly after she'd had me, pretty much in the hallway of the hospital I've been told, either because I came too quickly or because she'd had lots of practice, my mom underwent a total hysterectomy. It was now certain that I was going to be her last child. That was it for her child-birthing years – finally and I know that she was secretly very grateful.

Families of seven kids were very common for a good practicing Catholic family, perhaps even a bit small. We had many friends when we lived in Portland, Oregon, who were one of ten or twelve kids. I remember a family, who lived just down the road from us there, who had fourteen children including two sets of twins. It seemed the Rhythm Method didn't work well for a lot of Catholics. My parents were definitely not alone.

Even though my mother had been pregnant or nursing (another one of the supposed "safe" periods) for more than a decade during her fertile years, there still ended up being a lot of us, including me who was definitely unplanned as were all the others. As kids we used to jokingly call my mother "Fertile Myrtle". She even conceived me while she was on her period, a definite "safe time" according to the Rhythm Method! Mom really didn't have a chance, did she? She was perennially pregnant.

Only a few months before the seventh anniversary of my mom's death and my unofficial decision to come out about what happened before, during and after it, I was interviewed. A newspaper editor, John Nurden, wanted to do a feature about me and my first book, *It's Your Choice: Uncover Your Brilliance using The Iceberg Process*. I thought the interview was going quite well and then he asked me about my family. When I said I was the youngest of seven, his ears perked up. Much more animated than he had been from the start, he went on to tell me that this birth position was supposed to indicate strong psychic potential. "The seventh child in a family of seven," he said, "was quite auspicious." The line of questions changed immediately after he'd heard this. He then proceeded to ask me questions like, "Have you ever seen a ghost?" which had nothing to do with my language theory and my methods for personal growth covered in my first self-help book he was supposedly writing about. But Mr. Nurden was also writing about me, the person.

What surprised me most though was not his interest in my birth order or if I were psychic but that I found myself being honest with him. I knew full well that he would publish this feature article in our local newspaper along with a photograph of me holding my book. Everyone I knew and tons I didn't would possibly read it. I was stunned as I heard myself answering, "Yes," to his ghost questions and even more shocked as I calmly recounted my odd experiences when my mom died and just after.

You might not think much, if anything about this, but to me it was significant and pivotal. Not only had I blurted out my secrets around my mother's death but I'd never before heard that a seventh child of seven was thought to have increased psychic abilities. After having gone through the last seven years, I now had to agree with him even though my psychic *gifts* were maybe latent and only surfaced after my mom's dramatic passing.

Now let's get back to my original query about the importance of the number seven at the very beginning of this opening chapter. Apparently every cell in the human body is replaced within seven years. Automatically, outside of your awareness, your cells are replicating and renewing your entire body all the time, continually every day. You're essentially totally refreshed every seven years and as it turns out, nature does many things in patterns of seven. Yet probably the most critical factor for me about these last seven years is that I feel so very different this time. Physiologically, psychologically and even emotionally, I'm just not the same person anymore.

I'll never be that person that I was before my mother died. Although there's a part of me that logically understands that I can't go back to that time, there's also a part of me that wouldn't want to go back to that previous version, the me of seven years ago. I've grown so much from my experiences surrounding my mom's death that my life has expanded beyond my expectations.

Chapter Two

A little about my mom and me

I remember certain things from my childhood with extreme clarity including the honest and open conversations I had with my mom, especially those we had once I was an adult living with her by myself. She told me of some of the challenges of being my father's wife and of being a mother.

I remember her vehemently speaking about the time her doctor told her that it was essential that she did not get pregnant for awhile. I also know that she and my father failed at this recommendation. She fell pregnant again in her usual interval.

I was close to twenty when I listened to her tell of how she'd summoned up the courage to approach her priest, again, but this time under specific doctors orders.

We were living together then, almost as peers or roommates rather than mother and daughter. It was just after she'd broken up with my father, after their second and final divorce. I was going to college then and she was working fulltime for a bank in Seattle in their personnel department. We'd moved together, out of my parents' large home with 26 acres and into an apartment closer to my school and her job. I had chosen to live with my mom rather than my father. Although my dad wasn't at all happy about this and I ended up feeling his wrath later when he reneged on financing my final two years of university out of anger for my mother, and perhaps for me, I made the best choice.

It didn't take me long to decide I preferred to live with my mother. She was much calmer and I knew she needed me more than my dad did. Within a year my father was remarried. He never intended to live alone without a wife and cook. My mother, on the other hand, neither remarried nor ever dated again. She never wanted to be controlled by a man again.

After my mom's doctor had made it clear that she mustn't have another child right away, as a converted and devout Catholic, Betty went to visit her priest seeking special permission to use contraceptives. Her doctor had said her body desperately needed a break, both for her own sake and for the health of any future children. He was worried after she'd had her third child, my eldest sister, who had been born handicapped with spina-bifida. Shockingly, the priest roughly rejected my mom's request and said that it would be God's will if she died in childbirth.

I remember too, hearing how she'd lost all of her teeth after she had my brother Tim, her sixth child and fourth son, born just three years before me.

Thinking about it now, it was some sort of miracle that she'd had enough energy to successfully carry me after the many drains on her body. I was born easily and in perfect health.

Adding me to the picture, she was now raising seven kids essentially on her own, Monday through Friday. My father's work required him to travel constantly. He was gone a week or even two weeks at a time. He was working very hard to

earn enough money to support all of us and pay both residual and continuing doctors' bills for my eldest sister's surgeries and health care.

It would have been very difficult for any woman to take care of seven children
by herself. However, it was especially tough for my mom because of my handicapped sister and my third brother who was born just after her with undiagnosed
bi-polar disorder. The sheer volume of children with these added complications,
along with my parents fighting made for a very wild, unpredictable environment,
to say the least.

As long as I can remember I was either referred to as the baby of the family or
the runt of the family. In my brother's and sister's eyes I would always be twelve
years old. It didn't matter what age I was. I would always be the youngest and
as it just so happened the most petite. I hated the runt reference. I didn't like the
image it conjured up of my mother being an animal that had a litter of kids like
a dog or a pig. However, I'm sure the runt label was more to do with me and not
my mother. I was small and blonde, and the last born. Possibly I was more like a
toy or little kitten that my brothers and sisters could play with than a sibling or a
human baby. My other sister, the fifth born and the middle girl, Claire, confessed
that she used to pinch me while I was in my bassinette or crib until I would cry
loud enough for my mother to hear. She'd then yell to my mom and ask if she
could pick me up. Most of my life I've had trouble sleeping soundly, maybe she
had something to do with this.

Being the seventh child came with some inherent issues. In my family, my
brothers, my sisters and my parents were all stronger and more in control of my
life than I was. I remember when I realized as a teenager that I didn't even have an
opinion of my own. I must have subconsciously or even consciously determined
as I was growing up, that it was best not to express any differing ideas in my
household. But this is deviating from my story.

When my parents divorced, the first time, after 33 years together, I was only
thirteen and in eighth grade. My brother, Tim, and I were the only two children
left at home by then. The others had left the house as quickly as they could once
they'd finished high school. Tim and I found ourselves moving from a gorgeous,
wooded, huge country estate to a double-wide trailer in a somewhat trashy or low-
end part of town.

The trailer park, although it had a pool, which I remember having fun in, was
situated almost next to my school. It was way too close for me. Even at thirteen
my reputation in this very white-bread, middle class, university town suffered. I
had no chance now of fitting in with the "in crowd".

I recall Tim used to have the same repeating nightmare. He'd dream that someone with a giant can-opener would come along while we were sleeping and open
the top of our trailer. We'd be exposed, then ripped apart or even eaten alive!
Much to our distaste, even worse than hating living at the trailer park, we were
more concerned when my mom and dad started dating each other. Both of us

13

secretly, and without the other knowing, used to wait up in our bedrooms until we heard my mom's car pull into the metal covered car park next to our unnatural aluminum house. Unfortunately, mom and dad didn't listen to our input and decided to remarry each other after less than a year apart. My mom later told me when we lived alone together that they did this because of us. She thought Tim really needed a father figure as she'd discovered that he'd been smoking pot. So, although we were adamant that we didn't want them back together and were willing to trade off the embarrassment of living in the trailer park for the peace and quiet and predictability it offered, they thought getting back together was best for us. They were wrong.

My parents divorced again in 1980 after six more extremely turbulent years. Tim, however, had to leave home long before then when he was only 16. He hadn't even finished his high school years and had two more to go (just like Claire, who'd left home before our "trailer trash" stint) but Tim's departure was under much more extreme and threatening circumstances.

Five years before my parents' second divorce, and less than a year after moving back to our lovely house in the woods (and out of the synthetic trailer park) my father tried to shoot Tim right in front of me. I never understood what could have prompted this but knowing my father it might have simply been that Tim had spilled oil on the driveway as he worked on his car. Almost anything could set my dad off and land you in deep shit. He had a bizarre mantra for a father of seven; anyone hearing him would think he hated us. If we annoyed him or did something he didn't like, which seemed to happen constantly, he'd be heard loudly repeating, over and over, "God-damn, son-of-a-bitching, f**king kids."

After that horrendous day though, the day that Tim left running through the woods as my dad fired three shots at him, I was the only one left with my parents. My memories of what happened once I was with them alone are a bit sketchy, until the last year when they finally broke up. I actually only recalled the shooting incident itself a couple of years ago, four years after my mom's death and almost thirty years after it had happened. Not only had I totally blocked out the attempted murder, but I also blocked out the fact that Tim never came back home to live with us. He left me there by myself. I'm sure I would have done the same thing under the circumstances. He ran as fast as he could through the underbrush and trees, while my dad fired real bullets at him from a Smith and Wesson pistol, while I tried ineffectively to stop him from shooting at Tim. He never returned home after that except to get some clothes while my dad was away and I was at school.

While fortunately a lot of the things I experienced during those final years after Tim left are blurred, I do remember a couple of ugly nights. There was the time I stupidly tried to hide the vodka bottle from my mother. She'd resorted to drinking to handle what was going on with her and my father and perhaps why Tim left. She must have known even though I'd forgotten until recently. I hid quietly with the half gallon of vodka, shaking in my bedroom closet, thinking she wouldn't look there. I was wrong and she was livid! We battled over the bottle and I lost. She almost broke the closet door down – she wanted it that badly.

Another night, I took all the alcohol I could find and poured it down the sink. But the final time I attempted to stop my mom from drinking alone while my father was away, I covertly slipped out the garage door, loaded all the bottles into the trunk of my 1965 Mustang and drove over to my boyfriend's house crying. His parents let me sleep on their couch that night. That's when I first heard about a support group called Al-Anon, it taught people who were living with an alcoholic or problem drinker (or two!) survival strategies. I started secretly going to the Al-Anon meetings after school and learned there that I couldn't stop my mom or my parents from drinking and that I shouldn't get involved in trying to control it.

Oh and I can't forget the night she drunkenly pushed me out of bed. I woke up as I fell painfully onto the floor. Apparently she'd come into my bedroom and crawled into my bed by mistake. Also, there were the many times I helped her into her own bed after she'd fallen down, drunk, late at night. Although my mother drank to excess she always made it to work and I realize now after her death just how abused she really was. I can't really blame her. My dad drank too, just as much and even without alcohol he was downright mean.

My parents were from what I call, "The Martini Generation." Now that I'm older I understand more about just how difficult my parents' lives must have been, especially my mom's. I've forgiven them both for escaping in this way, numbing out through alcohol and acknowledge what they endured throughout their lives. I may have done the same.

So there I was, so very much alone. I withstood another six years of my own version of Hell without Tim or Claire for mutual support. I was reluctantly forced into the unexpected and terrible role of mediator or marriage counselor as well for my violently feuding parents, until I finally cracked and couldn't stand it any-more. It certainly never felt like their staying together was for my sake or benefit. Those years were filled with possibly the heaviest drinking and fighting I had seen yet. Night after night, there was no let up. My mother would drink quietly by her-self, vodka in a coffee cup, until she'd either pass out or go to bed while my father travelled from state to state selling stuff. Then again on the weekends they would drink quite sociably together, to start, and then the fighting would take over.

It seemed if they weren't fighting or screaming at each other during those years, they were drinking in preparation for a fight. Often they did all of these, all at once and threw things at each other to boot. As the only child left in the house by then, I spent much of my time just trying to stay out of their way. And then it got worse. When I was seventeen, the summer before my senior year, my parents moved from Oregon to Washington, taking me away from the town where Tim and Claire had their apartments. My dad had decided to start working for himself and had bought a 26 acre wholesale nursery. He was now home every day and every night. There were no business trip reprieves. It was unbearable.

15

Beyond Goodbye

Only I went through both of my parents' divorces, including the buildups and the final battles before they decided each time to call it quits. My three eldest brothers and sisters (the first born) weren't at home for either of these divorces. Lucky them! I'm still convinced that I was in no way spoiled. Even though most of my family always said I was, it wasn't actually true.

I remember when I was taken in by the family of a girl in my college French class. I hardly knew her and had never been to her home. During the final months of my parents' last divorce, I started uncontrollably shaking and crying in my lectures. I guess I was having what you might call a breakdown. This one particular classmate noticed me and took the time to find out why. That's when I realized I couldn't manage anymore. She discussed my situation with her parents and they very kindly offered to house me while my mom and dad worked out the details of their divorce and finally split up, this time for good.

I can't recall, or maybe I just don't want to recall, how many times my parents' fights reached those lofty heights, high enough to cause them to separate or consider separating, let alone divorce each other. But there were enough to frighten anyone and all seven of us as kids experienced at least one separation. No one really had it easy in the Cap family. The fighting had been going on since before I was born. I entered life in fear. It was rarely comfortable or felt totally safe in our house, particularly if dad was home. When my parents fought or my father was upset about something, even very minor or trivial, like one of us spilling a glass of milk or using too much toilet paper, or God forbid spilling the milk and breaking the glass (which happened often when all nine of us were at the dinner table together) all hell would break loose.

Those times, all the years my parents were together, were far from pretty. And I certainly never felt lucky or privileged to have experienced them, including the many years I had alone with my mom and dad. But I'm at peace about them now, finally, I think and it's a lot to do with the connection my mother established with me as she died and after.

Chapter Three

I can't stop thinking about her

If I'm honest, I'm sure I know why I waited seven years before talking about what happened between me and my mom as she died. It took me all that time to stop viewing my experiences with her as *abnormal*. I'm sure that's the main reason I waited this long to share my story and write this book.

Over these past seven years, I've experienced major challenges in my life which were all mixed up with the fantastic and the fabulous. The combination has ultimately allowed me to see my mother and life in a very different and positive light.

I'm comfortable now with whom I've become. I find I'm ready now to reconcile and understand the many unexpected events that went hand and hand with my mother's death, after it, and even before it.

It was seven years ago, this January – January 2nd, 2004 to be precise. Almost to the very day of that memorable anniversary, I've found myself preoccupied with repetitive thoughts of my mom. It's as if the experiences, the loss, and the love we had was somehow amplified and enhanced. It's like someone has turned the volume up on my experiences and they can no longer be ignored.

Just the other day, I burst into uncontrollable, gasping tears. I'm sure you know the kind, the type of tears that shake you deeply and bring you down into your core. They were like those tears that I felt in college when I temporarily moved to my French classmate's house and those that I shed when I found my husband had been having an affair less than a year after my mother had died. They were the kind of tears that won't let up, until you reach a personal conclusion previously obscured, or a long forgotten painful memory like the day Tim left home.

I was in my car when it happened. Suddenly, I realized that I was watching for her. I was looking for my deceased mom as I drove home from work! Seven years on, I was wishing so hard that I could see her again, that I found myself peering through the windscreen expectantly.

I was actually thinking she'd be there. I was truly looking for her, watching and fully expecting to see her standing there on the side of the road. I was so sad when I realized what I was doing AND when I didn't see her. I can't adequately explain how overpowering this desire and expectation had been. It was so strong and so utterly surprising, and emotional, that I broke down. I quickly pulled the car over to the side of the road, almost exactly where I'd been looking for her, and balled my eyes out.

Oddly, I've been missing her much more than usual these last few months since the seventh anniversary of her passing. No one in my family mentioned it this year, but I felt it take hold of me. Those tearful moments at the side of the road convinced me that I had to look into what actually took place between us. It seems so strange that I'm now on a mission to understand how her dying act catapulted me into the unknown and how with each experience that followed my reality was inextricably changed. Only now that she's dead have I discovered what a truly courageous and durable woman she really was. I'd never known very much about my mom's childhood or her family until after her death. My relatives on her side had been absent in my life.

On reflection, I suspect that I closed up and never revealed the finer details of what occurred on the day my mom died and in the weeks and years that followed. The initial responses I received from my immediate family when I said how mom had connected with me were pretty mixed and negative. They were heavily tainted with disinterest or maybe distrust. My experience of feeling my mom's dying physical symptoms was even laughed at.

I'm not sure how to describe how I initially felt when I attempted to tell them. I remember though that it felt kind of surreal, just talking about it. It was as if I had this fabulous thing to share, which I sincerely wanted to talk about in great detail, but no one could hear me. I felt I had some kind of wisdom to impart or that I knew a special secret. Somehow, I wanted to allow them to share in it, as I had. I longed for their opinions as well, but I saw in their eyes and heard in their voices that this personal experience was just for me. I guess they weren't to benefit from it, not then anyway. It was apparently all and only for me. Although I'd mentioned what I'd felt when mom died to the whole family, no one ever asked me about it again. If anything, I think telling them made them feel worse, because they realized it hadn't happened to them.

To be fair though, one or two of them thought what happened between me and mom was very special, but most showed no interest at all, and others expressed jealousy, sadness or even blatant doubt. I think some may have even thought that I had made it up, or that it was another one of those experiences which proved to them that I was *a spoiled brat.*

Along with being called the runt, I was constantly accused of being spoiled. Supposedly being the youngest of a family was always easier. I never understood that theory. I wasn't spoiled. I was frightened. I was frightened into being the best behaved kid that you'd ever want to meet. I was quiet as a mouse and able to sit as still as a statue. I did whatever it took to avoid drawing attention to myself or getting hit. I watched, I learned and I hid. I knew when it was best to keep my mouth shut and I obeyed ALL the family rules. I'd figured them out. Keeping quiet and not provoking my dad, and even my handicapped sister and some of my brothers was the safest thing to do in my household. Consequently, I think I didn't get beat as much as the others. Maybe that's why they assumed I was spoiled.

I guess I've grown up a lot over the past seven years after mom's death. Having to face the many challenges and encounters brought about by the odd experiences with her, helped me muster up enough courage to now reveal everything. Even though keeping quiet was always such a good strategy in a big dysfunctional family, it's no longer necessary for me.

I give full credit to my mother's departing gestures, for my personal positive transformation. So, better late than never, as they say – I'm finally ready to speak openly about what many may find unbelievable.

Some of you reading this may have had similar experiences to mine but for personal reasons have kept your stories to yourselves. Or maybe like me, you hadn't realized the catalytic effect that sharing or participating in a death can have on you. Although this is my journey, it may be similar to yours. I hope by reading this book you will be reassured that you are not alone. Maybe by hearing my story you can acknowledge your own unique spiritual experiences and allow them to be a positive force and influence in your life.

Chapter Four

Propelled to understand

When I caught myself looking for my mom by the side of the road – I knew it was time. I had to do something. I had to put all the various pieces from the past seven years together to make sense of them. There was no denying their importance, value and relationship to the death of my mother any longer. As I looked for her outside the car window, I recognized and acknowledged that I was a very different person today than I had been before she had died.

It was as if the memories of my supernatural experiences and the love I felt from her were being thrust at me. It was just like the day it all started, the day she died. I decided that very night, or more accurately, I was pushed into deciding that night or couldn't stop myself, that I had to find out if anyone else had experienced what I had, when one of their parents had died.

I realized I didn't really know how to go about this. How was I going to find out if other people had been changed in the strange ways that I had by the death of their mother? I wasn't talking about grief. I was talking about what I thought was abnormal, supernatural changes. I didn't even know what to call what had happened to me, both when she had died and what happened after.

What the heck happened to me anyway? Had I imagined it? No! I knew that much. I even had witnesses to some of the experiences. But I'd never heard anyone else in my entire life talk about feeling the way I had when their mom passed away. Most people cried a lot, but they didn't have what I had happen – I thought. Not even one of my six brothers and sisters had felt mom die the way I had.

Then I noticed, out of the corner of my eye, a book on my bookshelf. I'd picked it up in a charity shop (the Salvation Army store) with my English husband, Matthew, on one of our trips back to the states to visit my family. It might have even been the trip we took to attend my mom's memorial the summer after her death. For some reason today, it seemed to stand out as if it were glowing. The book was *Life Before Life* by Dr. Raymond Moody and Paul Perry. I had purchased it and *Closer to the Light* by Dr. Melvin Morse (also with Paul Perry) at the same shop near the Oregon coast perhaps five or six years ago. These two books contained the stories of adults and young children who had died and come back to life to tell of being "in the light" of a divine presence.

I decided to start my search by "googling" these authors to see what they were up to. Maybe I'd find some similarities in the events that they studied and my own personal experience when my mom died. Although it seemed like a long shot, I didn't know where else to start. These two doctors and this researcher, had written about adults and children who themselves had actually died for a short time and experienced something extraordinary during their moments of death. They had not written about the family members' experiences in the two books on my shelf.

Part of me hoped that these three experts, if they were still involved in this area, might have encountered a relative or two who'd had something very odd happen like I had, even though they hadn't died.

So off I went to my little notebook computer to see what I could find on the World Wide Web. God, I love the Internet! Within minutes and only a couple of quick keystrokes later, I sat in front of the screen open-mouthed and stunned. Talk about accelerated synchronicity, which I would find out is also one of the more common after-effects of dying and coming back to life also known as having a near-death experience or a NDE. The very first thing I encountered was a video on YouTube of Paul Perry interviewing Dr. Moody about their new book, *Glimpses of Eternity: Sharing a loved one's passage from this life to the next.* It was all about what Dr. Moody was calling, "a shared near-death experience," a beautifully special event in which a member of the family or someone with strong emotional ties, or even a doctor or nurse in the room, participates in the after-death experience before the person is resuscitated.

Eureka! I was onto something. Although it wasn't exactly what had happened to me, there surely must be someone who had been miles away when their loved one or parent had died and they somehow shared in the dying event, like I had. So I kept reading and listening. With each click and link, I was led to other websites, articles or videos. I read or watched various presentations and forums on near-death experiences, always hoping to find a common thread. It was like a treasure hunt. I just kept following wherever the trail took me, always hopeful that it would lead me to the gold.

That was when I came across a recent press release which said that it was Dr. Moody who had in fact coined the term near-death experience (NDE) in his first book *Life after Life* published in 1975. He had been a medical intern at the University of Virginia School of Medicine working under the supervision of Dr. Bruce Greyson at the time.

Then I read about the commonalities of a near-death experience. I suspected that they would be the same for a shared near-death experience as well. That was when my mood dropped. They all supposedly "saw the light". I hadn't seen any light! Dang it! I'd missed the light! How come I hadn't found myself bathed in brilliant light? My mind was racing in circles now. I started to think that I was on the wrong trail and perhaps this was just a wild goose chase after all, but then I thought again. I questioned myself. Maybe not everyone who shared in a near-death experience saw the light? Maybe some did and some didn't? And because what I was reading I found so fascinating, I just continued following along, clicking on the many links presented.

From what I could deduce, it appeared that for your experience to be clinically classified as a shared near-death experience (SDE or S-NDE) or a near-death experience itself (NDE) in which you are the one who died and came back to life, you had to tick most of the boxes on a list of common and primary elements or characteristics of a NDE. Maybe I could get away with missing the light after all?

21

Hum. I reviewed the list of critical commonalities again. This time I focused on other aspects, rather than just the light people saw. That's when I found I couldn't tick very many of the boxes at all of a proper near-death experiencer.

I couldn't tick the *being in the light box*. I hadn't sensed a Godly presence with me when mom died, and I didn't remember feeling as if I had left my body either. So there it was. I hadn't experienced some of the most important, key components of these so-called expanded states of consciousness. I didn't appear to satisfy the criteria of a shared, or an actual near-death experience. But again I heard the little voice in my head which said, "Keep looking. Don't give up." It spoke to me strongly, and editorially added, "But mom actually died. Maybe the characteristics are different when someone really dies, for good and doesn't come back to life? Or maybe she had me join her death just before she saw the light?"

For some odd reason, beyond this logic, I only felt deterred for a couple of minutes. What I'd said to myself seemed to drive me forward. I continued reading. Then I found something. I was so excited. I ticked most, well actually almost ALL the boxes of the after-effects of someone who'd had a near-death experience! So something extraordinary had happened to me, even if it didn't fit the classic mold or *average* experience.

I learned that the amazing one-off event itself, was not only what determined whether a person had a clinically recognized near-death experience, or some other type of profound experience. It was the event combined with the after-effects – they were both important. These two things, the experience and the after-effects must be considered together. They went hand in hand. The after-effects, the changes within the person afterwards, almost validated the original event and made it authentic in the eyes of the experts.

After reading this, I knew it wasn't time to stop hunting. I mustn't give up on my search. I'd found enough anecdotal evidence to know that I was looking in the right genre even if I hadn't found the exact title for what I'd shared with my mom as she'd died.

It was also evident that what had happened between us was special. As it turned out, I'd had almost every one of the psychological, physiological and attitudinal after-effects of someone who'd had a near-death experience (NDE) or near-death-like experience (NDLE) them self. Although I certainly had not died, in the years that followed my mom's death, I was exhibiting all the common changes of someone who had.

I decided then that I needed to somehow access the actual research papers, or better yet, the research personnel themselves who had many years studying these profound events. That was when I broadened my search from "Moody", "Perry" and "Morse" to "NDE Research Experts". This led me to IANDS website, the International Association for Near-Death Studies (www.iands.org), as well as Barbara Harris Whitfield and P.M.H. Atwater. These were all names I'd never heard of before that day.

It was a link on the IANDS website that connected me to The Virginia School of Medicine where I realized the importance of Dr. Bruce Greyson. It was like someone switched on the lights again in my head. I knew immediately that I needed to get in contact with this man. However, I strongly suspected Dr. Greyson might have retired by now as earlier I'd read that he had been the supervising professor over Dr. Moody in the 70's when Moody was studying to become a doctor.

Only moments later I read that Dr. Greyson is referred to as "the father of research in near-death experiences" and that his team were still researching this phenomena and other experiences surrounding death including (and I held my breath) similarly intense states of consciousness that stimulated perceptional changes in a person. This was cool! I knew then that I was very close to finding out what had happened to me. The Virginia School of Medicine's website indicated that their Department of Perceptual Studies was actively looking for people who'd had what Greyson calls a, "deathbed crisis," or "deathbed apparition." The text on the site explained that this was when someone AT A DISTANCE sees or in some other way experiences an apparition of a dying person. This was almost what happened to me.

Although I hadn't seen a vision of my mother in the moments before her death, I'd felt her. Then in some kind of hyper-speed or time suspension, I found myself emailing Dr. Greyson as well as Dr. Moody, Dr. Morse, Paul Perry, Barbara Harris Whitfield and P.M.H. Atwater (all the people I had encountered in my search that day). Without a second thought I pressed the send button each time, fully expecting each of them to be interested in what I had to say. I requested an interview and asked them to help me understand my experience.

Only after it was too late to amend any of my emails, did I reread the messages I'd sent to these doctors and experts located around the world. I was surprised at how, without the slightest amount of concern, trepidation or regret, I had typed the following.

Dear…

I am currently writing a book (my second book) about the experiences I had when my mother died and the after-effects. I'd be honoured if you would grant me an interview (with yourself or someone you nominate). I'm gathering expert information to be included in my book.

I have had a very different sort of NDE or perhaps it's not a NDE but a deathbed shared experience, a sort of linking together with my dying mother who was thousands of miles away. I don't really know what to call it but it too has changed my life and my beliefs enormously including many paranormal occurrences and abilities since. It may be a distant 'crisis' announcement with the physical sensations of her death to get my attention and it certainly did and I've never been the same.

Let me know if you might be able to speak with me over the phone or Skype. I'm an American living in England near Canterbury. I look forward to hearing from you.

All the best, Annie Cap

I'd obviously read enough on my mini blitz of near-death and shared near-death experiences on the internet to know that my psychic abilities had been stimulated by my mom's "death touch" (as I sometimes call it). This email showed that I was really prepared to tell everything to someone other than my husband and not just a few anecdotes, but what had actually transpired.

I was sincerely baffled by what I had typed and sent so quickly in these emails. I had easily announced to complete strangers that I'd had and was still having paranormal things happen to me! I was honestly startled when I read how clear and honest I had been.

Looking at them now, I wouldn't deny or change a thing in these emails. My life really *has never been the same* since my mom's death, but I still find it very interesting that I could say what I said to Dr. Greyson and the others without any consideration. Perhaps it was because I trusted that he and the other doctors and researchers had heard these sorts of things before and wouldn't think I was crazy. (By the way, feeling that your life can never be the same, as it was before the event, is also one of the most common consequences of a near-death-like experience.)

The very next day the first response to my emailed requests came in. Barbara Harris Whitfield was willing to be interviewed by me! Not only is she a world renowned researcher of near-death experiences, she experienced two NDEs herself. Therefore, she has first-hand knowledge that may help me reconcile my own odd experience. Additionally and surprisingly, I discovered that Barbara had worked as a research analyst under Dr. Greyson (there was his name again). Also she had been the first woman on his staff who'd had her own near-death experience (NDE). Whitfield is also the author of *Full Circle* (the story of her two NDE experiences) and *The Natural Soul*. I felt I'd scored a major goal here. My research was now officially underway.

Only a day later, I received further replies to the emails sent to the experts in the United States. To my amazement, P.M.H. Atwater also agreed to be interviewed. Atwater is the author of *Beyond the Light, Coming Back to Life* and more recently, the book *Near-Death Experiences: The Rest of the Story*. She's one of the original NDE researchers, having begun her work in the field of near-death studies in 1978. Like Barbara Harris Whitfield, P.M.H. Atwater was another of the few top NDE researchers who'd had a NDE herself.

Then Dr. Greyson, the man that I had intuitively known would supply the many answers I needed, sent me an email. I was excited as I opened it. His email was very kindly written. He even apologized for his late response. Regretfully, he wrote that his current commitments meant that he wouldn't be able to talk with me, but he suggested I contact Peter Fenwick, Penny Sartori, David Rousseau, Allan Kellehear and David Lorimer. I hadn't heard of any of these experts. None of my searches had come up with their names. I was intrigued and flattered that Dr. Greyson had taken the time to reply with these experts names, who apparently were located in my own time-zone.

I immediately emailed the contacts he'd suggested and the first to respond was Dr. Penny Sartori, who is known for conducting the largest and longest near-death investigation so far in the UK. She's also the author of the book *The Near-death Experiences of Hospitalized Intensive Care Patients: A Five-year Clinical Study.* Dr. Sartori, Penny as she allowed me to call her, would also allow me to interview her and much to my surprise she was also interested in hearing about my personal experience with my mother. During her research she had come across two individuals who had experienced something like what I had happen but they were physically in the room with the dying person.

It appeared the gates were opening and the heavens conspiring to help me write this book, as more responses came in each day. I was stunned by the ease at which I was making contact with extremely busy and prominent experts. I was in the flow, there was no denying it. One by one, almost everyone I reached out to either agreed to be interviewed or recommended someone else that I should not overlook including Yolaine Stout, head of ACISTE (American Center for the Integration of Spiritually Transformative Experiences) and a previous president of IANDS. Even near-death experiencers themselves and clients who'd just lost their parents began to show up in my life without any effort on my part.

It felt as if I'd opened the door to something amazing and it began to have a life of its own. My calendar was filling up with dates and times to interview researchers, doctors, professors, scientists and experiencers – and my mind was being blown away by what they were telling me.

Before I share with you what I've found out through my many interviews and research, the latest scientific understanding and spiritual understanding of what happens when someone dies, including whether there's an after-life, I wish to tell you my story.

Chapter Five

My mom dies

There's no nice way to tell you about the day my mom died. No matter how many times I read through this, I still end up crying. I'm somehow transported back to the intensity and feelings of that very day.

I also distinctly remember how uncomfortable I was as I watched and listened for the reactions of my siblings when I told them what had happened to me in England, as mom had been dying so close to them in the United States. None of them had an experience like mine and although what I went through was difficult and emotional, it was very special. It was a turning point in my life which I'll never regret. I feel extremely privileged in a peculiar way and very grateful to my mom for sharing this time with me.

I suspect my brothers and sisters may have even wondered about my some-what odd fascination about mom's death. Maybe they'd thought I was being too morbid, questioning them about her final hours and minutes. I remember thinking that they must have sensed an undercurrent of inappropriate elation in me as I dug for details to compare with my own experience on another continent.

I don't think any of them really wanted to talk as much about it as much as I did. They may have wanted to just forget about it and get on with their grieving. Not even my brother, Peter, who'd had his own unique experience as she died wanted to talk much. On the one hand, I knew I had lost my mother that day, but on the other, I knew I had felt her with me as she left us. It was an odd sensation, yet very reassuring somehow.

Peter, who had been in mom's room when she'd died, said something beautiful happened. He's kept it all to himself but maybe someday he'll share it with me. I'll understand though if he never does. Maybe, like me, he'll reach his own point of acceptance (or maybe he already has) similar to when I hit my all important seven year mark and found myself looking for mom alongside the road, unable to dismiss my experiences any longer.

I want to be as accurate as I can in telling you what happened to me. Therefore, I must highlight from the start that my life was turned upside down. Not only because of what happened on the day my mom died but because of what happened and continued to happen, after her death – as I've been hinting.

Within a week or two of mom's death many of my fundamental beliefs were simply melted, like a Salvador Dali clock. My transformation was well on its way in just over a week. Without knowing it, I was being led through direct and personal experiences to a new understanding of my own reality and life in general. I was shocked into believing in the unseen and the power of a divine force, which I had never previously believed in.

I was to quickly gain a first-hand understanding why some people insist on using phrases like "she passed away" or "she passed over" when they talk about death instead of using an abrupt and final statement like "she's died".

It all began about twenty minutes before her death and while I'm positive that the death of anyone's loving mother is bound to have a massive impact on them, the death of mine was like some kind of initiation. I suspect without knowing it, my mom left me a priceless parting gift, a kind of booby prize of limitless value, although there's never been a day that I haven't wished for her physical presence instead.

It may sound trite but my life truly has never been the same since that cold day. It was the 2nd of January 2004, four in the afternoon at my house in England (GMT, Greenwich Mean Time) – almost 8am (Pacific, west coast time) in Portland, Oregon where my mother was.

I was busy working upstairs with a client in my in-house therapy room, when suddenly out of the blue I began uncontrollably gagging and coughing. I could hardly breathe and I felt like I was drowning or suffocating. It came on without warning, from out of nowhere, so extreme and intense. I was wheezing and had a strange gurgling cough. Nothing I did seemed to stop it fully. Tears ran down my face as I tried to catch my breath in front of my client. I excused myself and rushed to the downstairs bathroom. I was trying to get as far away from my therapy room as I could. I didn't want him to hear me as I attempted to cough up whatever it was that was causing this.

I'm not sure what I had thought I could do about it, but I remember feeling a bit like a cat trying to vomit up a hair ball. I had no luck. My deliberate attempts to cough something up didn't help much.

It was strange, especially because I didn't have a winter cold or anything wrong with me when it started. In fact, as far as I knew, I was in perfect health.

I began to feel quite scared when I realized that I couldn't ease the gagging sensation. The coughing wasn't so bad but the feeling of suffocation was horrible. My face was visibly wet with tears when I returned to my therapy room and I felt myself getting more and more upset in front of my client. I was now feeling very emotional and overwhelmed. I continued to struggle to catch my breath, although I knew I wasn't actually choking. I'd choked once in the past in a ski resort cafeteria. Luckily I received the Heimlich maneuver from someone who had witnessed my choking. After the ordeal, my life-saver informed me of one very important distinction – you can't speak if you are truly choking.

As I couldn't effectively clear whatever was going on with my throat and lungs, but I could talk, I knew I had no option but to stop the session. This had been my third appointment that day. However, when this client arrived, I recognized that my heart wasn't in it. As soon as I made that decision to postpone the session, I sensed it was the right thing to do. Immediately, my mind then shifted to thoughts of my mother. I wanted nothing else but to be with her.

Sunrise was getting closer and closer to my mother as she lay in her hospital room in the states. We'd agreed to talk again as soon as morning had reached her bedside. I'd promised her the night before that I'd ring as soon as she was awake.

I did the best I could to regain (and maintain) my composure in front of my client. I found it quite difficult because this peculiar choking felt like what I'd always imagined drowning would be like. All my life I'd always feared suffocating even though I'd never known why and had just attributed it to some sort of birth anomaly or some swimming accident I'd forgotten about.

As I climbed the stairs to talk with my client, I felt an incredible urgency and I knew that I had to call my mom right away. The coughing increased and I cried silently, but openly in front of him. My mind was now focused on only two things: my mom and how to get this client out of my house – fast!

I had planned the apology in my head while in the bathroom downstairs coughing. I'd apologize first for how we had been abruptly interrupted, ask him if he'd be willing to come back on another day, and offer to give him both sessions for free. I figured that should do it. However, it had been so obvious to him that I wouldn't be able to continue that he'd already put his coat on and was preparing to leave when I reentered the room. He'd seen the color leave my checks and the discomfort I'd been in while trying to breath and suppress the coughing. I stopped any attempt to hide what I was feeling and told him that my mother was in the hospital and she wasn't expected to survive the next few days.

Although he was leaving now, I knew it would be another few minutes before I could pick up the phone to call her. For some reason, even though I'd just cried in front of him, I still felt I had to remain as professional as possible. I wished then that we didn't keep sheep in our field, as this meant I'd have to walk down the driveway and open and hold the gate for him before he could exit with his car. I began to sense quite powerfully that I needed to hurry him out of my house, although I still felt that I must appear calm. I was feeling very concerned and although I was trying to act like everything was fine, inside I was calculating how long it would actually take before I'd be back in the house and able to use the telephone.

Covering my mouth as I continued to cough, we slowly (and much too casually actually) descended the stairs. We crossed the lounge passing the settee (which will be important later in my story) and we exited my home through the French doors of our kitchen.

Once on the drive, I walked as briskly as I could, without appearing ungracious. I opened the gate and as his car turned onto the lane, I closed it slowly behind him. Then, trying to look the part of the serene and consistent holistic therapist and counselor, I gave a little good-bye wave and smile, as always.

As soon as his car moved behind the hedge and I knew he couldn't see me, I sprinted as fast as I could for the house. I made it inside the kitchen in under ten seconds and grabbed the phone along with the piece of paper that had the long international telephone number to my mom's hospital room on it.

My mom must have decided to die then

Exactly seven days earlier, on the day after Christmas, my mom had been admitted to the hospital feeling unwell. It was just a week (seven days again) after Matthew, my boyfriend at the time, had surprised both my mom and I by asking me to marry him on my birthday, December 19th.

Both of us had been married and divorced before. We had openly discussed (many times) that neither of us felt comfortable about remarrying. We had agreed that we'd just keep living together. However, when Matthew asked me to marry him I heard myself saying, "Yes," with no hesitation at all.

My mom was the first person to call and wish me happy birthday that day. Matthew took the phone away from me to tell her the good news and simultaneously asked her for her permission. She cried with happiness and I could hear her saying, "Yes," parroting exactly what I'd said earlier. She proceeded to tell him, "Take good care of my daughter," with an audible lump in her throat, which I could hear myself, as Matthew held the handset between our heads.

As soon as I found out mom had gone into the hospital, I instantly wanted to buy an airline ticket and be with her. I had a sinking feeling about this one, probably because of what she'd said to Matthew about taking care of me. It was such an odd statement for her. I hadn't been able to stop thinking about it all week. Part of me knew something was up which she wasn't telling us. Her comment had sounded more like a command than an off-handed quip or request to my new fiancé to be good to me.

Perhaps she'd decided at that moment, upon his announcement, that she could go. In her mind, maybe she thought that now that I was going to marry Matthew, I didn't need her anymore? She loved Matthew and maybe felt she didn't have to worry about me any longer, assuming he would take over the role of watching over me for her.

When I spoke to my sister, Stephanie, and told her I was planning to fly over and was looking for a flight, she told me I shouldn't bother and it wasn't anything serious. She thought I'd be wasting a lot of money and there would be many more trips to see mom in the future. She said that there appeared to be nothing wrong with mom but that she'd passed out or fainted. The doctors just wanted to keep her overnight and run a few routine tests. Stephanie assured me that there was nothing to worry about and mom would be out of the hospital the next day. She repeated that she really didn't think I should come over, "just for this." Of course I know now in retrospect that I should have listened to my gut and gone immediately.

The test results showed that my mom's organs were failing and quickly. Her kidneys were shutting down and the doctors told her she must go on dialysis to stay alive. Mom's heart, too, was worn out and really struggling. To top it off, her liver wasn't functioning properly either. Everything was packing up. This was serious! She was in real danger this time.

Although mom had suffered a heart attack in her late fifties, when she finally had to give up smoking (one of her great loves) she was now 78 and had been dealing with symptoms of congestive heart failure for at least six or seven years by now, even if we hadn't been aware of it. I remember how difficult it had been for her to catch her breath when she came over to visit me in 1999 after I'd first moved to London. I thought she was just out of shape and hadn't realized that she wasn't able to get enough oxygen to her muscles because of a weak heart. But no one, except maybe her, expected this to happen now.

Mom had been using a walker for (perhaps) the last five years, after using a cane. She'd been living with either one of my two sisters, Stephanie or Claire, or my brother, Tim, and his wife Fleur for close to seven years. In the last three months of her life, it had become necessary for her to move into a residential nursing care home. My siblings and their spouses all worked full time jobs and my mom needed help now during the day. It really wasn't safe or comfortable for her to be left on her own. She was falling a lot and wasn't able to get up by herself when she did.

After a few days on dialysis, my mother boldly told the doctors and nurses that she was tired and wanted them to stop it. She said she was ready to die.

While she was in the hospital, all of her children were with her off and on – except me, her youngest. I made a dreadful mistake not buying an airline ticket when I had the chance.

What seems both odd and unfortunate now, is that I know I spoke with my mother every day that she was in the hospital, from the very first day on December 26th (Boxing Day in the U.K) until the day she died – seven days later. However, I can't remember much, if anything, of our conversations except the very last one. We spoke numerous times each day over the phone, including New Year's Eve and New Year's Day, but the only conversation I can fully remember was the last telephone call when she could no longer speak.

I know we both expressed our love for each other many times over those days, but I can't help focusing on the fact that when it became clear that this was serious and that she might actually die, I couldn't find a flight that would get me to her in time. There were no flights available to Seattle or Portland. I even looked at flying into other cities like San Francisco or Los Angeles and taking a domestic internal flight to Portland or Seattle and renting a car, but nothing was possible. There weren't even any flights into Vancouver, Canada I could take.

New Year's Eve was closely approaching and the brief quiet times for the airlines, just after Christmas leading up to New Year's Day were over. I'd waited too long. The Christmas and New Year's celebrations and holidays meant that nothing was available. Maybe I might have been able to go on standby, but I was advised that it was highly unlikely that any seats would open up in time.

The realization hit me hard that by following my sister's initial advice and waiting those first twenty-four hours for the test results meant I couldn't be with my mother as she died. I felt awful. I was stuck in England, so damn far away from where I wanted so badly to be. All I could do was keep myself busy, even though I knew my mother had been taken off the dialysis machine and her kidneys were not functioning at all. It was just a waiting game now. The doctors said it would take a few days, as much as five for her to finally die, as her body filled up with toxins and all her organs shut down.

Reluctantly I went to a 007 James Bond themed New Year's Eve party at our local pub where Ian Fleming had taken the number 007 bus from Canterbury to The Duck pub where he had written *You Only Live Twice*. I had New Year's Day off, like most everyone else, but had clients on January 2nd which would keep me busy and preoccupied while I waited for my mother to die.

I had many unsettling hours working before morning arrived in the Pacific Northwest, which is eight hours time behind England. My plan had been to go ahead and see my clients as previously scheduled. I hadn't expected my mom to die for a few more days anyway.

My sister, Claire, who is closer to my age than Stephanie, had taken time off from work to be with our mother during her final days. She'd stayed the last few nights with mom, sleeping by her side and holding vigil.

Once the dialysis had been stopped, mom's body was unable to filter her blood. Instead of the toxins coming out via her urine, they inefficiently could only come out through her pores and breath. Her skin itched horribly; it hurt and it burned.

According to Claire, mom was becoming more and more bloated. She was extremely swollen due to the buildup of toxins which her kidneys and liver were unable to process and clear any longer. Claire told me, the last time we spoke on New Year's Day, that mom's heart was still working but that the doctors had said that it was very weak and it would slow down gradually or she'd go into cardiac arrest. They informed my family that my mother had instructed them not to resuscitate her in this case. She was to be left to die.

Although my mother was extremely uncomfortable during this time, I expect it may have been even more challenging for my brothers, especially Tim and Stan, as mom's decision was out of their control. My mom had decided to die. They disagreed and of course did not want it to happen.

In the final days, mom restricted Stan from being in her hospital room. He had apparently been wailing and throwing himself all over her and mom found it too distressing to bear. I was told that mom asked the others not to permit Stan to come back into her room. She must have wanted a more peaceful setting as she progressed into what now appeared to be the inevitable.

Tim and some of my other brothers (I have four in total) fought with the doctors and nurses to try and force my mother back onto dialysis. Apparently, although I'm relaying this second hand, they'd felt that she hadn't fully understood what she'd instructed them to do when she told them to discontinue the blood cleansing procedure. They tried to convince my mom that she should keep fighting and shouldn't give up like this. It was so unlike her. They really disapproved. They even accused the nurses of putting the idea into her head and suspected that one of them had talked her into it.

My brothers were so upset and angry. They thought our mother was inappropriately shortening her life and that she didn't need to die yet. They kept telling her that if she just stayed on dialysis she might be able to beat this or at least extend her life a bit longer. I'm sure they were in shock and denial about the reality of the situation mom was in. Maybe they just weren't ready for her to die. But she was ready and it was, after all, her choice. They didn't want their mom to go, neither did I, although I'd accepted that it was her time.

Counselors were sent to talk with my family members about their impending loss, especially my brothers who disapproved of mom's decisions. They explained to my brothers that it was her right to decide whether she wanted to fight any more or not, not theirs'. She was prepared to die and they needed to honor her decisions, both to stop the dialysis and to decline resuscitation attempts. My brothers needed to come to peace with this. The counselors explained that mom had made it clear to the doctors and nurses that she didn't want to prolong her life any longer. She was really tired and had accepted that it was her time but for some reason they didn't really want to believe it. To this day they still express some disbelief and anger, saying that it hadn't been totally mom's idea. I wasn't there, so I may not have a right to an opinion on this but it sounds like something my mother would be strong enough to do. She was an amazing woman after all.

Once the dialysis was stopped, my mother's pain (as well as the other symptoms of organ failure) increased until the discomfort became too great. That was when my mom was put on morphine to help her cope until she passed away. The administration of morphine was the beginning of the end. I was aware that it was common for morphine to actually contribute to the dying process. While it made it more comfortable, the high doses also meant it was almost guaranteed that she'd die soon.

My morphine-high mom and I said goodnight to each other through tears the night before she died. I assured her we'd speak first thing in her morning and we both said, "I love you," before Claire took the phone back from mom's ear and spoke to me. She told me she would again sleep in the chair next to mom's hospital bed and then she hung up the phone only after promising to ring me if there were any changes before the morning. I arranged to call about 9 a.m., the time when mom had been waking up each morning since she'd been in the hospital.

The doctors expected she would last at least two or three more days. It can take a long time to die apparently once the process has started. Unfortunately, it's rarely quick or easy. There was nothing more any of us could do now to change the outcome. All we could do was wait and pray.

I'd told mom that I loved her many times and had long ago reconciled any issues we'd had with each other. I felt good about where we were in our relationship. We were clear and had no remorse. If anything, I respected her, although I'd accused her of not being a very good mother on occasion more than once. I tried to prepare myself for the coming days. I knew, full well, that each time we spoke on the phone that it might be the last time. Each time we said goodbye to each other, we both knew that we might never speak again. It was terrible not being there. My heart was being ripped out of my chest. I didn't know how I'd get through this. I'd never before experienced what it was like to have someone you love knowingly dying and being unable to be there, made it doubly worse.

Calling my mom

My hands were shaking by the time I completed dialing the last digit of the telephone number to my mom's hospital room. I prayed Claire hadn't left the room to go to the bathroom or for some other reason, or that she wasn't already on the telephone.

As Claire picked up the receiver, what was left of my coughing and gagging miraculously totally stopped! She answered with an unmistaken-able sadness in her voice, yet so pleased and surprised to hear mine. She told me she'd stayed awake again all night watching over our mother and never let go of her hand.

Almost whispering now and with a frog in her throat, Claire was crying softly and seemed to be struggling to talk. She told me that our other sister, Stephanie, was on the other phone. She'd called in only moments ago on Claire's cellular. It seemed fitting that all three of us, all of my mom's daughters, were now gathered. My brother, Peter, was in the room with Claire as well.

Claire had called everyone earlier that morning, as soon as she realized mom was actually dying. She called everyone – except me. She would have called me she said, but she couldn't. She didn't have an international calling plan on her cell phone and the hospital room telephones were restricted. They were limited to local calls and only national calls at a premium but no international calls could be made. Peter was the only one who made it to the hospital in time after he received Claire's call. My other three brothers were apparently on their way but had a greater distance to travel.

While Claire quietly greeted me, I couldn't help but hear the gurgling and choking in the background. It was unbelievable and sounded exactly like what I had sounded like only minutes earlier. A chill ran though me. I had pins and needles up and down my spine as I made the association of what had just happened from so far away.

Claire said, "She's been waiting for you. The nurse has just told us that this is what they do just before they die. She has only a minute or so left we think. She wants to hear you. Do you want to say good-bye?"

Holding back her heavy heart, her words broken and strangulated by her tears, Claire said, "Mommy, Stephanie's on the cellular and Annie's here now on the phone. They want to say good-bye." Mom's gurgling and rattling then stopped abruptly for a time and then started up again.

Claire then quickly explained to me that mom was having long gaps between labored breaths as she was drowning in her own fluids. Her heart was no longer beating strongly enough to keep the fluid from accumulating in her lungs.

Beyond Goodbye

She then held both handsets (the hospital telephone and her cellular phone) up to my dying mother's ears and I whispered, "I love you mom," over and over as I heard her take her last gasp. Quiet tears raced down my face as I felt her drift away.

Although my breathing had returned to normal, I'd lost my mother. We all had lost our mother. I sobbed.

I explained later to Claire what had happened to cause me to call at just the right time. She told me how badly she had felt when she realized she couldn't contact me to tell me mom was dying and how relieved she had been when I'd called on my own accord. I don't know why no one else thought to call me but I'm not going to worry even a moment about that because they were losing their mother – besides my mom got in touch with me anyway!

I told Claire how I'd started gagging and choking just out of the blue and how I'd had to ask my client to leave so abruptly.

Claire had never left mom's side that last night. She said that mom had been going in and out of consciousness. She thought it was due to the morphine and she had wanted to be there to comfort mom each time she awoke. They'd spoken during one of mom's more lucid periods during the middle of the night and mom knew she was dying then. She told Claire that she was going to try to wait until morning came so more of her kids could be there with her.

I was amazed at this conscious determination and the strength it must have taken for my mom to keep from dying that night. I felt honored, too, as Claire informed me about their intimate discussions and told me how much effort it appeared my mom had put into holding off her own death. She'd done everything she could to wait as long as she could and not because she was scared of dying but because she was our mother. She was the mother of seven very amazing and different children. She had dedicated her life to us and I expect she wanted to say her own last goodbyes to each of us. Or maybe…I've just had a thought. Maybe she wanted to wait for me to get there. Maybe she thought I was flying over?

Unfortunately, she didn't quite make it until everyone was with her, and only Peter got there quick enough to be physically by mom's side along with Claire. But at least Stephanie and I were on the phones. While the rest were stuck in traffic or in transit, we got to say goodbye to our mother.

Because of the morphine, I'm not sure whether mom realized that I was still in England when we spoke the night before. She may have thought I was by her bedside then or on my way. Either way, what I'd like to think is that when she realized that she could hold death off no longer, and that it was her time to go, that she could feel the lack of my presence in the room.

I believe that she recognized that I hadn't been able to physically reach her and when she didn't hear my voice, she decided to come and get me. Her desire to have me with her and her will were so strong that she reached out to me as she began to suffocate. Perhaps she was fully aware that this was the only option available to her to contact me.

Somehow, her energy then connected with mine overshadowing me physically as she succeeded in touching me, regardless of the distance. In contacting me in this way, she unknowingly or knowingly (I can't know which is true) caused me to mirror her dying symptoms. Ironically, coughing was a kind of a signature of my mother anyway. As a girl, whenever I'd lost her in the grocery store (or anywhere else for that matter) I would simply listen for her cough. We'd all done this and even commented on it. She'd always had a distinctive cough. Ever since I can remember she'd coughed, or hacked, as we called it. It was either from allergies but more likely from smoking so many years before people knew it was bad for them.

I believe, she rapidly sent the strongest message she could to me. My mom was very smart. Knowing my work ethics, if she were going to die out of sequence with her plan, she would have to interrupt me in a big way or I wouldn't have called until it had been too late. Aware that her death was imminent, I suspect that she did everything within her power to reach me, and possibly the only thing she could do which I would not be able to ignore.

I feel now that she had attempted to link her remaining, drowning, energy in with mine to say goodbye and to hold me one last time. She must have truly wanted me to be with her as she was dying. That thought makes me even more sad and regretful that I hadn't flown out immediately. I should have gone. However, I'm sure because of this experience that she knew how much I wanted to be with her too. In this very unique and special way, she helped me be there.

I still don't understand how she did what she did – linking in with me – but she did it. So much more is possible than we know or can prove scientifically. Our experiential knowledge must be taken into consideration. It was so obvious to me what had happened once I heard my mom's breathing and gagging when I called. This was confirmed again when I listened to what Claire had to say about my mom's long last night, as she struggled and postponed her death. I must have died a little along with her, feeling what she felt physically as she bridged time and space to get to me. And again, if she hadn't reached out to me, extending her consciousness in such an extreme way, I wouldn't have been able to say goodbye. I would have been too late when I called as we'd previously planned.

My brother, Peter, also watched as my mom died. He told us only that it was the most beautiful thing he had ever seen. Although I don't know what he saw, perhaps my new mysterious compulsion to research near-death experiences will shed some light (pardon the pun) on that too. Maybe I'll find some clues to understanding both of our experiences and why mine has influenced my life the way that it has.

The angel light – a deathbed coincidence

When Claire heard the results of mom's organ function tests, she knew she'd be spending some nights with mom alone. She wanted to have candles in the room but the hospital staff couldn't allow this.

Beyond Goodbye

Knowing how much my mother, Betty, loved angels, Claire decided to see if she could find an angel statuette or something along with a night light at The Dollar Store which she passed on her way to the hospital. Her thought was, if they couldn't gaze at the flicker of an actual burning candle, at night in the darkened hospital room, maybe she could find an electric candle or another pretty light.

Claire felt really pleased and lucky when she found a little plastic, glow in the dark, disposable light – in the shape of an angel! She brought it into mom's room and turned it on immediately. She left it on day and night, never turning it off even though the packaging cautioned against this. The instructions said that leaving the little angel on for any great length of time was detrimental. It was to be used only occasionally for short periods of time as the internal battery could not be changed or recharged. It stated clearly that it was only intended for short periods of use and if left on uninterrupted that it had a total battery life of approximately 24 hours.

Magically, the little glowing angel lasted much longer. Rather than lasting for twenty-four hours, it lasted all the days that my mom was in the hospital – almost a week! Only as my mother passed away did the angel's light finally go out. It stopped shining exactly as my mom died. Observing this and seeing both the symbolism and synchronicity, Claire wept even more.

She told me how extraordinary it had been. The angel light had been turned on since the second day mom was in the hospital, after they'd received the test results and realized she would die in the days to come. It had been glowing delicately, illuminating the room for Claire and mom each night, and day, until the very moment of mom's death. Only then did the little angel light go out.

I remember my mom had always talked about the angel that had hovered over her bed as a child. She'd been sick with measles and had almost died when an angel had appeared above her and told her it was not her time. It was so beautiful and comforting. She wanted to follow it but was told that it was not her time and to go back to sleep. She had a lot of living to do still. It sounds like my mom had her own near-death experience, when she was young.

Mom had been a believer in God and angels for as long as I could remember. Maybe it was because she'd died briefly before and had her own transformative encounter, when she'd been sick as a little girl? In my opinion, she'd always had an amazing amount of faith and durability for someone who'd had such a tough life. It always intrigued me how she could just keep going in the midst of turmoil or upset. Unlike me, who's best friend recently said she'd always thought I was a bit fragile.

I remember how it had always saddened my mom that I didn't believe in God at all. She could never convince me otherwise when she had been alive.

Even with her extraordinarily difficult life, including being sent away from her family during the Depression years of the 1930's and the many challenges our volatile, dysfunctional family life presented, she never stopped believing. She may have wavered in her religious practice at times but she never stopped believing in a higher power. She always hung onto her faith.

Secretly, I suspect I longed for some of what she had – her unmistakable faith in the unseen forces, but I couldn't allow myself to believe. I thought that if you believed in a good force, or God, that it was a package deal. If I believed in God, then I had to believe in the opposite of God. That's how it worked in the Catholic religion anyway. Believing, for me meant that I had to believe in evil as well. So, I preferred to shut the door to both.

Although I longed to find the comfort that she must have found from this and wished I had such strong resolute beliefs, I thought I'd never have the relationship she had with her God. It just wasn't going to happen for me. Instead, I chose to believe that when you die that it was the end of everything. It was easier and safer to be an atheist or agnostic in my opinion. That kept the devil or evil complement out of the picture totally for me.

Chapter Six

She comforts me…after-death contact

After mom died, I cried the rest of the day and throughout that night, and the nights that followed. Even in my sleep, I cried. Matthew held me while I slept. He tried to comfort me in this way, hoping that it would stop me from crying, but it didn't.

I didn't realize that it was possible to cry like that and still stay asleep – but apparently it is. I thought I'd wake up, like I do when I've had a nightmare or a bad dream.

Each night thereafter, I'd cry myself to sleep and then just keep on crying. Then I'd wake up sometimes in Matthew's arms and cry some more. This extreme response to my mother's death was totally unexpected. Neither I, nor my husband, could have anticipated that I'd be in such grief over my loss. Matthew had never seen me like this and was afraid to leave me alone.

Maybe it was because I was unprepared for mom's death, but we all were unprepared. Or maybe it was because I couldn't be there that I felt such sorrow and confusion. Or could it be because she bridged time and space to emotionally and physically connect with me before and as she died?

I still don't understand the whole dynamics of what happened but I felt it and it was certainly real. I missed mom so much. It was unfathomable that she was gone. I didn't know grief could feel so bad and be so all consuming. There was a hole in me, in the shape of my mother. I honestly hadn't thought it would be this tough. I even found myself distancing myself from her in the months before she had died. Maybe that's natural but I hadn't been calling her as much as I had the weeks and months before. Maybe, I sensed I wouldn't have her for much longer and was making the break early on.

Seeing how inconsolable and distraught I was, my husband called his work and asked for some days of compassionate leave to take care of me. They gave three days off for the loss of a family member and allowed him to work another few days from home. So instead of flying back to Germany that first week after my mom's death, Matthew stayed with me.

Back then Matthew normally worked four to five days a week away, but he knew he really shouldn't leave me alone like this. By the end of his time off, and few days working from home, I was still crying in my sleep but it had generally lessened, especially during the daytime. So when Matthew's compassionate leave ended, he felt more confident that he could go back to his work in Germany.

The night after he'd left for Paderborn, I again cried myself to sleep. My face was so puffy and sore around the eyes from so many days of crying that it hurt to open them and the salt from my tears stung.

I was hoping things would calm down soon. But not having ever gone through the death of a parent, especially my mother, I didn't know what to expect. The tears at night were back with a vengeance as soon as Matthew wasn't there to hold me.

On the third very distressing night of crying after Matthew had gone to Germany, I was awoken by someone stroking my hair. My first thought was that Matthew, knowing how tough a time I was having, had flown back from Germany and was home now to help me. I laid there feeling the hand on my head and relaxed a little, but then suddenly, I knew intuitively and without opening my eyes that it wasn't him who was touching me.

Instantly, I was petrified. I was not just sad now – I feared for my life. Someone, other than Matthew, had entered my room! I thrust my arms up in the air, striking out as hard as I could at the intruder in my bedroom. I was dreadfully panicked and wondered who was in my house and in my bedroom. Shit! It was my worst nightmare coming true.

All my life, I'd always been afraid of being attacked or raped. So I kept the door to our bedroom locked whenever Matthew was away. Even if I knew he was expected home sometime that evening or night, or if I'd already gone to bed, I'd lock the bedroom door from the inside and he'd have to knock to wake me up before he'd be let in. He much preferred this routine than having me slug him or kick him with my feet, like I was known to do if he woke me unexpectedly, even if I'd just gone up to bed before him.

I'd never really gotten used to sleeping alone in my bed at night. Now I screamed and swung my arms and fists around my head as I tried to push whoever it was away from me, but my arms met no one. I kicked my legs up under the duvet forcing myself to a seated position and reached for the light. I was afraid to see who was standing there. But when I turned on the light, there was no one. I rubbed my eyes and really looked around the room, even in all the dark corners. Surprisingly and thankfully, it appeared, I was actually still alone.

The door was also still shut and securely locked. But…I'd felt someone stroke my hair. How could this be? I was dreadfully confused. I was shaking and crying now with fear rather than sadness.

It was three in the morning, four a.m. in Germany, but I rang Matthew anyway on his mobile phone. I was so pleased to hear his groggy voice when he answered. I told him what had just happened. He reassured me that I was safe and I fell back to sleep only minutes after we hung up from each other.

Again, I started to cry in my sleep, and again, someone stroked my hair. I screamed out, "Stop it!" and whoever it was, did. They stopped abruptly.

I turned the light on again, and checked the room once more, even looking under the bed for someone who might be hiding there. The door and lock were again just as I'd left them. So, I tried to calm myself and told myself to go back to sleep. I must be imagining this.

Each time I started to cry, the rest of that night, while asleep or awake, I felt a hand stroking my hair. I was uncomfortable with it at first, but after I made it through that first night of being touched invisibly and the week went by, I began to understand that it was my mother trying to help me. I realized she was attempting to comfort me in Matthew's absence and I need not be afraid – not of her anyway. But she was supposed to be dead and non-existent? What the hell was going on here?

As a child, when I was upset or overwhelmed, my mother would stop whatever she was doing and sit down with me on the couch. I used to cry a lot, often without even knowing why I was crying. Once we'd both sat down, she'd then have me lay my head in her lap and she'd begin to stroke my head and my hair. Starting from the crown of my head, she repeatedly and slowly stroked me, like she was petting a cat. Touching me, gently but firmly, from the top of my head until she'd reached the ends of my hair. She would do this soothingly for as long as it took, until I was calm and had stopped crying.

She was doing it again for me, but this time she was dead! She was trying to support me and calm me. She was "mothering me" now, even after we'd said goodbye. Yes, it was confirmed that she had died but she certainly wasn't acting like it. She was with me again.

Once I allowed this awareness to sink in, acknowledging that it was her and could be no one else – an amazing thing happened. I no longer could dismiss the idea of an after-life. I took my first real step towards believing that there is more to us than just flesh and bones. I even decided that maybe it was okay to pray and start entertaining the idea that there is a God. I felt my mom was trying to tell me something very important and lasting, and the events that transpired over the next few weeks seemed equally unreal and magical.

Chapter Seven

Undeniable confirmation

Maybe my mom had thought that touching me from beyond the grave hadn't been enough. She knew, better than most, just how stubborn I can be, especially when it comes to religion and other things that I don't believe in, understand or fear.

I'm sure she would have anticipated how I would quickly and naturally decide that I must have imagined her touching me. She'd know, too, that there'd be pressure from others to disregard it. My brain certainly wanted to deny that it had happened, while my heart knew it was true.

After all, my mom had died rather unexpectedly and I was now over-tired and exhibiting visible signs of emotional and physical stress. Anyone could see that I was obviously in the throes of heavy grief. It didn't take an exceptional intellect to figure that out. But my heart knew somehow that she clearly had a plan for me. It couldn't be a coincidence that I felt her as she was dying and now after her death. Could it? It seemed mom wasn't going to leave me alone to deny her contact just because it was easier. She was going to persuade me and even Matthew, that she still exists and we need not be sad.

I believe she wanted there to be no doubt in my mind what had really happened and the implications of it. I had a witness to the coughing and gagging part, but there was no one with me – except her – when she'd repeatedly stroked my hair those nights while I was crying. My mom seemed determined to expand and radically shake up my narrow views on life after death, once and for all.

I'd always been afraid of dying and never liked the idea of being buried in the ground. I didn't want to be cremated either. I'd thought hard and often about what was going to happen to my physical body when I eventually died. I thought I was this physical body and there was nothing else. I was perversely very concerned from a young age about what would happen to my body after I'd died. As a child, I used to visualize how worms would eat my brain and bore holes in my skull as I laid underground, petrified and frozen in fear. I could see myself scared beyond belief and alone in a dark, dank grave, in some long-forgotten cemetery.

Perhaps that's another reason why my mom made her next move. I can see it now very clearly. Her after-death behavior was performed like intelligent and strategic chess moves. What she did next not only helped me feel more confident with my experiences of her during and after her death, but also shattered my current limited views for good.

Her follow-up display was rather like putting the proverbial icing on a cake. Stroking one's hair might have been enough evidence for some, but even after repeat performances, I still attempted to deny it. Her next move, though, proved her continued existence to me and to my husband. Although each of my experi-

41

ences thus far had been amazing, what happened next was irrefutable. Proving it was real did not just rely on my personal feelings when I was alone in my dark room.

She convinced us

How does someone who's no longer in physical form bring things into your home? Is there some kind of transporter that dead people can use or some other means to jettison things into this dimension? How does someone who's only in spirit form go about moving their personal items into your world? Or moving your personal things or household belongings around for that matter? I don't know the answers to these questions as I write them. But my queries became even more complicated than these. How do they go about getting things from their old home and move them into yours? When they're dead?

My mother had never been to my home after I'd moved in with Matthew. She'd been too frail by then to make the journey back to England although she really wanted to. So when I began to find some of her things in our house, I could rule out the remote chance that she might have left them here over the years when she'd visited. She'd never visited us in Kent.

How do I explain that in the weeks that followed her death, after she'd stroked my hair, that we started to find what appeared to be her bobbie pins conspicuously left around the house? Bobbie pins are what they call hairgrips here in the U.K. where I've lived now for more than a decade. I found the first bobbie pin in my therapy room, the same place I'd been when I began to cough and gag as mom was dying. It was dark brown or almost black, the same color of my mom's hair much of her life. It simply appeared on my couch one morning, from out of nowhere. It hadn't been there when I'd gone to bed the night before, but was there in full view when I entered my work room the next morning.

My mom had always used this exact color and style of bobbie pin, even after she'd gone almost totally grey. She never bothered to replace them with grey pins. My mother had always set her hair in rollers after she'd washed it. Like most women of her generation, she used bobbie pins to secure them. Also, each night before she went to bed, she would use these same bobbie pins to make pin curls around her face and at the base of her neck, so her hair style would look good in the morning. My mom was from a time long before there were curling irons or hair straighteners.

I'd never owned any bobbie pins in my entire life and there weren't any in this house that I knew of. I'd worn my hair very short for more than 15 years, longer than I'd lived in Kent with Matthew. Until I'd moved to England, I'd always thought that bobbie pins were only used by *old ladies*!

When I found the first bobbie pin, I checked with Matthew to make sure that his ex wife or an old girlfriend hadn't been in our home and left it there for me to find. I'm not sure what exactly I was thinking when I asked him this because the hairpin appeared overnight while Matthew and I were both sleeping together. I was obviously grabbing at straws. No one had been in the house after we'd gone to bed. Even if he'd had an old girlfriend who'd worn hairpins, that could only explain how a hairpin might have originally found its way into our home. It didn't explain how it had ended up on my therapy room couch overnight. Matthew assured me that I was the first woman he'd brought to this house. He'd owned it less than a year before I'd moved in with him.

We discussed all the possibilities of how this hairpin could have appeared. Although we rationally speculated that the previous home owner may have used hairpins, it still didn't explain how one had found its way onto my cream couch. Even if there had been some forgotten hairpin lodged somewhere in the bottom of a built-in wardrobe or cupboard, how had it been moved from wherever it had been hiding to my upstairs therapy room?

Over the next three or four weeks hairpins were being left one at a time strategically in full view for us to find. Coincidentally, they always showed up when we were 100% certain that no one else could have been in our house. I even contemplated that I'd taken up sleep walking and was placing them around the house myself but Matthew insisted that he would have noticed it if I'd gotten out of bed.

Just like before, when my mother had touched me, the doors to our home at night had always remained locked. No one had crossed our threshold to place bobbie pins for us to find! It wasn't like we had some rogue Easter Bunny or Tooth Fairy visiting us. My mother had to be doing this.

One of the most wonderful things about finding the bobbie pins was that it didn't just happen to me. I wasn't going crazy, at least not alone anyway! Matthew and I had both found them, independently. It was as if they were being deliberately placed so we would have no doubt in our minds that they were from her.

Usually we found them in the mornings. I remember after I found the first one, that I made a point of checking that nothing was left out of place on the kitchen counters or my dresser before I went to bed each night. The very next day, after I'd started this practice, I found another one when I went down to make the coffee. There it was, another dark bobbie pin left right in front of the coffee machine. It was in such an obvious position I simply couldn't miss it, or disregard it.

Although they were mainly moved or *placed* overnight and found when we first got up, I also found one that had been placed on my dresser when I returned to my bedroom to put my earrings on. It hadn't been there when I'd been dressing only a few minutes earlier.

We found them in the kitchen, the bedroom, my therapy room, on the bathroom floor and on the coffee table in front of the settee in our downstairs lounge. It became accepted that my mother was doing this. There really was no other logical option. We didn't even have a cat, back then, to blame. In the prime of it, whenever I'd find one if Matthew were at home I'd holler out, "She's left us another one!" or I'd text him on his mobile to let him know.

We both came to believe that by leaving these bobbie pins, my mom was providing solid evidence of her after-life existence. I still have the first bobbie pin of hers that I found. I don't know what happened to all the others. Perhaps she was just moving the same one around the house but I hadn't realized it.

We often smelled her presence

Many mornings we woke with the smell of cigarette smoke in our bedroom. My mother had adored cigarettes. She had smoked until she had been forced to quit in her late 50's, after she'd had a heart attack. Matthew and I both smelled the cigarette smoke and immediately realized it represented her. She was signifying that she was around us and it was wonderful. It was very comforting, even more so than the bobbie pins. Their undeniable presence was a bit disturbing to me at first, but the smoke was nice – even though neither of us had ever smoked. Right from the very start, we knew it was her, and felt pleased about it.

It had been almost a month since my mom had died and my crying at night had almost stopped. I was crying more during the day now, so my mother's stroking of my hair had ended. I'd already guessed that being asleep or being almost asleep must have meant that I was more receptive and could feel her touch more easily. I realized that I missed her stroking my hair now, but more to the point, I missed her greatly.

One afternoon, I was walking up the lane we live on, trying to come to grips with my loss, when once again I was overwhelmed by uncontrollable tears. I was overcome by an unexpected wave of grief and began to weep. I continued to walk up our lane crying, entered our gate and went directly into our field. I climbed the fence at the very top of the paddock, which overlooks our fantastic view. It was something I'd never done before.

Sitting there awkwardly perched on the fence, I cried out or almost wailed to my mother, "You never got to see this!" Then, I felt her so strongly. I sensed her arms wrap around me, even though I couldn't see her. I felt her give me a huge bear hug. It was as if she were just behind me all the time, sitting with me, looking at the view and now she was holding me, to let me know with no uncertainty that she had been here and that she was here right now. She'd seen our beautiful place. She'd experienced it. And she was not gone, not really. She was just out of sight. She had just transitioned to another place where I couldn't see her but I could feel her and smell her if she chose.

As I felt her arms so tightly around me, I was reassured. I stopped crying right then and there. From that day on, when I cried about my mom, I shed just little tears. They were nothing like the tears I'd cried before. I knew then that she was with me and perhaps would always be with me, even though she had physically or visibly left my side. She'd done enough now to convince me. I no longer doubted her and I no longer doubted whether there was an after-life. I was certain of it now.

I knew then that we, my mom and I, and everybody else, and love, continues after death. There's no question about it anymore. I'd been wrong all along. There really was more than this. I didn't need to fear worms eating my body anymore.

This was a huge change in beliefs for me. It was massive, in fact, and so very important. What a significant gift my mother had given me. I had stopped believing in God long ago when I was a child. I couldn't bear the inconsistencies between my home life and what I heard in church. It seemed so hypocritical. Even as an eight year old, I had rejected the Catholic churches' teachings. I especially hated the idea of "confession" and being able to be forgiven for whatever you've done simply by confessing to another man, a priest, and then saying a few short prayers in penance. I had stopped believing in God, Heaven and any kind of after-life entirely back then, but my mom's efforts were to change all this – eventually. She'd planted the seeds, now time had to work its magic on me.

By now I'd had my own first-hand spiritual experiences, including evidence which my husband could collaborate. My mom's *survival* and contact after-death were undeniable to me, finally. She proved that she still existed and wasn't really gone. She was still around me and she was still there for me.

I began to pray again in those early months. It had been so long since I'd sincerely prayed that it seemed weird and peculiar to me. But during those weeks after my mom had first touched my head and hair, I closed my eyes and attempted to talk to God. It was quite different than before, much less regimented. Partly, I think, I began to pray because I was confused and frightened by all that was happening, but mainly I did it because a deep belief was rising up within me.

I didn't just have faith now that there was an after-life. I had my own proof and knew my mom had entered it. What more could I ask for? Well, if I'm honest, I still lacked evidence that there was a divine benevolent God. But I can't ask for everything, can I? The fact that my mom had *survived* death and could contact me from "the other side", as so many call it, was enough to remove my slightly atheist views but not my agnostic position. I was still confused about who or what was up there orchestrating all of this. And how much direction and free will we really had.

It was an amazing feeling, to think, no…to know, that no one could take these experiences away from me. No one will ever be able to convince me that they didn't happen. I'd felt my mother. She'd contacted me before and after her death and not just once but repeatedly. It was fabulous and I know now that these acts of her love opened the door for me, to so much more.

As I allowed myself to fully believe that my dead mother, or her soul, was able to continue to comfort and communicate with me (in whatever way I could receive it) the concepts of other beings like angels and spirit guides became real for me. The existence of angels, especially guardian angels whose purpose I'd heard is to keep us safe, was now a real possibility. For some reason, it was easier for me to consider that angels existed than God. Remember, though, that in my upbringing, if there is a God, than there has to be a devil, and he's a nasty piece of work.

The thought of guardian angels being there for me, along with the spirit of my mother, was very satisfying. It meant that the world didn't have to be such a lonely and frightening place. I started to believe that I wasn't really ever alone. (I'd forgotten that angels were supposed to be created by God!)

Chapter Eight

A spiritual doorway opens, sensitivities increase

Following my mother's after-death contact (which I've learned now is referred to as after-death communication) there was a definite increase in my sensitivity. I began to experience even more of what I'd call the paranormal. It felt like I was playing some kind of a game of psychic building blocks. With every new event I experienced, I was being lifted a bit higher, high enough so that I could reach the next level. Instigated initially by mom's deathbed contact, each of these unexpected encounters enhanced my awareness and prepared me for further surprises.

I felt changes not only in my psychic abilities but also in my sensitivity in my physical health. Soon after mom died, maybe even immediately, I started having digestive problems. It got so bad that I decided to be tested for food intolerances. All of a sudden, it seemed, I was now lactose and cow protein intolerant. How did that happen?

I remember thinking what an interesting metaphor it was to be milk intolerant after losing my mother. The tests also confirmed why I was reacting violently to MSG and could not handle eating anything with yellow food coloring or a lot of preservatives. It was as if someone had turned up the volume or intensity of all my sensitivity knobs.

Food was not the only area that I was having trouble with. I could feel other people's emotional and physical feelings very strongly now. I was sensing their pain when they were with me and even from a distance. Perhaps I'd always had this ability but it now was quite noticeable. My husband and I seemed psychically linked now. When he was traveling, I knew when his knees were hurting him. I began to send text messages telling him to sit down whenever I personally felt his knee pain.

I had learned Reiki healing a few years earlier. When I used this technique on clients, since my mom's death, I began to know things about them and their past. For example I might sense that they had been raped or their relationship was in trouble. I just knew things and I found that they were accurate 100% of the time. I also realized that my healing abilities were more pronounced. People were having more significant experiences in our sessions together. They were getting much better very quickly. I felt their physical symptoms within my body more now than I had before my mom had died. I realized, too, that when I felt their problems that if I could handle it myself, and not pull away, that it would clear from them either totally or partially. The pain or other physical problem which they arrived with would frequently be resolved, at least for a time.

Lights were also turning off around me. My computer would often restart for no apparent reason and I could no longer consistently keep a watch running.

I seemed to have enhanced hearing capabilities as well. All my senses were heightened to some degree especially my senses of touch, sight and sound, including a noticeable change in my perception of light and temperatures.

Beyond Goodbye

As unsettling as it was, I was beginning to feel other invisible energies, or beings, if you will, hanging around me – other than my mother! This was really distressing for me. I was living totally by myself from early Monday morning to late Thursday or Friday night most weeks. Matthew had returned to his normal schedule of traveling and was staying in Germany midweek as he'd done for years. I only saw him on the weekends.

I was really scared again to be alone at night. The very thing that I'd never wanted to happen, and what I'd always tried to avoid, was happening to me now. It began to dawn on me that something major had changed within me ever since my mom had entered my bedroom those nights to comfort me after she'd died. She must have left some kind of spiritual doorway open to the other-side!

I was barely used to the fact that she was continuing to contact me, when I suddenly realized – if that were possible (and it was certainly happening), I now probably had to believe in ghosts! Isn't that essentially what someone else would call my mother's spirit right now?

I didn't feel she was a ghost for some reason. I figured, of course, that she was in a spirit form but what's the difference? What's the technical distinction between a ghost and the spirit of one's mother? Maybe I preferred not to think about that. Somehow it had never even crossed my mind that her touching my head was perhaps equivalent to being contacted and touched by a ghost! I struggled with whether I needed to determine the difference between a ghost and a spirit. I'd just glossed over that whole issue because I hadn't wanted to lump ghosts and the spirit or soul of my mother into the same category.

She is my mother after all, even though she's no longer in her physical body. I felt that her stroking, or holding me, was okay and even appropriate. In my head, I insisted that her contact was different than that of any unknown ghost. But that subtle differentiation didn't stop me from feeling the other presences which seemed to be lurking around me now.

My senses, I suspected, had been honed through mom's repeated contact from beyond the grave and the connection she established from her deathbed. I was feeling so much more around me now – that I just couldn't see! It was staggering and uncomfortable, and it was pushing all my fear buttons. Although, it didn't feel like the spirits or whatever they were (or whoever they were) were dangerous, I was disturbed by the fact that I was sensing their presence. I felt very jumpy and anxious. I wondered why all this was happening to me and what I could do about it. How would I ever be able to sleep alone in our house again?

Coincidentally, after mom had died, I started reading about guardian angels and archangels. I intuitively thought that I needed the protection they were supposed to offer, if you remember to call on them. I certainly wasn't interested in any negative spirits, poltergeists or other spiritual forms who might want to harm me, or at least annoy me. Or was I? I started to believe (because of something I read) that when you are fearful, for any reason, that you create or imagine terrible things called "thought forms". They're not supposed to be real but are created by fearful thoughts.

My hearing and my other senses seemed to be operating in overdrive at night. I was hyper-sensitive now to subtle changes in my environment, especially in the dark. I heard every bump and creak of the house.

The extreme fear I had as a child, when I thought that something was hiding under my bed and trying to get me – was back. And it seemed even worse. Because now, I knew from my encounters with my deceased mom that locking my bedroom door and the doors to the house is insufficient to keep out those who don't have their bodies anymore! When Matthew was away midweek, I began praying in earnest, not so much to God because I still wasn't sure about him or her (or it) but to the angels. I asked them to keep me safe through the night. That's when I remembered the prayer we'd been taught and used to say as children every night before we went to bed. It went something like, "If I should die before I wake, I pray the Lord my soul to take…" How the heck would the words of that prayer comfort any child who was already afraid of the dark and fearful of whoever might be out there lurking in it?

I still felt it was okay for my mom to "visit" me but not whatever or whoever else I was now sensing. It began innocently enough. I started to feel as if someone were sitting next to my legs on the bed. After I'd turned the light out and was under the covers, I'd feel someone (or something) push my legs over and sit their butt right down next to my legs. I'd feel the weight of their invisible body leaning up against me. It was freaking me out! I became extremely careful not to put my feet out from under the covers because I was worried that I might feel whoever it was touch me. This was exactly how I'd behaved when I was little.

I was also now seeing sparkles in the air. They were appearing both in full daylight and at night by this time. I liked seeing the sparkles. I'd read that they indicated angels were around you. Then I found other articles by a spiritual writer who thought that these sparkles represented spirits moving from their non-physical plane (or dimension) to our physical plane. I thought of the transporter on the Starship Enterprise and I began to feel even more scared. Depending on how you investigate anything, or how you "google it", the answers can be very different.

Then I encountered one of my first openly spiritual clients named Erica (the first of many to follow). She told me that if you open yourself up to spirit, you open yourself up to everything – good and bad. Although I wasn't sure what she was telling me, as I didn't know the definition of spirit. I wondered, if spirit meant one spirit, i.e., one deceased person's soul like my mom's or one angel, or if opening up to spirit might mean that you were opening yourself up to all the spirits that were out there. Either way, it didn't help relieve my concerns. If anything her comment elevated my fears.

Beyond Goodbye

I had to be careful, Erica said. She then told me about *closing down,* so the spirits (the ghosts, I guess) couldn't get in willy-nilly! She didn't use that exact term but the general meaning was the same. She talked about chakras and how I should put myself in a protective bubble. I remembered something about this from before, when I'd taken a course in Indian Head massage. Erica believed there was both divine goodness out there and evil. Shit! I was done for! She went on to say that I now appeared as a brilliant sparkling beacon of light, now that I was opened up. Apparently everyone could see me and many spirits would be attracted to me, some safe and some not safe in her opinion.

This was around the time that I began to find hangers in my hallway at night. If I woke and had to get up to pee, I'd first turn my bedroom light on and unlock the door. Numerous times when I stepped out onto the landing (which leads to the upstairs bathroom and my therapy room) there would be a hanger or two on the carpet just outside my door. My mother might have been leaving the hangers there for me but I wasn't sure about that. The bobbie pins had a personal significance - but hangers? Hum, I didn't know. I was quite concerned after hearing Erica speak about all the nasty or playful spirits that would be drawn to me like moths to a flame. I remembered she'd said, "Just because someone dies, doesn't mean that they automatically become wise and gentle."

I thought if a spirit or ghost could move hangers, maybe they could throw a chair or something. My mind darted around my memories at the speed of light. I recalled some of the horror film trailers like the one Linda Blair was in, *The Exorcist* and *Poltergeist* in which little Carol Anne was taken through a portal to another ghostly dimension. I'd never even seen either of these movies. I'd always been too afraid. I'd only watched parts of the trailers if I couldn't avoid it. Even then I covered my eyes while trying to plug my ears at the same time. But everyone either knows or has heard about some of the famous scenes in these two movies, including when Linda Blair's head turns around in complete 360 degree circle.

Again, I used the Internet. This time to find out how I could keep spirits out of my house, or get them out of my house, if they'd already found their way in after *seeing my light.*

I renewed an old habit of carrying rocks, crystals actually, in my pockets, in my bra and even in my purse. I selected crystals that were meant to act as personal barriers, almost like pepper spray for the invisible ones. This was something I'd learned about when I lived in Seattle from my old spiritual roommate, Katrina. Crystals apparently could raise your energy levels and your vibration. The higher your vibration, the more positive and angelic encounters you'd attract. It was all about repelling or attracting the right kind of spiritual energies and experiences. I recalled too that together, Katrina and I had bought dried white sage, used by native American Indians, to clear our home of anything untoward. This is called smudging.

All these things that I had been exposed to and somewhat interested in ten years before, now became my rescue and hopefully my solution to my growing problem. I started wearing pendants day and night to clear me of any negative unseen energies that might be calling negative spirits to me and I smudged my house repeatedly when Matthew was away. I also renewed the daily policy of putting myself in a protective bubble of light, another thing Katrina and my friend Diana from San Francisco had told me to do regularly, many years ago. I was invoking every ritual I could find to keep the unseen away from me. Still according to the conversation with my current spiritual client, Erica, I was shining like a lighthouse and needed to do more to dim or camouflage my light, or else! I knew now why it had been simpler for me to just not get involved with this stuff before.

Things were actually getting pretty ridiculous. I was sleeping with rocks on my belly, under my pillow, in my bra and now even in my panties. I'd also placed them under each corner of my bed and strategically positioned crystals outside the threshold of our house. Even with all the bubbles around me and asking the angels to guard over me, I was still feeling things around me at night. Then it happened. I was touched, well tapped actually, on my shoulder while I'd been asleep. I knew it wasn't my mother this time. The crystals and angel requests had been worthless. Whoever it was had made it through the gauntlet I'd laid easily. I actually wondered if I had to put crystals on the roof of the house. But weren't the angels clever enough to handle that end? This was silly. There had to be a better way.

When I felt the tapping, it was very firm. It was almost like light slugs from someone's fist. I felt in my head that they, or he, or it, whatever this was, was indicating that I needed to "wake up". That's why they were tapping me so hard. "I had to wake up!" I think I may have even heard those exact words. Only later did I realize what they meant.

I opened my eyes and as I had expected, I saw nothing. I turned the light on and checked around the room. I got out of bed and really looked around, although I was frightened by the prospect of finding someone there this time. I satisfied myself that the door was still locked and there wasn't a robber or rapist inside my room. Then after genuflecting like a good ex-Catholic, I turned the light off and closed my eyes again. As soon as I'd fallen back to sleep, it, or he, tapped on my shoulder again! I could sense that something or someone very large was hovering over me by the side of the bed. I screamed at it to go away and leave me alone. I turned the light on again and stayed up the rest of that night.

I knew that I needed to get some help but I wasn't sure where to start. Did I need a counselor and anti-anxiety medication? Or maybe I'd have to call in a spiritual expert? Did I need an exorcist? I'd heard about people who charged to *clear* your house. Maybe that's what was in order?

Chapter Nine

Invisible boundaries

The insistent pounding on my shoulder, my unavoidable wake-up call, was delivered every few nights for about two weeks. It didn't seem like it was going to let up and I wasn't willing to consider that I'd gone off my rocker. So I decided to go ask some questions at *my local rock shop*, as I like to call it, where I bought crystals.

I was now certain that whatever or whoever it was who was tapping on me was not my mother. I sensed it was a big, huge, bloke who was trying to get my attention or intimidate me, or both. I was dreadfully concerned, to say the least. Someone other than my mom was forcibly touching me "from across the veil". I recall how I'd sniggered when I'd first come across that term on the web. It sounded all lacey and much too delicate for what I was feeling. I was being incessantly poked and pounded. There was nothing dainty or refined about it.

I went into Canterbury to the shop called *Pure Magick* and spoke with the owner, Janis. Before I had a chance to explain why I'd come in to talk with her, she said, "He's not malevolent. He means you no harm. But he's big. His energy is huge. He doesn't mean to be frightening you."

I hadn't known, but Janis was a medium or what she liked to call "a sensitive". Apparently she could feel spirits. She could talk to them and to her invisible guides, whom she said were like personal aides. That's how she knew I was having some trouble with this particular spirit before I'd even opened my mouth.

I told her of the firm tapping I was feeling on my shoulder while I was trying to sleep at night and then she told me my rights, so to speak, in the spirit world. This was amazing and all new to me. I listened intently to what she had to say. She clearly had experience in this area and knew much more than I did.

I shared with her a bit about my mother's after-death contact and she said (just like my client, Erica had said before) that I was now "open" and spirits could now see me.

They must have read all the same books, because, she too, said I was like a little beacon in the night. My light was shining brightly for all who cared to see it. She continued saying that the visitor who was tapping on me was not trying to frighten me but I needed to set the ground rules with him. I had to let him know what I expected of him. As I heard her say this, I almost swore. I wanted to say, "I didn't invite him into my house and I don't expect anything from him!" But I stopped myself.

Almost reading my thoughts, she said that I was basically broadcasting an unwritten invitation with, "my lovely light." That was a very pretty thing to say to me but it didn't feel safe. Although I didn't understand why my "light" was transmitting so brightly now, apparently I had no choice but to believe her. After all, she had correctly told me that some big guy was bugging me before I'd even shared my problem with her.

She said that as it's my house, they (those in spirit form) had to play by my rules. There are universal rules that spirits have to abide by. Hearing this was comforting and it was certainly worth a try. Janis suggested, "Talk to him, as if you can see him. Talk to him directly and firmly. Tell him you don't want to be woken up at night and that you are a human and you need your sleep. Also tell him the conditions with which you will talk to him." This was interesting. I didn't think I wanted to talk to some big ghost at night, under any conditions!

She went on to explain that I set all the rules. I could tell him, or them, to leave. Or I could tell them that they could only talk to me or bother me during the day time. Or I could choose to direct them to talk to someone else, if I felt too uncomfortable dealing with them myself. She kept using the plural word *them* which I found a bit distracting and enormously distressing.

Evidently, whatever I decided that I was comfortable with, I had to tell them. She reckoned that I might need to be tough with them or at least with this one. She meant that I had to be verbally tough. I had to command them to do as I wanted. I had to be in control of any contact rather than letting them control it.

She then said that it was imperative that I was firm and not wishy-washy, because more would come if I were. Dang! This was not what I wanted to hear. Feeling my mother's loving touch and presence was fine, but more spirits? Just any unknown spirit could come to see *my light*? Why was that? What was this all about? I didn't like the sound of more spirits coming to visit me. Who'd opened me up anyway?

I was starting to wonder if I should be as thankful to my mother as I had originally thought. She'd left the spiritual door open and my light on as well. I didn't know if I wanted this and wondered if I could close it down or turn it off. But apparently once you're *open*, you're open! I had to learn to deal with it. I didn't have a choice in the matter.

I had naively or stupidly enjoyed the sense of security my locked bedroom door had provided. However, if they could come straight through locked doors and walls, how was I going to handle this? I wanted to be given an option. I didn't want them to just appear and start bugging me whenever they wanted. So I had to try Janis' instructions.

Janis also graciously and freely told me that she believed that this particular spirit was trying to give me messages for my clients who couldn't sense spirits for themselves. Well, a few months ago I couldn't either. So how did he know that I was prepared for this? Did my mom's contact brush off the dust or grime from my light? And how was I supposed to deliver his messages?

After thinking about it for a long time, I began to recognize that I'd been receiving limited messages already in a way. I'd empathically and accurately been sensing other people's feelings lately and maybe I'd been sensing spirits since I was little. But now, it seemed that I was being primed for more direct reception of information and knowledge. Atwater was right. There was more to come.

Another uninvited visitor

If the invisible guy at night who was tapping on me wasn't enough, I began seeing a part of a man (don't ask me how or why) sitting on our settee during the day time. For some reason the presence of this man, or his legs to be precise, his bottom half, did not even remotely bother me. I wasn't frightened by him in any way. It just seemed peculiar.

I began catching a glimpse of him. I saw his trousers and feet on my couch (or settee as we call it over here) when I entered the lounge (our living room) from our kitchen. Out of the corner of my eye, I'd spot his legs inside some sort of old fashioned blue colored trousers. They weren't jeans but they were casual, perhaps made of a blue polyester or cotton fabric. He was, or rather the bottom half of him was, reclining always with his feet up. I couldn't see anything above his waist. The rest of him, except his legs, was totally transparent or just not there.

He came for months (or the bottom half of him did anyway) and would randomly appear on our settee when I'd walk into the lounge. I always saw him in the same position. He'd just be there when I entered the room. It was one of those, out-of-the-corner-of-your-eye, kind of things. You know what I mean, something that's visible in your periphery but gone when you approach it head on and in full critical sight. I'd see him to the left of me as I'd walk into the lounge but when I'd turn my head to look straight at him, he would disappear from sight.

My wedding week

Six months had passed since mom had died. The bottom half of the man was still showing up on my settee occasionally but the other spirit that had been waking me at night by pounding on my shoulder had gone away for awhile. I had *talked* to him, or talked to the air at least, saying that I didn't want to be woken up in this way and that he should deliver his messages directly to my clients, just as Janis had recommended. I guess that had been enough. It had done the trick.

My sister, Claire had flown over to help me with the catering for my wedding to Matthew. We were having a marquee in our field and Claire and I were going to make all the food for the guests. She had owned her own deli and catering company previously and thought we could do it all ourselves.

We were working in my kitchen talking. The last time we had been together it had been to divide up my mother's things between us kids. We both were saying what a shame it was that mom hadn't made it, meaning that she hadn't lived long enough to come to my wedding. That's when the phone rang.

We stopped our conversation and I picked up the receiver. On the other end of the line I heard a gentle American accent say, "Ann, this is your Aunt Mary. I'm married to your mother's youngest brother, Tom. You don't really know us but we're here in England and would like to come to see you this week, if that's possible." My mouth dropped open in shock and then I composed myself and replied, "You can do more than that, you can come to my wedding. I'm getting married on Saturday."

Claire and I couldn't get over it. It seemed like only seconds had passed or maybe a minute at most since we'd commented on how sad it was that mom hadn't been able to be with us at my wedding. Then the closest thing possible to her showed up, her younger brother. I hadn't seen him or my Aunt Mary since I was about four or perhaps I was only two years old and now they were not only here in England, they were coming to my house the next day and going to attend my wedding on the weekend! It seemed like my mother was going to join in on my wedding after all. She just sent us her proxy. Claire and I knew that this was a sign from her to all of us.

The very next day, my Uncle Tom, who ended up looking distractingly like a male version of my mother, arrived to help us cook, make cakes and pies, and arrange flowers. He'd even been a florist at one time and as we were doing all the flowers for the church, marquee and wedding party he was a great help. We talked almost non-stop about my mother and our lives, while we all worked together in the kitchen over the next few days. I was delighted beyond words.

Uncle Tom and Aunt Mary sat where my mother and father would have in the church and at our family table at the reception. It was wonderful.

A few days after the wedding, Matthew left to attend a conference in California. It was only thirty miles or so away from where Aunt Mary and Uncle Tom had just traveled from. The coincidence was amazing. What a small world we live in.

We'd postponed our honeymoon due to Matthew's conference and planned to take a vacation later in the year. Perhaps, not too unexpectedly, I couldn't stop crying a few nights after he'd left. I was very disturbed. I hadn't cried that much since that first week after mom had passed away. I tried Matthew's mobile with no success and when I wasn't able to reach him, I telephoned his hotel. They said he had checked out. The next day when I finally contacted him on his mobile, he told me that he'd just moved to another hotel after the conference before his other customer meetings in San Jose. He said he'd just forgotten to tell me that he was going to do that. I had no reason not to believe him until a few months later.

In September, only three months after our wedding, I was crushed. I slid to the ground without a sound, paralysed by what I saw. The shock caused my legs to give way. It was the oddest feeling. The wind had been totally knocked out of me. The impact had been that great. My lungs burned and the pressure on my chest was immense. I was unable to breathe, speak or even lift myself from the floor where I had collapsed. I wondered if I'd die right then and there.

I remember watching myself from above, sliding down the wall in slow motion. Somehow I was viewing myself from another perspective. I was outside myself. I'd split into two. There was a surreal numb feeling about this moment. I was scared and I was cold. I was shaking uncontrollably. Was I about to die myself? My heart told me I should. It would be easier.

The impact had pushed me backwards so strongly that I melted into the magnolia paint on the plastered wall. I didn't know if I could move ever again. I saw myself as a fly that had just been swatted to death. I felt I wanted to die.

A few minutes after I'd crumbled onto the floor, I regained some cognition. I slowly pieced together what had just happened. But my chest hurt so much. I looked down and was surprised that nothing was on top of me. It felt so heavy and difficult to breath. There could have been an entire car on top of my chest. It felt that bad. I struggled under the invisible weight while something burned in me like acid. I'd never felt anything like this before. Even after I'd survived the initial impact, I thought my heart was going to explode and I'd die right there from a heart attack or stroke without anyone knowing.

As I tried to slow my pulse down, the situation came back to me. I wasn't going to die. I wouldn't be that lucky. I took the deepest breath that I could and looked again at the words in the text message. Only moments ago I was convinced my life was charmed. But now I knew that I had been deceived and I was in for another divorce.

You see I'd picked up the wrong identical NOKIA mobile phone. Matthew and I normally had different styles of mobiles but Matthew's more current model had broken and he'd been using one of our older phones for the last few months.

Casually, with my morning cup of coffee in hand, I had grabbed his mobile by mistake. Both mobiles usually sat on either end of our silver microwave oven in the kitchen. But this time I'd picked up his without realizing it. Happily sipping my coffee, I opened my messages to find Deirdre thanking my husband for their wonderful and romantic time last week. She went on to say it was so special that she decided she wanted it more regularly. She understood he had work commitments but why must their time together be so erratic and infrequent. She wanted him all the time and she wasn't going to accept his work commitments as a valid excuse any longer.

Just like I didn't know about her, she obviously didn't know about me! "They were right for each other," she'd said. She wanted to keep repeating what she'd been enjoying and was trying to convince my husband that there was no good reason, no valid reason at all, why they couldn't be together more.

Part of me wished I hadn't picked up his phone by accident and had just stayed in my oblivious cocoon of love, but I couldn't rewind time. I'd read the messages and they had knocked me for six.

I struggled to hurriedly pick myself up off the floor. Then I went up to my therapy room and locked the door behind me. Still shaking, I quickly forwarded the text messages I'd found from Deirdre to my own phone so I could read them again later or use them in court. I sat there dazed trying to figure out what I was going to do. Then I heard Matthew coming up the stairs. He was looking for his phone!

As he tried to open my door, I suspect he instantly realized that I had his phone. I'm sure he understood why I had locked the door and locked him out. He wanted me to let him in. But he seemed to want his mobile phone back even more.

I wouldn't do it! I couldn't open the door. I explained how I'd picked up his phone in error and that I knew about Deirdre. He could tell I was crying and pleaded with me to open the door, but I refused. I made him talk with me through the closed and locked door for more than an hour. I felt broken. I wept and wondered what was wrong with me, when I should have wondered what was wrong with him or with us as a couple.

Is that Matthew on the settee?

A few months after I'd picked up the wrong phone and been surprised to find that my husband still had a girlfriend even after he'd decided to walk me up the aisle, we were still together for some reason. It even appeared that he'd seen her in the states the week after our wedding and that's why he'd changed hotels and perhaps postponed our honeymoon.

He'd convinced me that he had been trying to call it off with her for a long time. He'd tried to use his work as an excuse once he'd decided to marry me, but she hadn't wanted to stop seeing him and had made breaking up very difficult. She'd never known about me, you see. He was single and a great catch as far as she knew. She thought he just had an intense schedule because of all of his business travel and high level role.

He professed his love for me and said he'd finally end it. In essence, he said that he'd been scared to put all of his eggs in one basket when he *committed to me* through marriage. I guess I was some kind of chicken now rather than the runt of a litter of dogs or kittens! We were going to try to rebuild our relationship. I was very understanding, maybe too understanding. Helping clients, I'd read that when someone had an affair that it meant that something was lacking in their relationship. I was willing to do the work to identify where we'd gone wrong so we could repair ours.

Blinded by love, I thought I could fix whatever had gone wrong. I suppose I thought it was my fault. I suspected he liked professional women more than work-from-home therapists. He'd convinced me to quit my job and feeling secure for perhaps the first time in my life, I had gone back to school leaving my big career behind. I could have supported myself and easily left him if I hadn't given up my telecommunications job. I felt lost. And for some unknown reason I couldn't, or felt I shouldn't, kick him out. I went back and forth in my mind about this decision many times, thinking that I should have.

It was midday, when I came into the lounge and saw Matthew reclining on the settee. He was working from home that day as he had an early morning meeting the following day in his company's English office in Winnerish Triangle near Reading. It was the same office that I had worked in. In fact, when he visited there, he used my old desk. He was working more and more from home now, when he could, to help me regain my trust in him. Now if he had to be at a meeting in the Winnerish Triangle office, he'd drive home no matter how late it was instead of staying at his uncle's home near the office which was very close to where Deirdre lived as I later found out.

I said, "Hi Matthew," as I approached him. Then I heard Matthew call from his office, "I'm in here honey." Wow! I turned quickly to take another look at the man I'd seen and had thought was Matthew, and of course, you guessed it, he was gone.

This was the first time I'd ever actually fully seen a ghost or spirit (that I knew of), although I'd seen this guys legs now for months and I'd felt my mother touch me. He had been so solid and real looking that I wondered if perhaps we all saw spirits but weren't aware of it. How do we really know that everyone we see is alive, if they can look like he did and are capable of caressing you as my mother had?

This man looked so much like my husband and so genuine that it was only after I'd heard Matthew's voice come from his office that I made the connection. It had to be his father and I wondered if Matthew hadn't been in his office that day if I could have sat down and talked with him.

My husband's father, James, had died many years earlier when he was only 56. I'd never met him when he was alive, but for a few months now it seemed he'd been coming to visit me. Often he'd show up when Matthew was away but this time he'd come when his son was home with me. I'd been seeing his legs and then his torso along with his legs until now, when I finally saw him completely. I'd never realized it was him. So again, I wondered why? Why was I now able to see Matthew's dad and feel other spirits around me? What was really going on? And why had I only seen part of him so many times and now I could see the whole man? Was I learning to see spirits or was Matthew's dad learning to move between invisible to visible? I figured the most likely thing was that he had always been coming to see his son but that neither Matthew nor I had been able to sense him – until my mother triggered changes within me.

Even before I'd seen this man's face, I'd started to speculate that it was Matthew's father. I'd already told Matthew that I was pretty sure that his father was visiting us now (or visiting me actually when he was away) just like my mother. I remember how I'd often giggle as I would tell Matthew on the phone, "I saw your dad's legs again." or "He came to visit me again today." And now that I'd seen him completely, I knew that what I had deduced on my own had been right. It had been James all along.

My dead father-in-law, who looked so very much alive, looked almost identical to how my husband looks right now. It was uncanny. I had known that they had similar looks, and even seen photographs confirming it but I hadn't known just how much Matthew looked like James in his prime.

I ran into Matthew's office to explain what I'd just seen and reminded him how I thought I'd been seeing half his dad in the lounge for some time now. Luckily for me, Matthew had seen a ghost for himself a few years back, not his father but someone outside the manor house at Higham Court, where the real Chitty Chitty Bang Bang car had been built. He'd also experienced my mother's smoke in our bedroom and saw the hairpins she'd left so I didn't need to do anything to convince him. He immediately believed me.

When Matthew had lived in one of Count Zborowski's properties, the creator of the actual car that the movie Chitty Chitty Bang Bang was based on, he chased an intruder across the lawn until the man disappeared in thin air, right in front of him. The current owners of the home had taken a picture of the suspected thief just before he had disappeared to give to the police as evidence, but when the film was developed (this was before the age of digital cameras) only an aura, a sparkling electrical outline of the man was visible. The camera and photo were both checked by Kodak and the picture was found to be accurate.

That very night after I'd seen my father-in-law, for the first entirely sitting relaxed on our settee, Matthew woke upset after having a dream about him. When he opened his eyes, he saw his dad standing over our bed. His father said, "Don't screw this up." Matthew told me that he was sure that his father was really there. He wasn't still dreaming. His dad had woken him with the dream so he could then talk with him. The experience brought Matthew to tears.

Ever since my mom died, both of us have come to accept and even honor her visits. But Matthew, until that night, hadn't ever seen or felt his father's spirit around him. It was an emotional experience for him, just as my mom stroking my hair had been for me. It meant so much to Matthew to see his dad again. Although at this point, I hadn't actually seen my mother after her death, she had made it known that she was there in so many other tangible ways. It was becoming more and more impossible for me to maintain my agnostic views.

Chapter Ten

The turning point

A year had passed and Matthew and I were celebrating our one year anniversary, much to both of our surprise. It was June 2005. His dad's legs were still visiting me occasionally and I had become really interested in *the unseen* as you can imagine. You could often find me trolling the Internet for information about spiritual things. Although my knowledge was increasing from what I was reading, it could not compare to what I was gaining through my experiential knowledge.

Amazingly, everything that was happening to me was being verified. If I doubted an experience, I would receive some synchronistic confirmation (often within twenty-hours) to neutralize my doubt. My faith in the spirit world was consistently growing, as you might expect – even if I still couldn't bring myself to believe in God. That was apparently going to be a big hurdle for me. I wasn't sure I could ever clear it. I'd have to work on that one or it would just have to sneak up on me unannounced.

Matthew was to attend the same annual conference that he'd gone to the week after our wedding the previous year. He invited me to come along so I wouldn't worry. My good friend Diana and her husband Sean (whom I'd met when I was in my early twenties) still lived in San Francisco, the same city where the conference was being held. We arranged to stay with them for a few nights while we were there. I was delighted.

Diana and Sean had always been into *the spiritual stuff* – ever since I'd met them, just like my best friend Katrina in Seattle. This was great. I finally had something spiritual to talk about. For once, I would be able to contribute! I guess I'd been around spiritual things, or at least my friends had been into it for quite some time, but I'd been purposefully closed off to most of it, except, I suppose for my love of rocks. There they were, right under my nose all the time. My best and dearest friends had been almost like spiritual gurus compared to me, but it took my mom's interventions, her little after-death acts to get my attention and *open me up.*

I spent my time with Diana and Sean while Matthew was at the conference each day. They worked for themselves and were home most days and evenings. We were cheerfully talking non-stop in their living room when all of a sudden I realized I felt someone was in the adjoining room. The man I sensed, and momentarily saw, was not a happy man. I told them what I'd thought I'd seen and I remember distinctively hearing Sean say quizzically and impressed, "Oh! She's seen our wildlife." He explained, that like me, they had their own little "visitor" in their apartment. Apparently that building had burned down during the San Francisco fire of 1906 and many people had died there.

They were surprised that I'd picked up on him. I'd been to their apartment before and I'd never noticed him. We spent that evening drinking wine and getting caught up on my crash course in spiritual development. I told them of the visitations and after-death contact I'd been having, along with a necessary quick update on my relationship. Matthew was at a dinner function that night which I hadn't really wanted to go to, so this was my chance to talk with my friends openly.

That night, I dreamt that I killed the man I'd seen in their bedroom and then told him to go to the light. It was a freaky dream. It appeared that he hadn't known that he was already dead, until I stabbed him with a sword. Diana and Sean have since told me that he's never visited them again. They were pleased as he'd been a real nuisance. He'd been bothering their daughter for a long time when she was trying to sleep, in the room that I was now using.

A few months before going to San Francisco, I'd noticed that people were mistaking me for a Reiki Master (someone who was trained to teach Reiki healing). Now, it seemed, Diana and Sean also thought that I'd already been trained to the higher master level. I corrected them and they kind of nodded, as if they were saying, "Yeah right." It seemed like an inside joke, as if they knew something I didn't.

The very next night, Matthew and I attended a "by invitation only" dinner which was being put on by the company who had organized the conference he was speaking at and attending. We were asked to sit at the table with some of the company's executives because Ravi, the head of development, had brought his wife, Mishti, who was a Reiki Master! Ravi had assumed that I was one too and thought we'd enjoy sitting together.

Mishti and I couldn't stop talking the whole evening. She was fascinating. She's a Hindu from India and meditates every day and is in constant connection with her spirit guides. Although, she was trained to Reiki Master level, I had as much experience with it as she did. Before the dinner had ended we'd been invited to their home the next day for lunch and she asked me if I'd like to look around Berkeley University with her. There was an open day for a spiritual course that she was considering and she wanted my opinion! I didn't' know why, but she felt that I would be able to help her decide if it was right for her. She said she'd really value my intuitive thoughts about it. So it was agreed. They'd meet us at the BART (Bay Area Rapid Transit) stop closest to their home on Saturday and she and I would go to Berkeley while the men talked business. Then we'd all have lunch on their terrace together. It sounded great.

Matthew had been doing business with Ravi for more than a decade and in all of his trips to San Francisco, he'd never been invited to his home. He was amazed how doors had opened just because he commented to Ravi that I did Reiki.

We had a lovely time at Ravi and Mishti's. Not only were they gracious hosts but Mishti introduced me to some spiritual authors and concepts I'd never heard about before. She showed me a book on spirit detachment which shocked me. I had thought that possessions weren't possible after speaking with Janis at the rock shop, but Mishti thought they were. I knew that I'd have to get the real skinny on this because it was just too frightening to even consider. Mishti said there are entities, or what she calls negative spirits that are sometimes confused by the suddenness of their death and would *miss the light*. When this happens they find themselves stuck in some kind of in-between place. I told her about my dream the first night at Sean and Diana's and how I'd seen this man go into the light after I'd killed him with the sword.

We also talked at great lengths about the benefits of meditation and whether I should become a Reiki Master. Although neither of us liked the spiritual course that was being offered at Berkeley, we enjoyed each others' company tremendously. We vowed to keep in touch and we have.

When we left Ravi and Mishti that day I was still considering whether I should become a Reiki Master or not. I still hadn't made my mind up. The whole spirit detachment stuff and negative entity thing which Mishti had introduced to me had really thrown me a curve ball. So I decided I needed to think it over further. I'd also remembered that in the previous Reiki training courses I'd taken (beginner and practitioner levels) that both Reiki Masters had said that becoming a master was a serious decision. It became part of your life and they said, "It couldn't be undone." It seemed a bit dramatic but maybe there was a reason why they wanted you to be sure about whether you wanted to be a master before you embarked on the next training.

Mishti hadn't warned me about advancing to master level at all, quite the contrary. She had told me that it would help me maintain greater control in my household over the various spirit visitors I was encountering. It would, "brighten my light," she'd said and any lower vibrational entities, as she called them, wouldn't like that much light. They preferred the shadows and would feel uncomfortable in my space. One of the books she had shown me was exclusively on this very topic. It had instructions on how to get rid of these lower level spirits. Again I questioned myself about what the hell I was getting involved with. I remembered my spiritual client's caution about how you were opening up to everything when you opened up. I thought again about her and Janis' description of me being a bright beacon. Maybe my light was not as shiny as Janis had led me to believe but was just barely on and only the "darker forces" could see it. Maybe Mishti was right? I asked Mishti what she thought about the idea of me being a beacon that told spirits that I was supposedly open for business. I wondered whether she might actually advise me to try to shut it off instead of upping the wattage. But she assured me that the more light I expressed and the stronger my light – the better. Light was always a good thing and never bad according to her.

In our brief time together, Mishti had told me alot. She had scared me too. She'd explained that there were levels of beings and that I only wanted to be dealing with beings that were "of the light". She'd felt that the man in Sean and Diana's house hadn't gone to the light after he'd died and explained that these were not the sort of spirits that she contacted. She only dealt with higher level spirits "of the light", those that had "passed over" "into the light". All of this was a bit like a riddle to me being such a spiritual novice. I was being given another crash course, this time in spiritual hierarchy by Mishti and she convinced me that I needed to be clearer on what I allowed into my home. She thought I'd really benefit from the Reiki Master training even if I never taught any students. She suggested that I learn to meditate too.

I felt that Mishti was sent to help me, but not all of what she'd told me sat well with me. Although she seemed to know so much more than anyone I'd spoken with before, I'm sure it had a lot to do with her cultural background. One of the things I liked was that she said that I could learn to talk with my own spirit guides, just as she did each day, if I would only take the time to meditate. Her life was devoted to spirituality and enlightenment. Her husband Ravi meditated as well – as did everyone in their family.

Before our plane had touched down at London Heathrow, I had decided that I couldn't ignore the many synchronistic events that had occurred. I would find someone to take me to Reiki Master level and I would also learn to meditate. I also knew that I wanted a teacher who understood the spiritual experiences I was having. I needed someone who knew what Janis and Mishti knew, maybe even more. I determined that I wanted someone who could help me learn to talk to my guides and how to stop the invisible man from waking me up at night.

I was certain that it wouldn't be either of the teachers that I'd had for Reiki training before. The first one hadn't wanted to talk about spiritual matters at all and the second one, Frank Arjava Petter, would have been wonderful but he wasn't local to me. I needed to find someone closer rather than travelling to Germany to train with him.

My first Reiki teacher's response to me, when I'd called her for help after my initial Reiki training, was dismissive. I'd wanted to discuss the amazing experience I'd had on the twentieth day of my twenty-one day self-treatment program. After my first initiation into Reiki, we were told to treat ourselves every day for an hour, for a total of twenty-one days. On the penultimate night (the night before the final night) of my Reiki "self-cleanse", I saw a golden ball of light appear before me in my bedroom. It came mysteriously from out of nowhere and was racing swiftly towards me. It hit me smack dab between my eyes, landing right in the middle of my forehead – in the same place which mystics call the third eye. My head flew backwards in response and the room was filled with golden sparkling light. The third eye or brow chakra is meant to be linked to your intuition, insight and even your ability to have clairvoyance. My teacher laughed at me when I told her about it and commented on how silly it sounded. She said I was imitating the experience of the founder of Reiki, Dr. Usui. On his 21st day of meditating and fasting he had what is called a Satori. In Zen Buddhism this is considered a temporary state of enlightenment. This Satori experience was what led him to discover Reiki and become a healer. My Reiki Master at the time thought I had made it up. I certainly didn't want to train to become a Reiki Master with that teacher.

Finding Sally

I decided that the best place I could start to look for a Reiki Master, who would understand spiritual issues and could guide me through whatever it was that I was going through since my mom had died, would be the crystal store. Janis had been so helpful before. I was confident she'd know someone that would be perfect for me and not one that would laugh at my ball-of-light-in-the-forehead experience. I needed a master that wouldn't disregard my requests for help if more spirits ended up finding my upgraded light even more irresistible. I needed someone who'd help me as I progressed down this path I didn't remember asking to go down.

Janis recommended two particular teachers, one of them was named Sally Macgregor. I left messages for both of them and then proceeded to call all the other Reiki Masters I could find in my area. Out of the seven Reiki Master-Teachers I interviewed on the phone, Sally was the only one who I spoke with that felt confident and competent to combine Reiki teachings along with spiritual principles. Surprisingly many of the masters I contacted either had never trained anyone to master level or said that they felt there was nothing spiritual about Reiki healing. One actually sounded disturbed and turned off by my questions about "presences" and what I thought were wonderful after-death experiences with my mother.

Sally seemed totally comfortable and knowledgeable about what I had to say. She was the only one who I'd interviewed who had been. When I called her she happily answered my question. She didn't rush me, and she listened respectfully and intently as I described what had been happening in my house. She was touched by my mother's contact and visitations. She understood the aspects of empathy and wasn't bothered at all by the big spirit who was tapping on my shoulder at night. She was engrossed by my description of how I'd found the hair pins and hangers, and how Matthew's dad had been seen on the settee.

Thinking back, I probably scared all the others away, except Sally. Even though they hadn't said so, I knew they didn't want anything to do with me and my light! Maybe they thought I was crazy? Or perhaps they believed that I had a poltergeist around me that might harm them. Or both!

As serendipity would have it, Sally only lived a few miles from my house. That was amazing. Maybe I wouldn't have to travel for hours into London or over to France or Germany after all.

We arranged to meet. She wanted to interview me to see if I was truly ready before she committed to taking me on. Sally greeted me warmly enough, but when we sat down to talk over a cup of tea I felt she could see right through me and into my soul. It was both unsettling and encouraging at the same time. I found out that she not only was a Reiki Master-Teacher who was only minutes from my home, but she had been a professional medium at one time.

Sally was exactly as I had hoped. She continued to ask me things I rarely told other people and then conducted tests to assess my psychic abilities. When she put her ring in my hand, I was amazed as information unexpectedly shot into my head. She asked me what I felt or *knew* about the ring or the persons who had worn it. I told her boldly, although I didn't understand why, "They're your rock, your stability." She smiled pleasantly and then asked me why I wanted to be a Reiki Master. I explained how I'd never wanted to be a master until recently when so many people I'd encountered had thought that I already was one. She asked me more questions about my life and my attitudes. Then she ran me through the rest of her psychic tests before she agreed to train me. She also surprised me by inviting me to join her weekly meditation and spiritual development group which was starting back up in the fall. She said I was the most spiritually open person she'd been asked to train in many years and that she was looking forward to it. I'd make a wonderful Reiki Master according to Sally. I was so excited and honored. I'd not only found a spiritually experienced Reiki instructor but I'd found someone to teach me how to meditate.

We agreed to start our one-to-one training August 15th and instead of lessening my paranormal experiences, it would increase the unusual occurrences. Becoming a master would continue to exacerbate *the problem,* brighter light or not, and further accelerate my transformation.

Chapter Eleven

There's no going back

Looking back, that summer (and especially August) was an incredible period for me. My life was becoming nothing but one high caliber or high tension event after another.

Like setting up a column of dominoes, each step I took to understand, to avoid or control what was happening to me only acted to place another domino in the row. Unknowingly my actions and decisions were now probably encouraging additional and more extreme things to occur. Soon my understanding of the world would topple just like a perfectly aligned row of domino tiles.

I remember debating whether to answer the phone as I lay in bed enjoying my morning coffee. I always sound quite hoarse in the mornings until I've spoken for a little while so I wasn't sure I wanted to pick it up. It was early though and it could only be Matthew calling from Germany an hour ahead of me. So I answered it anyway. I was wrong. It was Rod, who was only an acquaintance of ours back then. He was someone who we occasionally saw in the pub and he came to see me professionally for a back massage and Reiki once in a blue moon. He sounded like he'd been crying. His wife, Margaret, was apparently in the hospital and she was in critical condition. She'd had a bowel blockage earlier that week and things had gone terribly wrong. He said they weren't sure if she was going to make it and he wanted my assistance as a healer. I'd helped Rod with Reiki after my abilities had increased since my mom's death. He wanted to see if I could help his wife now. She was in the Intensive Care Unit (ICU) at the William Harvey Hospital in Ashford. Rod could hardly be around her. The possibility of losing her was so scary for him. I told him I needed to make some phone calls to cancel my appointments and then I'd meet him at the hospital that morning.

When I arrived, Rod was waiting outside the ICU. He grabbed me and walked me purposely away from the nursing station and told me that I would have to lie to get in. He wanted me to say that I was their daughter who lived in the states. Only immediate family members were allowed into the ICU and this was the plan he'd hatched to cover my American accent.

Rod's description of Margaret's condition hadn't prepared me for what I saw. There was so much rubber tubing coming out and going into her that I quickly understood how serious it was. Even I was frightened. Margaret was pale and her face contorted with fear. I'll never forget the amount of terror and non-verbal pleading I'd seen that day in her eyes. She was awake but intubated. There were machines breathing for her and monitoring her vital signs.

One of the nurses told me later that they always heavily sedate people when they are "tubed" because it's apparently like torture and very frightening. But they couldn't sedate Margaret because the doctors suspected she would never wake up if they did. So her blood pressure and heart rate were through the roof and they were constantly concerned that Margaret would arrest, until I arrived.

Margaret had been in the hospital already for a few days by the time Rod had called me. Her bowel had ruptured while she had been in the hospital because of a horrendous mistake on the part of the consultant overseeing her. She'd come in with a blocked bowel but he'd left her for days without doing anything about it until finally it had ruptured. She then underwent emergency surgeries to clean up the mess this had caused. Margaret had almost died in the process and now was hanging on by a thread. She had to be stronger before they could open her up again or she wouldn't come out of the operation alive. The doctors had more peritonitis to deal with, caused by feces getting into Margaret's gut. Once they'd taken care of that they could perform a partial bowel reconstruction and finish with a temporary colostomy.

It wasn't looking good for Margaret. She'd developed a serious lung infection and couldn't breathe on her own. The doctors would not attempt another surgery until she could breathe unassisted.

I leaned over and kissed Margaret's head. She was unable to move because of the pain and all the apparatus they had on her. I greeted her softly and immediately saw that she desperately wanted to speak to me, but she couldn't with the tube down her throat. I looked around for some paper to write on, assuming there would be something within Margaret's reach, but there wasn't any. I couldn't believe it. She'd been left like this for more than twenty-four hours in the ICU and hadn't been able to communicate with anyone except with her eyes and facial expressions. All the while, she could hear all the horrible things they were saying about her predicament, and all the nasty alarms indicating she was in dangerous territory. But she couldn't ask any questions or tell anyone how she was feeling or what she needed.

I was stunned. How could this be? Why had no one including her adult children and husband thought to get something for her to write with? Why had they complicated the already terrifying position she was in? I wasn't sure which was worse, my anger or my levels of shock and surprise. Not even the nurses had bothered to get a pen and paper for Margaret and you'd think that they would have encountered this before. I kept going over the details in my head. It seemed simple to me. So, why hadn't her husband, or her real daughter or son done something about this? Her arms weren't damaged. They appeared to be working just fine, as far as I could see, and so was her mind. This was cruel and ignorant in my opinion and totally unnecessary. No wonder her stats were so bad! I went to the nurses' station immediately. Then thinking about it more calmly, I realized the family must have been in too much shock to see the obvious solution. They weren't to blame at all. They were scared that they were losing their mother or in Rod's case, his wife. But for the nurses and the other medical staff members, who dealt with this every day, this was inexcusable.

67

When I returned to Margaret's bedside, I handed her a clipboard with a thick stack of paper on it and a felt-tipped pen. I also made sure that she was watching me as I placed spare pens and more paper on the bedside table. Then I began to stroke her hair to calm her down, just like my mother had always done for me. The first thing she wrote was, "I need to get this tube out – I'm terrified."

Whenever the nurses and the doctor came around, I did my best to speak on Margaret's behalf. I asked them questions about why she had the tube in and when she'd be able to have it removed. Apparently they wouldn't even consider taking the tube out until her blood oxygen levels were higher. They said she needed the machines right now until her breathing was stronger. When they left, Margaret scribbled, "Can you help me with some breathing exercises?" She understood now that she needed to be breathing down into the lower sections of her lungs. She was determined to get that tube out of her throat and was so pleased I was there.

We went through tons of paper as she asked further questions and told me things she wouldn't have told her family, even if she could have. She didn't want some of them to visit her right now, but she feared they'd feel rejected. Apparently their visits were more upsetting to her than not. Their crying and frightened faces were disturbing for her. She could tell by looking at them just how bad things really were.

She only wanted me to be there with her, if that were at all possible, at least for right now while things were so gloomy. Her husband's presence specifically seemed to increase her anxiety. It must have been very difficult for him to see his wife in that state and understandably hard to appear calm around her.

She asked me to stay as long as I could and refused to let go of my hand for most of the day. I stayed seven hours by her side attempting to relax her. I massaged her legs and feet, I gave her Reiki and talked quietly to her while I held her hand. Later that day together with a couple of nurses and one doctor, they took the tube out of Margaret's throat and I continued to coach her on her breathing. She had to breathe very deeply in order to maintain the required oxygen level in her blood. If she were successful in doing this they wouldn't have to put the tube back in. She maintained proper levels for thirty minutes but then she was exhausted from all the effort and wasn't able to breathe deep enough any longer. We both cried when they reinserted the tube and turned the machines back on. Margaret's final notes to me that day were, "Please can I ask you to be with me tomorrow EARLY. The night staff don't give A1 and I can't speak or call. I don't want to write incriminating things. I need you to keep me calm. You go home now and come back." I agreed to clear my appointments again and come back first thing the next day.

I returned long before visiting hours had started that morning as I'd secretly agreed with Margaret. I convinced the nurses to let me in earlier than usual by reminding them (lying) that I had flown all the way from the United States to be with my mom.

As soon as I saw Margaret, I knew it had been a rough night. She looked worse, if that were possible and of course she was still intubated, just as she'd been when I'd left her the night before. She wrote in huge capital letters as soon as I came to her side, "ANNIE FREEZING." I arranged her blankets and went to find more.

Once that had been taken care of, I plugged in my CD player and played some soothing music to drown out the sounds of the machines a little. I proceeded to liberally douse Margaret with drops of neat lavender and tea tree essential oils. I put it all over her bedding and pillows, as well as on her chest, neck and arms. I was trying to limit her chance of picking up any further infections like the MRSA bug that was so prevalent in that hospital. Patients and even visitors were dying from contracting MRSA too frequently to ignore.

Again I stayed all day with Margaret. Throughout the visiting hours I did my best to keep her calm. I talked about lovely distracting topics. I read to her, gave her Reiki and more massages, and attempted to reassure her that everything was going to be okay, even though we both knew that might not be true. I wiped her face, and moistened her lips when she needed it, and wondered often why her family weren't doing this for her. I even got her son to read out loud to her rather than read silently to himself on his visit.

Margaret was a fighter. Before the day was done, she had convinced the doctors twice that she wanted to try to breathe on her own. Both times after having the tube out for almost a half an hour and being able to talk to me and her husband her blood stats were not good enough and they intubated her again while she was totally conscious. This was one of the most emotional things I'd ever been a part of. The sadness and disappointment was immense. The medical staff assured us that once her infection had cleared a bit more that she should have better luck. Instinctively, I then did the only thing and possibly the best thing I could have done. I helped her visualize her favorite place in all the world, her lovely park-like garden, while I stroked her head non-stop.

It was getting to that time when all the visitors were supposed to leave. I could see and hear from the alarm bells that Margaret was getting more and more agitated. Quickly she wrote, "LAST NIGHT NOBODY SPOKE TO ME AND I THOUGHT I WAS GOING TO CHOKE TO DEATH." She didn't want me to leave and was certain she'd die if I did.

I made my way to the nurses' station again. I've forgotten how often I went there over those two days. I pleaded with them to let me stay the night with *my mom*. I suspected they knew that I was lying but it was worth a try. What else could I do? I said I'd be content sitting in the chair by her side. They didn't need to attend to me. The first nurse I spoke to said, "No," and explained that they never allowed visitors to stay overnight in the ICU. I asked to speak to the ward sister (the head nurse of the ICU) and luckily for us she had been observing how Margaret's overall stats had always improved when I was around. The ward sister said I could stay.

Feeling reassured, Margaret's husband, Rod, went home to rest and I held vigil, so she could try to get some sleep. I promised I'd stay awake and watch over her all night. She could relax. If she had any difficulties at all I would be there and could be her voice to call for help.

The scene I found myself in seemed surreal. I barely knew Margaret then. Although we'd been invited over to her and Rod's house for lunch once or twice and I'd found it really coincidental that their old Ferguson tractor had a license plate containing my full last name (CAP), we were really no more than casual acquaintances. Nevertheless, I was there for her as I had wanted to be for my real mother. Ironically, too, just like my mom's body on her last days, Margaret's had blown up as if someone had pumped her full of air because of all the toxins and peritonitis. She wasn't eliminating her waste nor excreting her toxins properly since the rupture. Her skin was taut on her legs and abdomen, and she was in tremendous pain.

When the night staff took over, we both tried to settle in. I put two chairs together to make a quasi bed next to Margaret's. It was still close enough to be in constant contact with her, so I could give her Reiki and keep a hold of her hand to comfort her through the night. With the lights on the ward turned down, the sounds of the many monitors and patients' cries seemed pronounced. There was a relentless chorus of discordant and threatening bells, blips and pings tracking the vital signs of each patient. Even today the sound of an electronic bell will send Margaret into a flashback.

Even though the sun had set, the ward glowed with a strange green illumination coming from the many monitors, and there was one lone lamp on the frequently unmanned nurses' station.

Holding Margaret's hand through the bedside grill was rather uncomfortable but the tightness of her grip told me I would be wrong to bother adjusting it. I'm sure it gave her an improved sense of security. Finally for the first time since I'd come to the hospital I saw Margaret sleep.

The night took on a dreamlike quality although I never slept. I couldn't with all the noise but also I was going to keep my promise to Margaret. I listened to the sounds on the ward. A male patient, three beds to our left, whimpered nonstop and another patient two beds over from him arrested and died after a failed attempt to restart her heart. Finally about three in the morning all the patients were quiet and I think I was the only one awake when Margaret started making a very queer sound and was moving her neck strangely. She was gagging or something. All of a sudden her monitors showed that her heart rate and blood pressure were skyrocketing. I yelled for the nurses, set off the emergency call alarm and pushed the clipboard and pen into Margaret's hands simultaneously. She scribbled as fast as she could, "SICK. Tube pressing on air way." Then within seconds, her face and the bells told me how serious this was. She appeared to be choking or trying to regurgitate into her tube. There was a wild petrified look on Margaret's face and her eyes seemed larger than humanly possible. She was going to suffocate if I didn't get help fast. I screamed for attention again and as no one was there to hear me, I sprinted down the ward to find someone to help her. Just as I made it to the entrance of the ICU, a doctor and three nurses came through the doors responding to the alarm I'd raised when Margaret had first stirred.

I stood watching as they quickly put the bed flat and told Margaret that they had to reposition the tube. Apparently it had dislodged from its proper position. Now it was cutting off her air and causing her to gag and vomit. Then swiftly with no additional medication and with Margaret completely awake and me watching, the doctor pulled the tube out, only to put it back in the correct position a minute later. They secured it this time using an excess of gauze and surgical tape on Margaret's face and neck. It wasn't going to budge ever again. Margaret and I cried silently.

Once they were gone, I stood over her and took her hand. She squeezed mine as hard as she could and blinked her eyes firmly indicating her gratitude. I wiped her brow with a clean damp wash cloth and kissed her head before I sat back down by her side. She stuck her whole arm this time through the grill and patted me. We locked hands again and then both closed our eyes. The rest of the night thankfully was uneventful. When Margaret awoke in the morning she looked much better. She was over the hump.

I stayed three or four hours into visiting time overlapping with her husband's visit. I told him about our night out of ear shot of Margaret and before I'd left it was agreed that he'd be allowed to stay with Margaret on the ward that night. Margaret told me in front of her husband (in writing) that she knew that I had saved her life.

Feeling very numb, yet content, I drove home and immediately took a bath. That night I slept horribly with tons of nightmares and I awoke in the early hours covered with sweat. There was so much of it that it was like I was laying in a puddle. I'd never seen so much sweat. My husband had to give me a bath sheet to soak it up.

After two nights of having someone stay with Margaret, she was finally strong enough to come off the ventilator. When she was able to speak, the head nurse on the ward (the sister) came over to see her. Margaret thanked her for allowing me to stay the night. The sister had made an exception because she'd witnessed the positive impact that I'd had on Margaret's stats earlier that day on her shift. She then admitted that they'd thought her chances had been only 50:50, whether she'd live or die that night. That was another big reason why they let me stay over. It would improve Margaret's chances or I would be with my *mom* if she'd died.

The sister wanted to know what I'd been doing for Margaret. Why were there such significant and improved results when I was around her? Margaret explained that I was a friend of hers who was a healer, not really her daughter, and that even my presence had calmed her. Before leaving Margaret's bedside, the sister promised to rethink the visitor policy on the Intensive Care Unit ward.

71

Beyond Goodbye

Only a few weeks after Margaret's emergency, a friend of ours died in a mo-
torcycle accident. Arthur was only thirty when he crashed with his fiancée on
the back of his bike. He was cruising at some crazy speed and lost control. His
girlfriend survived, relatively physically unscathed with only a broken shoulder,
although it would appear for years after that she wished she had died along with
him.

More death

Arthur's death hit everyone who knew him very hard. He was a wonderful
young man who was full of life. Bizarrely, his brother, and only sibling had died
a few years earlier in a freak car accident, when a gazelle escaped from the local
zoo and darted in front of his car. Arthur's fiancée had also lost her only sibling,
when her sister committed suicide by jumping to her death off a multi-story car
park.

I lingered in the bath that morning (the day after Arthur had died), topping
up the water occasionally to keep it warm. I had a lot to think about. It was mid
August and my Reiki Master training should have started that day but Sally had
called to postpone until the next day. She was getting over a minor cold. My
mind was jumping around between thoughts of Arthur's mother, his fiancée, and
their family. I couldn't imagine how devastated his mom must be feeling after
losing her second son and only other living child. I tried to consider how terrible
Arthur's fiancée and her parents must also be feeling. I remembered being surrounded by death and dying with Margaret on the ICU only a few weeks earlier.
Then abruptly I found my mind preoccupied with my old childhood fears again.
The nighttime activity in my home had accelerated after my stay on the ward the
night when Margaret almost died.

As a child, I had always thought that someone, or something, lived under my
bed or in the closet with my shoes under the hanging clothes. I imagined that
whatever it was could come out at any time and attack me, when it was dark. In
order to fall asleep, I came up with my own protection ritual, way back then, before I ever knew the term. I'd attempt to go to sleep with my fingers crossed for
safety, but being a smart girl, I knew that as soon as I relaxed my fingers would
uncross and then I'd be unprotected. Somehow I convinced myself that many of
the hairs on my head, maybe hundreds even, were always crossed. That would
certainly be sufficient to keep me safe.

As I write this now, it's dawning on me just how strongly I believed in the
invisible when I was small. I had been only four or five years old when I came up
with all these safety procedures, all by myself. I knew back then that something
in the darkness could touch me, if I didn't take counter measures. And as an adult,
now that something was tapping on my shoulder at night, I immediately gained
a deeper appreciation for my *silly* childhood coping strategies. I no longer think
of my younger self as a fragile wimp who had too vivid an imagination. Maybe it

hadn't been that ridiculous or childish to have been as afraid of the dark all those years. I've come to realize that I must have been somewhat spiritually sensitive from the start.

I've even begun to wholly respect and understand my nightly long jump routine. Poised in the hallway each night, I'd leap as hard, and as far as I could, in order to land safely on top of my bed. I had to keep my feet and legs from touching the ground near it or I might be grabbed by the thing that I thought hid underneath. Not even my little toe could touch the bedroom floor I'd thought, if I were to survive the night.

While I soaked in the bath, I decided to close my eyes and simply focus loving thoughts on Arthur. As soon as I did this, I saw him in my mind standing and smiling in front of me. Behind him were clouds that started to form a staircase leading up to a heavenly light. I spoke to Arthur and told him to go to his brother. Then I saw him turn and wave as he climbed the steps and then he disappeared. It was a very pleasant vision.

More nighttime visitations

Only the week before, I was jolted back in time, when I felt someone touch my feet from the foot of my bed! I was four years old again for a few terrible moments! Matthew had been away as usual, and I'd been alone in bed, in the dark. Then I felt it, my worst childhood nightmare and fear happened for real.

Surprisingly, after my brief regression, I started to feel pissed off! Rather than letting my fear increase, I got mad. Everything I'd read recently had told me that this sort of behavior was not allowed in the spirit world. They weren't supposed to harass me like this. After I'd first spoken to Janis about the shoulder tapping guy, I'd made a sincere effort to learn all I could about spirit contact "etiquette" and being supported by angels, including my personal so-called guardian angel. I'd read by now that everyone had a dedicated guardian angel and that this angel was supposed to act as your personal doorman. It was meant to keep you safe and keep negative spirits away from you. So were the heck was mine?

Although the shoulder tapping and the hangers in the hallway had definitely reduced since I'd begun loudly *talking* to the spirits stating MY rules of engagement in MY house, I was feeling that my guardian angel wasn't really taking his or her part very seriously. My guardian was slacking in his or her responsibilities!

I shouted this time, angrily telling whoever it had been who had touched my feet that they weren't to startle me. I didn't want any surprises or physical contact without my permission. This had to stop – because I said so! I knew my rights.

I got out of bed and walked around my entire home. Thank God nobody was there to see me. I strutted around the place, speaking furiously at the top of my voice. I announced to the air my new instructions. I told everyone firmly (even though I couldn't see or sense them right then) that they weren't to scare me. They weren't to pop out unexpectedly or frighten me – ever.

There'd be no more Mrs. Nice Guy in this house. I also told them that if they had messages for me or wanted to contact me, for any reason, that they must do it in a pleasant, non-threatening way and preferably in the daylight. Still fuming I said, "I don't want to see any shadowy figures that will scare me. I've had enough of this."

For some reason, in spite of everything (which I don't totally understand) I was still willing to allow them to contact me, but only if done under my terms. I just didn't want them to frighten me, or harm me in any way. That was all. I didn't mind if they hung around, but if their contact scared me I told them that they would, "have to leave my house and never come back." Maybe subconsciously I knew that if I stopped them from coming, that my contact with my mom would end.

I reminded them, in my unrehearsed speech, that I knew that I could call on angels to bodily remove any spirit that did not adhere to my guidelines. Also, I told them I'd discovered that ultimately I was king in my physical environment and that they had to obey me. I really hoped that these things which I'd read were true and that I hadn't fallen into the deep end! Somehow, though, I knew that all this was accurate. I just had to become strong enough to declare my boundaries.

One of the most influential things I came across was someone who said that we had total autonomy at all times. We are always in charge and spirits cannot take over our bodies or harm us unless we invite them to do so. I found this fascinating to ponder and extremely comforting. I instinctively felt that it was true and I understood that somehow my fearfulness was unknowingly inviting disruptive contact.

Apparently there was little or no difference between establishing and maintaining boundaries within my personal, physically alive, relationships and setting and maintaining boundaries in the non-physical realms.

As you can imagine, I was startled and annoyed when I was disturbed again in my bed only two nights after Arthur's death. My recent dramatic speech and anger apparently hadn't been enough. I sat up in bed and screamed at the persistent spirit who was tapping on my shoulder again. I turned on the lights and loudly announced, in a threatening manner, my rules of the house once more. Just in case I was unclear before or too gentle, I strongly reminded them that they were not to make any approaches that would startle me or they would have to leave, regardless of whether they had a message to deliver or not. What was I, some bloody post office? I said, "None of you are welcome any longer in my house, if you refuse to abide by my rules." I calmed myself down and turned off the bedroom light. Irritated but confidently, I snuggled back under the duvet.

Later, that same night, I was awoken by a nice feeling on my right hand. It was tender. It felt cool, as if the fingers of my hand were in a gentle stream. The sensation was lovely. It was very pleasant. I opened my eyes and saw a set of eyes above me. They were beautiful. They were a fabulous greeny-blue color and they were just floating in the air in front of me, sweetly looking at me. There was nothing else there, only these two magnificent eyes. There was no face, no body – just the eyes separated and surrounded by air. We stared at each other, they blinked at me and then they were gone.

Awake now, I decided to get up to pee. I turned the key which unlocked my bedroom door, opened it and stepped out onto the landing where the hangers were sometimes scattered. Then I saw it. And it was gorgeous.

Directly in front of me was what I knew was an angel. Right there in the hallway, only a few feet ahead of me, just beyond the entrance to the bathroom, was a stunningly beautiful sight. It was an iridescent, see-through, sparkling angel. It was just wiggling there on the landing, pulsing with gorgeous energy and light. Every part of it was moving in and out in a dynamic and yet unpredictable, delicately fluid way. Light radiated from it as it continually changed shape.

I watched as soft waves of light perhaps best described as rounded, slow moving, peaceful lightning bolts, extended in every direction at varying intervals from its being. These tentacles or ribbons of light moved in concert yet were staggered in length. No two were the same or ever stopped changing. There was no obvious pattern or order to the movement. Nothing about it was ever still or solid at any time and the transparent, ever changing, sparkling colors it was generating were unimaginable.

It was big and moving like a pulsing star. It had a brilliance and clarity I'd never seen before. Bits of it were shooting out in all directions only a foot or so in front of me. It was somehow clear and see-through yet white and gauzy at the same time, with sparkling specs of light throughout. It was kind of like looking closely at sandblasted glass or through ice crystals on a frozen window. There were thousands of twinkling flecks of opalescent light shimmering on the landing in front of me.

The angel stretched all the way to the ceiling while constantly moving in all directions. It maintained the same general size and shape as it individually expanded and retracted its many light extensions. So delicately and smoothly it pushed and pulled its light about. It twinkled and sparkled continually while it delicately oscillated and perpetually pulsed.

I wouldn't say it had wings exactly – more like energetic extensions. It had many translucent, glistening, sparkling waves of light that came out from its core. These waves of pointed extensions or arms reached out in all directions. I suppose like a star's light would. They were in no way fixed or rigid. They were continually, gracefully changing. As some of the extensions were being pulled back into the center of its being, numerous others of varying sizes and lengths would grow to softly poke or probe the air around me. It was simply beautiful and in no way threatening. I only felt love and comfort from it.

There was no head per se, or eyes for that matter. But it felt to me like a being of extremely high intelligence and I knew it was benevolent. It took my breath away when I first saw it but then it was like we were both staring at each other, feeling each other's energy I suppose.

It didn't come any closer to me, yet I had no desire to move away from it either. I just stood there and absorbed what I was experiencing. It was so calming and beautiful. The angel continued to sparkle and pulse, moving its energy around me. I recall how thick it had been and how it somehow appeared to be more than three dimensional. It was perhaps eight or nine feet tall and six to eight feet deep at its center core or heart, although it was always changing in size. The tips of the many light extensions (I can understand how some might see them as feathers) were reduced down to an extremely fine rounded point. It's energy extended beyond the width of the second floor landing. I wasn't scared by it at all and I couldn't take my eyes off of it or turn away. It was that beautiful. I felt bathed in love and at ease as I observed it.

I watched it until it slowly disappeared, leaving sparkles of all colors hanging in the air after it had left. The colors, both in the transparent angel's body and the flecks of opal-like shading of its extensions were not like our colors. They were different and greater in some indescribable way than any colors that I had ever seen before on earth. Maybe they were multi-dimensional colors? I don't know. I had never really put much thought into the idea of multiple dimensions until my mom had died. Somehow these colors had added vibrancy and life to them, much more than our normal colors. They had more depth and impact. I believe I must have somehow "experienced" the colors and their beauty rather than just having seen them. I sensed these colors with more than just my eyes. I felt them. I also had the feeling of being very safe. My language cannot fully express or explain how wonderful this angel looked or how great I'd felt being near it.

Once the angel disappeared I knew I had come in to contact with something extremely special and that it would watch over me while I slept or engaged in any other activity. Although I didn't hear it speak to me or give me any verbal messages that night, and of course by now I knew that message delivery was one of the primary functions of angels, I did somehow understand that things would be different from now on. This angel would be there to keep unwelcome spirits from touching me. Maybe it let me see it because I'd doubted whether I really had a guardian angel helping me at all. Or maybe it came because I'd yelled at mine for slacking off? Either way, it didn't matter.

My fears, in general, dramatically diminished after this angel encounter. I stopped worrying so much about being bothered by spirits at night, and I happily imagined this beautiful and fantastic, sparkling being of light assisting me, keeping me safe by standing by as my loyal guardian.

The very next day after the angel had showed itself to me I started my Reiki Master classes with Sally. The one day postponement had been perfect and I felt becoming a master now was even more appropriate. Although the training itself didn't feel that significant, apparently the process of the master initiation and perhaps the concentrated discussions about spiritual matters must have acted like someone had stoked my fire. The *new* senses and abilities that had been awakened in me by my mom's death were now amplified even more.

Chapter Twelve

Receiving messages

September arrived and I started going to Sally's spiritual development group once a week. After the events of last month, the timing couldn't have been better. In fact, as luck had it, Sally had changed the night of her classes just so I could attend.

Every Tuesday, six or seven of us sat together in the tiny building in Sally's backyard and attempted to contact our spirit guides, angels and deceased relatives. Shockingly, here I was actively and excitedly trying to learn how to do what I'd previously been too afraid to consider. As you might expect, I downplayed the whole spiritual aspect of this group to my husband. I spent so much time alone while he was away, I hadn't told him everything about my new interest. Matthew thought I was attending a *normal* meditation class, whatever that is. I decided not to concern him with the broader details, worried he might think I'd gone over the edge or become one of those airy-fairy people we used to laugh about.

Once everyone had arrived and we were seated in the circle of chairs inside Sally's nicely decorated shed, she'd turn out the lights and begin. The evening was always started in the same way. Sally would light a candle and recite a sort of prayer, which she called a dedication. She'd ask for divine protection and welcomed any spirits of the light. She stated that nothing else was allowed to enter our circle. Once this had been completed, Sally, or one of the others, would lead us in a guided meditation. Sometimes we'd simply stare at a candle in silence and other times we'd try to imagine ourselves walking down a path to a meadow or woodland glade where we'd hopefully meet and talk with our personal spirit guides.

When I first started attending the group it was obvious that I was the beginner and the others were very experienced. Everyone but I and a lady named Lynn, also relatively a novice, were on a first name basis with their non-physical guides, guardian angels and something they referred to as their gatekeepers. They could recognize when these beings were near them and easily heard their messages.

The stories of their experiences during the meditations were magnificent, filled with angelic contact and beauty. Although I felt a bit out of place to begin with and embarrassed by my lack of knowledge and seeming inability, I knew I'd really seen an angel myself. However there were times when I wondered if some of them weren't making it all up.

In the first weeks and months in the group, I had great difficulty following along with the guided meditations. I wasn't able to imagine things as vividly in my head as the others could. After each meditation, when Sally asked us to share our experiences, I usually had very little to say. While Nick, her brother, might say that he'd spent his time, "saving lost souls," guiding them to the light, and Jenny had floated amongst the clouds while talking with her guides or swam with dolphins to Atlantis, I'd simply have felt a quiet stillness within me. Often though, I felt I'd been conversing with my mother. Mom and I had little chats during most of the earlier sessions I had at Sally's. Mom and I would usually talk about common everyday things. Once she'd suggested that I should make more meat pies for Matthew and sometimes I'd see a younger version of her with my mind's eye in her favorite emerald green dress.

Although I did my best to follow along during the visualizations, frequently my meditation results were very different than the rest of the group. I regularly found myself just contemplating my life or thinking I was talking with mom. I actually was having excellent success but hadn't realized it.

After meditating or *visualizing*, we'd spend some time each week doing exercises to develop our intuition and sensing abilities. I was pleased when I found I was quite good at these *games* and I always enjoyed what the others had to say as well. One of the most interesting practices was when we'd "read" an item like a ring or some other object that one of us had brought in that evening. (Just like Sally had asked me to do before she'd agreed to train me.) Sally called this psychometry, although I kept confusing it with psychometrics, the aptitude tests I'd had to take with AT&T and Cable and Wireless when I'd interviewed with them. On the nights that we'd planned to do this type of reading, everyone would bring at least one thing in with them and place it under the towel which covered Sally's tray without anyone seeing it. This way no one knew what anyone had brought or who each item belonged to. It was startling how accurate the readings were.

After our Christmas break, Sally started to have us chant before we meditated. This had a dramatic effect on me and significantly improved my meditations. My favorite was a Buddhist chant called Gate Gate (pronounced gah tay, gah tay). I found I was able to go deeper into my meditation whenever we chanted this particular one.

By now I'd been meditating with this group once a week for four months and like everyone else I thought I was in contact with my guide and gatekeeper. I'd learned that the gatekeeper was responsible for allowing or denying spirits access to me kind of like a guardian angel. They kept lower level beings away from you and only permitted contact by those they trusted and knew would be of benefit. Just like the others, I was now sensing more contact than just my mother in our sessions. I actually felt I was conversing with some kind of spirit guide in my head and had consistent physical sensations whenever it was around.

Then on February 14th, 2006, on my Grandmother Elaine Valentine's birthday (my mom's mother), I had something amazing happen. That particular Tuesday we'd started by chanting Gate Gate and then Sally led us straight into our meditation without stopping. For some unknown reason, things felt quite different that night.

Just before Sally indicated that we should think about finishing our meditation, I realized that I wasn't able to move my arms. I felt like I was partially paralyzed and when Sally prompted us to come back mentally to the room and instructed us to open our eyes when we were ready, I knew I couldn't.

Sally had been silently watching each of us while we had been meditating (one of the duties of whoever led the visualization each night, although I'd never understood why until then). Now her gaze was fixed on me alone. As she continued to watch me sitting there, I heard her tell the group, "I think Annie was about to go into trance and was going to channel." Although I could hear her, it was as if she were talking about me from a great distance. I felt I was somewhere else and wasn't focused or concerned with what was happening in the shed around me. Sally quickly convinced the group to go "back in" and she asked them to be patient while she worked with me.

I didn't have a clue what she meant when she said, "I was going to channel." I hadn't ever heard this term. Then with all eyes on me, Sally used her soft melodic voice to help me return to the deep mental state she'd somehow witnessed I'd reached. As I hadn't completely come out of it anyway, I was soon quickly back into my semi-frozen position. Sally then began to ask questions. Oddly she wasn't addressing them to me but rather to whomever it was that she thought was "with me". She seemed to be trying to get the spirit to converse with her using my voice box. It felt like whoever it was that was "with me" was now somehow sharing my body or my mind, as if I were just a shell or vessel for it. It appeared that Sally thought that somehow someone else was resident inside of me.

Only the week before something similar but not as extreme had happened also at the end of my meditation. I'd felt as if my husband's Uncle John, who had died only a few days earlier, had come to talk to me along with my mother. In my head I could hear them both speaking. My mother's dead older brother, Richard, was also there. They were discussing my Uncle Tom's health (the uncle I'd met the very week of my wedding last year). They told me that he was seriously ill and wanted me to check on him. Then all of sudden, everything went quiet and fuzzy within me and for the first time I felt this strange paralysis. Sally was just about to end the meditation when she noticed a change in my posture and my appearance. Before anyone knew what was happening she'd broken the silence in the room and was asking if there was a spirit with me.

Although last week I (or it) was unable to answer her and I couldn't open my eyes, my head had started to rotate in a small circle. Sally stood up, placed her crystal pendulum over my head and asked her question again. She explained to everyone later that she'd seen another face "overshadow" mine and that my body had taken on the appearance of a man's for a few minutes. Her pendulum confirmed to her that a spirit had "joined me".

Tonight however when Sally asked her questions, someone else's voice came out of my mouth! It was an extremely quiet, raspy male voice. The whole time he spoke through me my hands felt like they were burning up. My left hand jerked back and forth at my wrist and spastically twitched. Although it was difficult to hear him, when Sally asked if he could speak any louder he said, "She's not ready." Meaning me, I guess! Sally then asked who she was speaking with and, "Ramses," was the reply. Then she asked if he had any words of wisdom for us and he said, "Thank you. Thank you. Thank you. You are on the right path. Keep going. Keep going." Suddenly he was gone. He left so quickly that my neck snapped backwards as if I'd been whiplashed in a car accident.

Sally was very pleased and told us afterwards that she felt this spirit had come to be our new teacher. Most likely he'd lead the group once I was strong enough to accept his energy! Apparently she'd always expected this might happen to me and had been watching me closely for weeks. Nick was ecstatic. He told me Ramses was an Egyptian pharaoh.

Before we met up again, I spent every available moment I had finding out what channeling was. I emailed my two good friends in the states confident that they'd be able to point me in the right direction. Of course, as Diana has lived in San Francisco all of her life, a city known for its spiritual bent, she'd been exposed to channeling for some time. Katrina in Seattle seemed to know a lot about it, too. Apparently they both had read "channeled" spiritual books and had paid to see "channelers". Diana owned a whole series of audios by Jack Pursell, who channels a being called Lazarus. Diana said Pursell had been made famous by Shirley MacLaine's spiritual coming out book, *Out on a Limb*. She also mentioned Jane Roberts who channeled Seth. Katrina emailed me about a lady named JZ Knight who channels Ramtha, and Sanaya Roman who speaks for the entity called Orin.

When I arrived at Sally's group the week after the Valentine's Day which I'll never forget, it was obvious that not everyone was excited by my channeling. It was threatening to take center stage and might disrupt some of the others plans for their own spiritual growth.

My feelings were hurt and I felt slightly assaulted when Lynn boldly announced right before we started meditating that she felt Ramses would not come that night because our expectations were too high. She curtly declared that I wouldn't be able to do it again.

Lynn was right, at least that night, because after her comments my mood drastically dropped and I couldn't channel. Much to my surprise, I sobbed when I got home that night. That's when I realized if I wasn't careful this could become like an addiction. It had felt so wonderful when it had unexpectedly happened and my excitement and anticipation had peaked after hearing from Katrina and Diana. Just thinking about it made me feel a bit high. I made a pact with myself then that I would only do it if it were healthy for me. I vowed not to let it control my life in any way. If it were going to happen – it would. But I refused to allow myself to get all wound up about it if it didn't.

But the next week in our meditation, he came back. And he answered the questions that Diana had emailed to me the week before when Lynn's comments had put me off. Sally and Nick were equipped with printouts of Diana's questions and my microcassette recorder was turned on, just in case. Seconds before Sally started the meditation, Lynn again piped up saying that Ramses wouldn't come today because I obviously wanted it too much. Her deliberate timing and insensitivity annoyed me. However, when Sally started to verbally walk us down a set of stairs to the seaside, with each imagined step I took in my mind, I went so deep that I felt like I was being drugged.

By the third step, my head had begun to droop. I sensed I was going out very quickly. I stopped hearing Sally's voice and instead heard myself talking in my head. I was speaking about my guide and gatekeeper who'd recently identified himself as the Archangel Gabriel. It seemed I was talking to my *new friend* Ramses and to my mom as if they were in the audience. Then I asked Gabriel for help channeling. I told him about my concern that Lynn's comments would stop it from happening again. That's when I felt a poke in my ribs and heard laughter. I immediately guessed it was Tommy, Nick's young deceased nephew who often visited with Nick during his meditations. As my mood lifted my hand started jerking in that flinching and conspicuous way it had before. However by the time all this had happened, Sally was already bringing our meditation to a conclusion.

After she'd "brought us back", she said she'd seen my face change during the meditation to someone who looked like me but had a fuller face and dark curly hair. She'd suspected it was my mother and with that description, she'd be right. Before we started to take turns talking about our experiences, I asked to go last. I listened to everyone else while I debated if I should mention the effect Lynn's comments and negativity were having on me. Although I wanted to be kind, I knew I had to say something. When it was my turn, I asked Lynn as gently as I could at that moment if she could be more supportive and explained how her comments had changed my attitude and energy before the last two meditations. Lynn didn't take it very well and cried briefly in front of everyone.

Sally delicately calmed the situation and then started our next exercise without delay. As she drew a card for each of us from one of her angel oracle decks, I couldn't keep my eyes open. I felt the spirit was there again. The same thing was happening to Nick as well. Nick's eyes were closed now and when I saw his head bob to the right, I tapped Sally silently. I checked that my tape recorder was still on so if Nick channeled, whatever words came out of him would be recorded. Then directing her attention to Nick, Sally commanded, "Let Ramses in," but instead Nick came out of it slowly and said, "He didn't want me. He was for Annie." He was amazed how powerful it had been. Nick had never felt anything like it.

Nick and Sally, both intuitive and brother and sister, decided that I should try again. This time Nick helped me regain the meditative state conducive for me to channel. It was obvious as soon as I'd achieved it because my left hand went crazy. It jerked so strongly up and down this time that my hand repetitively slapped my thigh. When Nick saw this, he proceeded to welcome our visitor. When the odd voice came through me, the violent jerking of my hand immediately stopped. Instead my fingers began to curl towards my palm slowly and continuously. Starting with my middle finger and then followed by all the others, except for my thumb, my fingers rhythmically and elegantly furled and unfurled constantly at the same speed while he spoke. My body was bent over with my head bowed and my chin almost touched my chest. Then just like before, when he'd finished talking through me and had decided to exit, my head suddenly and forcibly was thrown backwards. It felt like my back and neck were almost being snapped or as if I'd been adjusted by a chiropractor. Sally told me that the next time he came she would be sure to ask him to leave more gently.

Although the microcassette recorder had been on, when I played it back at home the volume of Ramses' odd voice was extremely weak. I understood now why Sally had asked him to speak louder a few weeks ago the first time he'd spoken through me. After I heard Nick's voice on the tape greeting this spirit, I had to turn the volume all the way up to hear Ramses speak. Before Nick had even had a chance to say his first question out loud, Ramses began to answer it. It was as though all Nick had to do was think about one of Diana's questions and without it ever being verbalized Ramses responded. He must have been reading Nick's mind with telepathy or something.

First I heard him say, *"They're for me (pause), the chambers. They're for me. The (pause) passageway (pause) for movement. (Pause) It was our primitive way of thinking. We don't need it."* I guessed he was referring to Diana's question about what was under the Sphinx. I then heard Nick ask a few of his own questions that Ramses didn't seem to understand or didn't want to respond to. Then I heard Sally's voice ask a very general question. She wanted to know if he could share some advice on spirituality and he replied, *"Takes a lot of time. (Pause) Keep (pause, his voice fading), just keep (pause). It can't be said in one sentence."* Then abruptly he told them, *"She's tired,"* referring to me, like when he said I wasn't ready. Then he added, *"I'll keep coming."* Then before he left me he laughed very strangely. It sounded clipped and staccato. It sounded something like, *"Hum hum hum no."* Nick and Sally thanked and blessed him for coming and he said, *"And to you."* He paused again before saying, *"Thank you."* Then, after an even longer pause, he airily and very slowly said, *"Ra."*

This had been so incredible. Even though I didn't know why or how it was happening and what was to come, I found it appealing as well as stimulating and energizing. As Katrina and Diana were on the west coast, eight hours behind me, I emailed them with the news. I'd have to wait for the weekend to talk with them. I decided to call Erica, the client who had cautioned me about opening myself up without understanding the rules of the spirit world, after my mom's first dying or after-death contact had set me alight. When we spoke, I told Erica how it appeared Lynn had purposefully attempted to sabotage my efforts in our meditation group. Erica laughed at me and told me that I was very naive to think that everyone would be interested in helping me. She knew there'd probably be a lot of jealousy of my new gifts and that unknowingly I would push people's buttons. I would be surprised how few people would genuinely be interested in my development. Many would be only interested in their own growth. She also rightfully questioned my level of excitement and told me I needed to be clear about why I was doing this and allowing it to happen. Erica didn't want me to go off on some ego trip. Additionally she believed I would soon need to find a new group that specialized in channeling, as the current group would soon tire of me unless they saw some direct benefits for themselves. In her opinion, I needed to be with high caliber individuals to support me through this.

When I spoke with Katrina she gave me the best advice that anyone could. She told me to take notes, record my experiences and progress. And most importantly, she said I needed to ensure that I always felt safe and protected when I channeled. She was happy for me and understood Erica's comments about people potentially being jealous. According to Katrina this spirit apparently had picked me and she expected that a ten to twenty year relationship would develop between us. She said I needed to get my body ready to accept the energy increase. Apparently, my current energy level was why his voice was so quiet when it came through me. It would become stronger over the coming weeks, months and years. Katrina informed me that these high level guides normally came to teach, not just to help their "host", as she referred to me, but the many people the host or channeler shared their knowledge with.

She then explained that I would need to use my guardian (the gatekeeper, I guess) to monitor and control the channeling. She'd spent years in a development group where the leader was a channel for a being she called a, "master guide or high level master-teacher." The master guide provided general spiritual lessons or teachings at the end of their classes. He wasn't allowed to just come to play around or talk whenever he felt like it. He was focused on educating and they scheduled the time of his *lectures*.

I would need to manage this new relationship if it were to benefit those in my existing group or any new group I joined. Apparently, I shouldn't let this master guide take full control of me. I must control my body. Modern channelers, Katrina informed me, stayed conscious and in semi or light trance only. They weren't ever totally unconscious. I asked her about the jerking of my left hand and told her how it changed to slow curling of my fingers when he spoke the last time. She thought this was my body's response to his energy and that it would probably settle down once I'd gotten used to it and my energy had been elevated. She even assured me that I'd get used to him entering and exiting. It would get easier and more comfortable with practice. She said, "The voice will get stronger and louder as well with time and practice." Eventually I would be able to speak for him for hours! I was so intrigued and wondered what all I would be learning from him over the years.

Katrina continued by telling me about different spiritual energies she'd experienced in her group in Seattle and repeated that this master guide had picked me and my energy. I must be a good match for his. He had come down to meet me and I needed to raise my energy vibration to meet him, part way, to make it easier for both of us.

I'd circled what she'd said next in my notes, "Channeling always leads to something. There's no accident that he's channeling to you." I'd felt exceptionally honored when she then said that I was a special kind of person with special skills.

Although like Erica, Katrina suspected I'd need to find different people to channel with, she told me any questions asked of my master guide must be for my group. If he was willing to work under these terms then I should schedule his "appearances". He shouldn't interrupt the others meditations. I needed to tell him he had to wait for his turn to talk, just like anyone else. In the group Katrina had attended, they meditated together first and only afterwards would their leader channel for a half hour to answer spiritual questions.

The week after Ramses had come through me, I'd felt as if my chest and heart had been expanded. I felt broader and more open in my chest and shoulders. Even my neck felt better and my breathing had slowed and deepened. I hadn't physically felt this good since before my car accident in late August, only a few days after Margaret had come out of the hospital. A very distracted lady had rammed into me with her big four-wheel drive Discovery on my own lane. She'd been looking at her child in the backseat rather than the road.

Just after speaking to Katrina, I decided to read from a new book I'd bought on spirit guides and angels only that week, *Angels and Spirit Companions* by Leah Maggie Garfield and Jack Grant. I opened it to the table of contents and looked for the words "master guides" (another term I'd never heard before Katrina had mentioned it). I found it listed and quickly turned to the section to read, "Master guides rarely channel for the sake of just one person...but they focus on teaching those who will then go on to teach others. Master guides are spiritual beings who endeavor to implant seeds of higher knowledge on the next plane." This was fascinating.

The next day I went to see Sally. It was Monday and our group would be meeting up again the following day. After talking with Erica and Katrina I knew I needed Sally's input regarding my recent channeling and how it might affect our group. I wanted reassurance that it would fit in with the other members' goals, especially in light of Lynn's behavior the last two weeks.

When we met, I expressed my concerns and shared with her an uncomfortable discussion that had taken place with Lynn after the last class. She'd sort of cornered me outside Sally's home as I was getting into my car to leave. Lynn was very upset and felt my comments inappropriate and aggressive, which wasn't at all how I had intended them. Sally listened, almost knowingly and then recounted a conversation she'd had earlier with Nick, "We think Lynn may be jealous and was too sensitive to what you said regarding her negative comments possibly acting to block you. We've seen that she is overly sensitive to any criticism."

Then when I asked Sally if I shouldn't have Ramses come through, she said, "But that's what class is about. What will be, will be. That's what a circle is about. It's the amount of energy in the room that helps each of us." She commented that she believed that he would have come through to me anyway, meaning without the group's energy. Then she said, "Chances are he'll come to you alone. He's chosen you." She assured me that my channeling was a great thing for the group. She wanted him to come and talk. "This is why we do this and it demonstrates to the others that it's possible." She surprised me then when she said, "If they don't like it, they can leave."

Although Sally's intentions had been excellent and she herself clearly wanted me to channel for the benefit of all, after a few months I was still running into roadblocks. Just as I'd been warned by Katrina, Diana and Erica, my new found ability threatened some of the members. Even the idea of it frightened the occasional drop-in that sometimes joined us on Tuesday nights.

I was feeling frustrated. My "voice channeling", as I'd read some people call it, hadn't improved at all since the second time I'd succeeded in doing it, way back in February. In fact, it was non-existent in Sally's group or any other group for that matter. After a few false starts, when no one listened or heard me trying, I'd stopped attempting it all together. Although, Sally and Nick truly seemed to be encouraging me, it was evident that most of the group strongly viewed it as counter-productive. Sally herself ironically was very deaf in one ear and my low volume in the beginning was impossible for her to hear.

When I put myself in their shoes, I could see that my channeling would take the limelight away from everyone and as Katrina had said, it had the potential of disrupting their experience. Because it was so new to me, I didn't know how to predict when or if I would achieve the right meditative level for it to happen. Therefore, Sally had suggested that I just speak any words I received whenever they came to me, right in the middle of whatever was going on. It's certainly not difficult to see how this policy would have a strong negative impact on the others who might themselves be in deep meditation. It seemed selfish as well, to let my wonderful experience overshadow or even cancel out someone else's. I must say, too, that *voice channeling* frankly was a bit freaky and I'm sure that not everyone wanted to be around it. Even if we'd found a suitable solution to manage it better at Sally's, some probably didn't wish to witness it.

Over the next six months, not much happened in this area, simply due to a lack of practice rather than desire. I'd certainly wished that I could find a way to achieve it but Sally had vehemently discouraged me from doing it alone and I didn't want to interrupt the rest of our group. It seemed I was being forced to look for other groups or people that were interested specifically in channeling if I were to progress.

In the meantime, two important things happened. The first was that I decided I needed to tell Matthew about the unexpected odd voice which had come through me (twice now) and the real nature of the Tuesday group. I had succeeded in keeping this to myself while I tried to figure things out. Now, as I knew I wanted to do more channeling, I felt I had to be honest with Matthew.

I wasn't quite sure how or when I'd say something to him and I had no way of knowing how he'd respond. So I prepared myself for the worst. I figured he'd want me to quit the group immediately, call what I was doing rubbish and then I figured he might want me to see a psychiatrist. Although I knew I didn't need one.

Telling Matthew

The following weekend we went to visit two of Matthew's best friends, Steve and his wife Beth. We stayed the night and in the morning, while Matthew and I had coffee together in bed in their lovely guest bedroom, I spilled the beans! Without too much preamble and not exactly how I'd rehearsed it, I blurted out that something fantastic and a bit odd had happened to me in my meditation class. I wanted to get his opinion on it because he was my best-friend, my husband and also a scientist (geo-chemist). I said I wanted or maybe needed to hear his thoughts.

I began by telling him about what had happened the week before Valentine's Day when my mom, her brother and his Uncle (all deceased remember) had told me that my Uncle Tom in California was ill and how I'd actually confirmed that this was true! I'd called my Aunt Mary, Tom's wife, to see how he was and she was startled by my query. Only when I confessed that my mother and my Uncle Richard were concerned about Tom (who my Aunt knew were both dead) did she admit that Tom had just been diagnosed with prostate cancer and that they hadn't told anyone yet. She made me promise not to tell her kids, my cousins, before they'd had the chance to break the news to them.

Then I told Matthew about how the voice of Ramses had come through me. I wondered if he believed this could actually be possible. My heart was beating so fast and loud that I could hear it in my ears. I found it hard to think while I waited for Matthew to respond. We'd been working very hard at rebuilding our relationship and trust. I guessed that his response could be a tell-tale sign of things to come.

He hadn't laughed but he hadn't said anything either, for a few minutes. He just looked like he was sincerely contemplating what I'd said. Then he spoke, saying, "There are many things in this world that we don't understand but that doesn't make them less real." He said he believed me completely. He didn't think I was off my rocker, not even a little bit and thank God he didn't think I needed to talk to a professional about it either. There would be no mental evaluation for me! I was as sound as when he'd first met me.

I couldn't have been more elated. My smile must have been huge. I realized right then that this was one of the very reasons I hadn't left Matthew when I'd found Deirdre's text messages. I loved Matthew's unwavering, yet often quiet, acceptance of me and all the strange experiences we were encountering together since my mom's death.

Matthew then continued to explain that he believed the biggest advancements we would see in our life-time would be in the area of the mind and how the brain works. He said, "There's so much we don't know or can't comprehend," and there has to be much more that is possible. I appreciated his comments and thoughtfulness that day, perhaps even more than I understood right then. He hadn't dismissed me, nor this thing that I knew probably couldn't or shouldn't be stopped. Even though I didn't really need his approval, he was even giving me the green light to advance it further – if I wanted.

The second important thing that happened during this time was that I found a way to receive the information being offered to me without talking. Out of necessity rather than any instruction or method that I'd read about, one night at the Tuesday group I discovered that I could write channeled information, rather than having to audibly speak it.

By the way, the channeled material was coming to me in a substantially different way than the messages from deceased relatives, or the conversations I had in my head with my mom. In those cases, it was like either eavesdropping or just talking with someone. Channeling however, felt like I was some sort of transmitter, sending out one word at a time while not being totally aware of the content being delivered.

The first two channeled messages (or lessons) I partially received in my head, and then completed by transcribing them were, *"Listen to everything. Listen to nothing,"* and *"Don't stagnate. Watch those in stagnation and their misery. Keep moving. Change. Intuition."*

After I realized I could do this, I was pretty content. I felt I wasn't wasting my time now by staying in Sally's group and more importantly I wouldn't miss out on any knowledge being extended to me.

It was easy to write the words that were coming in and it didn't bother anyone. As long as I used a felt-tip pen no one heard or was offended by my scrawling. If I felt Ramses or one of the others that soon began to come to me this way, rather than stopping them because I felt uncomfortable speaking over everyone, I'd simply and quickly open my journal and write their words down, right there in the candle-lit garden shed. Occasionally I'd share it with the group, if I thought it appropriate, or if the information was intended for someone there. But often I just kept their messages to myself. I'd learned through trial and error that this was usually best as it frequently fell on deaf ears.

Although, it was a somewhat strange arrangement, I'm so pleased I figured it out. If I noticed that I was hearing the same words repeated in my head, cycling around incessantly, non-changing, I'd quickly pick up my pen. Around the same time, I comprehended that until I'd written these first words (or spoken them, as

I would do later) that no more would come. I'd only get the same two or three repeated if I didn't act on them. For some reason, they only provided me with the beginning over and over, as if they didn't believe I'd remember all of what they had to say accurately. Maybe it indicated the importance of it. Then once I'd written their initial repetitive words, they'd be off. Their words would just fly into my head and through my pen. I had to write as fast as I could to keep up or I'd miss some of the message. Unlike the first words, they didn't repeat any of the others that followed. They just flowed, non-stop. Later I started to get visuals too and added information in other forms along with the text.

On the 8th of May, that same year (almost three months after I'd channeled for the first time) I heard in my head, *"We are here, we are all here,"* over and over. I had just written in my journal that the music that night was especially loud, and although Sally had announced that she had invited me to try to channel for the group that evening, I knew I wouldn't be able to speak over the CD player.

Then my left foot began to stomp and my hands became frozen in place. I heard male voices singing along with our chanting to Gate Gate and then realized it was impossible because the only man in the room was Nicky and he never sang! Then I heard, as if in the lyrics, the words, *"You are safe. I am here."* But there weren't any English lyrics to Gate Gate on the CD, not that I could understand anyway. The Buddhist mantras we were chanting along to were in another language! I became very cold and felt tingling all over my head. It felt amazing and I wrote quickly while simultaneously listening to, *"You are safe. I am here,"* and *"We are here,"* in my head, that I believed that I was hearing and feeling God! After I wrote the words, *"We are here. We are all here,"* I received:

Know you are safe and loved and will always be a part of something bigger than you comprehend. It's about time to seek and seek you will, for you are a part of the solution. Teach, be yourself, make mistakes, make joy and make others think.

It's impossible to be all you might here on earth but you'll be all you can and will see more each day.

Be happy, be whole, [and] do not regret [mistakes] as that's how we impart knowledge. Be young, be old, all in one, in order to lead and inspire others to live fully. Do not struggle - let it happen. Right action, right time, right beings.

Accept your gifts and strength – it's not everyone who can blaze this path. Not everyone who can deliver messages to so many, to so key few.

Encourage all to seek and stabilize their lives. Positive thoughts, positive memory, clarity of heart and true, true passion is [sic] key. It's not what we do so much as what we strive to do. Never be said to have not tried. Be honest and screw up. Yes, I said, "Screw up." That's why you came here. That's the truth – you elected to do this – you just forgot. I'm here for you always and through life you live on.

Wait no longer for the sunshine, I'm here, now just open the curtains and see me!

It's lightning amongst the chickens sometimes. But it has to be to awaken many. Subtlety [is] no[t] good for everyone. Be sensitive to what it takes to make change and progress in some. Be calm and patient. Be breathtaking and exciting for others. Be what you know for each. People see contrast and shades of grey or darkness more than they see light if they have no comparison.

We have to experience extremes to appreciate the calm and peace of a meadow at dawn or a butterfly in-flight. [I'm not sure I wrote this word correctly may have been emerging rather than in-flight. I couldn't keep up!]

You too see things others don't because you look for pattern and blocks of... [I missed some here.]

See all there is and all there is not. Be one with nature and one with me. I'll prepare the space for you and yours to learn to migrate to other levels. Stick with it and you'll be rewarded with clarity of focus, love and empathy, as well as peace of mind and true ascension.

The possibilities of life are endless and without boundaries. Be that as it may, you must see the potential for this for it to even be an option. Remember thoroughness is important. To uncover true secrets turnover all the stones on the beach to expose new life. All is one and one is all there is. Be aware and transcend. Blessings and Thank you.

In my journal I had added a comment below this after I'd had a chance to reread the information at home. I'd written, "Dang, I forgot to ask whom I could thank for the message! I'll remember to ask next time. I felt it was an angelic source or the Holy Spirit due to the use of "I" and "we" but I expect many souls or ascended masters, or similarly evolved entities or souls would speak in this way or know these principles."

As you can see, only an hour or so after I'd received this wonderful message I'd already been trying to reject the possibility that it had come from God. Although I'd clearly indicated that I had thought that I was hearing and feeling God at the time, I was more comfortable rationalizing and considering any other option than that. From my notes, too, it's evident that I'd obviously been reading about "entities" while trying to teach myself about channeling. Why was I okay with them but not with God? I guessed that my childhood wounds and conflicting beliefs were too deep.

After receiving this message, I really wanted to start meditating and channeling by myself using this new writing method, but Sally was so dead-set against it that she'd convinced me I shouldn't. She had insisted that it was too dangerous for me to do alone, unprotected. Part of me didn't want to believe she could be right about this, as there were millions around the world who meditated by themselves every day. However my heightened sensitivities, and all that I'd dealt with thus far, since my mom had died, put enough doubt in my mind that I was persuaded to wait.

These were odd times

Immediately after my very first channeling experience, I noticed that clocks appeared to be playing tricks on me. After Ramses had come through me on Valentine's Day, I started to see the numbers 11:11 regularly on my digital clocks. Every day, actually, even sometimes twice a day, both in the morning and at night, I saw 11:11 for an entire week or more. No matter where I was or what I was doing, I seemed to glance at a clock at exactly that time.

Additionally, although the spirit who'd been tapping on my shoulder had stopped his antics, once I'd begun to channel I started waking up unprovoked to see 3:33 glowing brightly on my bedroom clock. I started to take these indications as signs. I didn't know what they meant but decided to appreciate and acknowledge them. I figured they must be indicating something because they had never happened before now. I understood that it was some sort of message or recognition of my new connection.

There were even days when on every occasion that I looked at a clock, repetitious digits were being displayed. One day, I noted waking first to see 3:33 followed by waking at 5:55 and then seeing 10:10, 11:11, 12:12, 13:13, 14:14, 15:15, 17:17 and then finally 23:23 (the equivalent to 11:11) on our twenty-four hour clock on the bedside table.

I came to realize that these visual displays symbolized that I was *in the flow* and that I was being notified that I had more access to guidance during these periods. Amazing synchronistic events and other unexpected fortuitous encounters appeared almost non-stop when I saw the number patterns.

Right now the appearance of 11:11 is prominent in my life, probably because I'm writing this book and because I'm writing this particular chapter about my channeling. The patterns I see have changed over the years. Some days I see 11:11 or 3:33, like when this all first started, while other days I may see 5:55 repetitively or some other combination like: 17:17, 11:33 or 21:21. When this occurs, it is almost guaranteed that I'll see triple, repeated or mirrored numbers repeated for a few days and often the same numbers every twelve hours. I pay close attention during these times to my intuitive hunches, ideas and impulses. It's always pleasant when this happens and I believe it's showing me that I'm on the right track, as information and the "right people" seem to flow easily to me during these times. I've learned that the numbers are indicating that I'm doing exactly what I'm meant to be doing.

Chapter Thirteen

Further confirmations

I was beginning to meet more people who were spiritual now and was invited to attend a talk by Doreen Virtue, on angels, with a new client named Fiona.

At Waterstone's in Canterbury, I listened intently while Ms. Virtue (What a great name!) said that although angels are messengers, "It was a dramatic occasion when you see an angel. They present themselves when only an angel will do." Otherwise, you may only sense them and their message, although she said they may intervene occasionally, especially if you've asked for their help. Doreen said it was rare, though, to see them.

I thought about the angel on the landing, outside my bedroom door. Doreen was right. That night I needed to see something with my own eyes, to dispel my fear and reassure me. I needed an angel then. She talked about receiving messages from them, smelling angelic fragrances and hearing celestial music. Then, as if just for me, she reiterated that actual sightings were uncommon.

The next day at work, I listened to Fiona. She liked to talk throughout her reflexology sessions with me about her spiritual beliefs and experiences. I was glued to her every word. It was like having Katrina or Diana sitting with me, in person, for an hour and a half each week while Fiona was seeing me at my clinic.

Soon I found myself sharing with her what had taken place during and after my mom's death. We talked about the spirit who had frightened me by tapping on my shoulder *to wake me up* and she laughed uproariously thinking it was a terribly humorous metaphor. I decided I could tell her about the angel. Normally, I mostly listened in my sessions, but Fiona's were somehow different. She wanted to know more about my experiences. I spoke tentatively, checking that she wouldn't laugh as I shared my very brief but intense experiences with voice channeling and how I'd learned that I could write the messages. She informed me that this was called automatic writing.

Much to my surprise, just like Katrina, Diana and Erica, Fiona also knew all about channeling. Where had I been when everyone else had learned about this? You'd think it had been a prerequisite in high school or something that I alone had somehow missed out on. All of them acted as if this was common knowledge and spoke about it so eloquently. Like Katrina, Fiona complimented me and seemed to feel it was some kind of a privilege which had been bestowed on me.

Fiona told me that day, that she now knew why she'd selected to come and see me rather than the other three ladies that offered the same things here. She believed that every encounter had a reason and that there was no such thing as coincidences. It wasn't just chance that we'd spoken of these things that day. Whenever Fiona met someone new or bumped into someone she hadn't seen in a long while, she thought there was a good reason for it. They would have a message for her or her for them. The engagement was to impart knowledge or pass on a message for one of them, or both. There was always some kind of exchange that took place in every encounter, in her opinion.

Today, she was there to tell me about the SAGB, the Spiritual Association of Great Britain, where she assured me I could take a course in channeling. For her, I was there to validate the experience she had with her mother after she had died. I was also to become the Reiki teacher she'd been seeking.

Confused by universal laws

While more and more of my clients, like Fiona, were divulging their hidden spiritual beliefs, one new client (who luckily only came to me once) really frightened me. As you know, I had taken on board this supposed universal spiritual concept which said that I was the master of my experience, especially when it came to spirits' access to me. When I hadn't felt comfortable with a particular spirit, or their conduct, I had been able to tell them how they must behave and that they would have to leave otherwise. That had been my understanding of this universal law. It said basically that they had to go if I said so.

This all fit very nicely into my radically new belief system, but then this client spent most of his session telling me that all his emotional or mental problems were down to negative entities! He talked about how they kept attaching themselves to him and how he could do nothing to get rid of them. I hadn't expected to be giving spiritual guidance to anyone at this point, being so new at it myself, but I tried to assure him that he was in control at all times. I told him about my new awareness of the primary universal law that assured me that nothing could influence him if he didn't want it to. He then shocked me by saying, "Creatures don't abide by universal laws!"

At our next Tuesday meeting we discussed how to go about "detaching unwanted entities". Although, Janis, Sally and Fiona were all confident that we are always safe during any spiritual contact (and my own personal experiences supported this), I recalled Mishti's worries that we could be attacked by an *unwanted entity*. I started to wonder if it wasn't all about the person's emotional and mental stability. Maybe those that are depressed or mentally ill were prone to spiritual abuse or imagined it?

Although, I hadn't been the one to bring this topic up, I was so glad when someone else did. I saw it again as serendipitous. Sally and Nick said all that we need to do is to ask for an archangel to help in these matters. Archangels are higher up the *angel hierarchy* (or *food-chain*) than regular everyday guardian angels (sometimes called soul angels). Guardian angels are those who help one person throughout their entire life. While archangels, instead, are able to help anyone and everyone, even if you they are called upon at the same time. Nick and Sally explained that they have the ability to be in multiple places at once. Nick then said that if that didn't work, you can always call in the Brotherhood of Light to help you. According to him, they are extremely powerful super beings that no spirit can resist. That night, they tried to reassure the new person who had asked the question (and me without knowing it) that if something bad had attached itself to her that she could have it removed. Sally then had the young girl stand up and smudged her with the smoke of her smoldering sage bundle she kept on hand just for these occasions. I noted that I'd better check my sage stash again!

All the while Nick and Sally were discussing this, they tried their best not to use the terms *bad* or *evil,* but instead used the words, "lower vibrational," "less evolved," or "not of the light," and even "confused souls." An entity was just another name for a spirit and did not denote whether it was a *bad* being or a *good* one.

I was unsettled by this conversation. Coupled with the concerns of my new client last week who'd thought he was under attack and plagued by "dark entities", the whole discussion really bothered me. Then the new girl, that night at Sally's, said that she'd also heard that "darker" or "lower" energy entities could jump from one person to another. Attracted by the more lovely light of someone who was innocently walking past them on the street, the entity might decide to attach itself to them. Damn, it looked like I had more research to do to verify that my previous working theory was in fact accurate and that this attachment stuff was just hearsay and scare-mongering.

Luckily for me, Waterstone's seemed to be having many spiritual authors speaking at the café in their bookstore lately, and my questions were soon answered. I went to hear Gordon Smith speak, a well known medium. All his life he'd been able to see and hear ghosts (spirits). He made a career of speaking to and relaying messages from spirits to their living relatives. He is said to be the most accurate medium in all of the U.K.

I learned in his talk that the Tibetans believed that the spirit of a person who dies stays around us for seven days before passing to the next part of their journey. He told of their rituals, at death, to help the spirit on its way. I didn't understand it all totally, but he mentioned seven sets of seven days, and that on the 49th day, how the spirit made its way to where it was going in the after-life. Here, again, was the number seven being discussed. I was mesmerized and impressed by him.

I'd written in my journal that night, as I listened to Gordon Smith's opening statements, that he'd emphatically said, "There was nothing to fear!" I was so pleased. Then he went on to tell some true stories of loving contact and messages that had helped the living. It sounded poetic when he said, "The nature of the spirit is to expand, ripen and refine."

I had come armed with questions for him and as soon as he'd finished his talk and opened the floor for Q and A, my arm shot up along with almost half of those in the audience. I found every question presented to Mr. Smith helpful but when he pointed to me, I realized no one had asked him directly whether there was ever a need for protection from spirits. Most of the questions had been about making contact with them and not protecting yourself once they'd found you. He repeated pretty much what he'd said at the beginning of his talk. He assured me that, "There was nothing to be fearful of," but then he added, "but some need trust and comfort." He seemed to recognize that I needed more and prompted me to say why I had asked my question, "What exactly was I concerned about?" I told him as quickly as I could how I'd heard that no spirit, no matter how evolved or not, could mess with me or control me and then told him how only recently I'd been told that this was not true. He leaned forward, looked me straight in the eyes and said quite definitively and slowly, "Nobody can be in your space if you don't want them to be." He continued, "They have no more power in your house. Define the boundaries in your home." This was excellent news! This is a man who has been able to see spirits since he was a young child, and he confirmed that what I'd originally heard was true!

San Francisco, *The Seth Material* and the pattern of light

A month and a half after I'd heard Gordon Smith speak, I flew to San Francisco to attend one of the largest mind, body, spirit shows in the world. Diana had convinced me that I must go with her to the New Living Expo. She'd been going to this event ever since it had first started when it was called the Whole Life Expo more than two decades ago. I was guaranteed by Diana that I'd have a blast over the three days of the expo. There were over 150 lectures by well-known spiritual leaders and authors to choose from and more than 250 exhibitor stands to visit. She hinted that we might even take in a workshop or two. The best thing, though, was that we'd have a lot of time to just hang out and talk. We had no way of anticipating that once I arrived, many synchronistic and mystical things would begin to happen.

We spent our first evening sat around Diana's kitchen table talking over a feast of carnitas, roasted fresh jalapenos and homemade guacamole. Although Sean is blonde (as you might expect because of his name), Diana is a Latina and the most magical cook you can imagine. The thought of her mole sauce with thirty-five spices and chocolate can still make me salivate. Once you've eaten at Diana's, you won't ever forget that she's often heard saying, "Cooking is my alchemy."

Over dinner and a few gorgeous glasses of buttery Sonoma Cutrer, I described what had been happening to me since I'd seen them last year. First, I told Diana and Sean of my sadness over my unsuccessful, rather abortive, attempts to voice channel in Sally's group these past months and how I'd learned to write instead.

Then I excitedly recounted the true highlights of my year, knowing that they may seem far-fetched. I explained how I'd received an accurate message about my uncle's health which made me confident I wasn't making this stuff up. Then I shared my implausible idea that I had the Archangel Gabriel acting as my primary guardian or guide, before I told them about the spectacle of the beautiful, translucent, sparkling angel I had found in my hallway.

That's when I remembered that I'd brought a few framed prints of my new angel paintings, inspired by my sighting, for Allegra's room. I'd thought that Leggie might like them for her bedroom which she always gave up for me when I came to visit.

After Sean had listened to my update, he told me how he'd taken a course years ago that had used *The Seth Material* by Jane Roberts as their textbook. It was all about how she'd unexpectedly began to channel, like me, and it detailed her progression over those first years. Sean found the book easily and we spent the rest of the evening, until we were too tired to continue, reading it out loud and comparing it with my experiences. The parallels were both amazing and reassuring. It had taken Jane Roberts some time before she could speak the messages through her. In fact, I was astonished that mine had actually started with direct voice channeling, as Jane's had not. That developed later for her.

Although Diana had to work the next day she worked for herself from home as a marketing and P.R. consultant. While she made her phone calls and replied to emails, I spent my time reading from *The Seth Material*, and a few other books that winked at me from the shelves. I felt I was in metaphysical book heaven, and then Diana reminded me that she had the complete set of the channeled Lazaris tapes in her office where she kept her "better stuff". I ended up sitting on the floor of Diana's office in my pajamas, drinking herbal tea and lemon water all day reading *The Seth Material* and sharing bits of it with Diana in between her calls. I was totally content. I was in my great friend's home office, petting her cat Luna and feeling completely substantiated.

Diana remembered to tell me that the spirit I had seen that had been bothering Leggie last year had never come back. Leggie was sleeping much better, and in her own room, rather than hiding between Sean and Diana in their bed.

We spent the entire next three days at the expo meeting up with Sean and Diana's close friends off and on. I'd flown 5371 miles to attend this and I'm so glad I did. It was worth every penny and hour I spent sitting in the plane and in the airports. I'd never seen anything like it!

As we wandered around the many booths, people seemed to gravitate to me just to tell me things. Things I'd wanted or even tried to understand, without success before, were being freely spoken about around us, topics of lectures, or simply presented to me unequivocally. I thought again of Fiona's comment about the exchange that happens between people and paid close attention to what was being said to me. I wasn't sure anyone was gaining anything from me but I decided not to worry about that. Maybe it wasn't necessarily always a two-directional or reciprocal arrangement. It felt like the whole expo experience was just for me, oh, and for Diana. There was so much to see and to be inspired by that I could hardly stand it. Although much of our time there was incredible, three very significant things stood out.

My aura reading

I had my aura photographed and it included an analysis and reading by a clairvoyant. If you were prepared to wait, someone would interpret the meaning of the colors and patterns in the photo for you. There were three or four psychics doing the readings but I'd hoped I'd get the lady who Diana and I had listened to give a few readings while we'd waited patiently in the line. When it was my turn, sure enough Martina was available. She held the Polaroid showing what I thought were very lovely colors around my head and upper body.

After staring at me silently and smiling for what seemed like ages before she started, she stopped herself and looked again at the photo. Then she began by pointing out something with her fingers while she spoke. She said she'd identified and recognized a few key things, other than the coloring of my aura, which she wanted to tell me about first. What came out of Martina's mouth caught me off guard. She said, "I see you are a channel," pointing to the column of light coming out of the top of my head in the photo. I'd totally missed that one. I'd been gazing at my picture for close to thirty minutes, while we waited for my reading but I hadn't seen it. Then she pointed to another area by my shoulder and emphasized, "And here, I see that you are being influenced by an angel who's sitting in your aura." Diana was standing right next to me listening to Martina as I'd asked her to take notes of what Martina said. When we'd registered what we'd just heard, both of our mouths dropped open and we turned to look at each other in shock.

Only two nights before, I'd shared with Diana how much I had doubted all these months that I could really have an angel talking to me and acting as my personal guide or gatekeeper, even though I'd actually seen an angel! Now I realized it was probably the same angel that Martina was pointing out in the photo. I'd refused to believe it was possible, for me anyway – until now.

Martina went on to say that I was obviously going through tremendous change but that I was also very frustrated with one of my projects. She then counseled me on how to work with this angel. She wanted me to tell it that it was to communicate with me from outside of my aura. She wanted me to tell it to come to the back of my hand for some reason. I couldn't understand why she didn't like the angel *sitting* there, if it really was that close to me. How could that hurt anyone? I thought again how lovely it had felt being in the presence of the angel before.

After the aura reading, Diana decided it was time to break her secret news to me. She had a little surprise planned for us. She'd bought advance tickets to a workshop as soon as she'd found out that I was really coming to the expo with her this year. We were going to spend much of the next day with a lady named Kira Raa who, apparently, channeled the Archangel Zadkiel. I didn't know how to react. Part of me was excited, but another part of me thought that it was impossible for a woman to have an angel come through her. I was surprised at myself. Even though I was personally experiencing these odd things, I still wasn't a hundred percent certain they were real and not delusions. I wondered what had to happen before I would fully accept them. How much confirmation did I need?

I felt a bit numb and in a daze as I moved about the stalls after Martina's comments. Diana appeared a bit fuzzy and far away when I looked at her. I must have been in a bit of shock after hearing how Martina could tell from the photo that I was a channel and had an angel with me. Her confirmations were destabilizing, although they should have been comforting. I needed time to let this sink in. I walked around in my own little world for a while lost in thought. I remembered the times I'd felt Archangel Gabriel talking to me and even asking him to help me channel at Sally's. Maybe all this was real after all, just like mom's spirit coming to me.

Diana then led me to the area of the expo that had the larger crystal vendors' displays. She knew how much I adore rocks and that I was on the hunt for a few beautiful pieces to take home with me including, if I could find them, natural octahedral (eight sided) fluorite crystals. I'd been attracted to them for almost twenty years, ever since Katrina first took me to the East West Bookstore in the University District of Seattle in the early 1990's.

F. Joseph Smith had the best collection and although he didn't have eight sided fluorite he had tons of others that caught my eye. Soon I spotted the most beautiful crystal clusters I'd ever seen. They were a sparkly pastel periwinkle blue. I immediately picked one up and planned to buy it if it wasn't too expensive. Holding onto my find and feeling extremely light and happy, Diana and I continued to look around the stall finding more we loved. Then, patiently, we waited to ask about our particular stones and negotiate. Joseph told me that the crystal I'd selected was, "Celestite, which resonates with the angelic realm." As soon as I heard this I gave an unmistaken-able look to Diana. She could tell that I was positively blown away by this further comment about angels. Then I asked the price while thinking as long as it wasn't more than $30 that I would treat myself and wouldn't have to put it down. Again, like minutes before at the aura photograph booth, I couldn't believe what I was hearing, "For you, the Celestite is $5 a piece, although normally I sell it for $25." Everything Diana and I were interested in he offered to us for a quarter or half of the marked price including a big piece of Citrine I also bought.

Although for some reason Joseph Smith had decided to give us almost whole-sale rates, I was further baffled when he picked up a set of ugly brown balls and placed them in my hand. They were slightly smaller in size than ping-pong balls and a very deep muddy opaque color. There was nothing sparkly about them and I wasn't attracted to them at all. Joseph said casually, "I think you should have these. They're my gift to you. You're going to need them. They are North American Indian Mochi Balls. Shamans use them for journeying to the spirit world."

With his explanation, I understood why he wanted to give them to me. Obviously like Martina, he also knew things just by looking at me. I giggled to myself and thought, "Too bad they're so ugly though." I wondered how it was that I was so transparent to these spiritual people.

Beyond Goodbye

Diana gave me another mysterious grin, one of many I received from her on that trip, followed by a wink to acknowledge the crystal man's quirky inferences. She seemed to be enjoying my bewilderment and for a moment I thought I'd observed admiration in her face.

Additionally, I couldn't get over how Joseph kept commenting on my luminosity and how he'd said that I matched the light in the pale Citrine I'd selected. Maybe it was normal crystal vendor banter to butter up prospective clients but it seemed genuine. I was a little uncomfortable with his compliments but didn't believe he was hitting on me. Either way, Diana and I were getting a bargain and both accepted his generosity with grace.

The day's events had caught up with me. Everything was feeling a bit dreamlike and surreal. When Diana suggested that we have some lunch and find a quiet place to sit, I was all for it.

That night when we returned to Diana's apartment, with its panoramic view of downtown San Francisco, I happily entered it carrying an entire box of crystal rocks! Sean almost fell over laughing. It became our little insider's joke, kind of like a knock-knock joke. For the rest of the expo and the remainder of my visit with them, for that matter, one of us would randomly call out, "What do you think we should do at the expo today?" and the reply would be, "I don't know, maybe buy another box of rocks," or someone might throw out, "What does everyone need?" In unison we'd each respond, "A box of rocks!" Although they teased me incessantly, I couldn't believe I'd only spent $35 for a box of crystals worth easily $250. My bargain "box of rocks" filled the apartment with laughter and amusement for days.

After dinner that night, Diana placed a large bowl of water onto her glass kitchen table and stirred in a half cup of pink Himalayan salt until it was dissolved. The salt, she told me, would cleanse our new crystals of other people's energies overnight. Once all the stones were submerged, without notice, Diana waved her hands gracefully over the bowl. I wasn't sure what she was doing but she had a huge smudge stick, almost ten inches long, in one hand and was saying something about calling in the energies of the North, East, South and West. I couldn't quite hear all of it, or maybe I didn't think it was important at the time. I remember thinking nothing of this as I'd come to expect Harry Potter-styled behavior from my good friend.

As Diana came to the end of her little *white witch* ritual, she began to tap on the edge of the bowl with her smudge stick. I was still standing next to her, not thinking of much really, but merely quietly being there as she did her thing. Then just as she made her final soft tap, with that massive string wrapped sage bundle, we suddenly heard a loud crack and saw a brilliant, almost blinding, flash fill the room.

An electric circle of white light blasted outwards from the center of the bowl. It came towards us rapidly. It moved as quickly as a lightning bolt as it cut its way easily through the air in its path and Diana and me. As it moved, it left a level film or trail of light behind it which hung like some kind of frozen flat cloth or sheet waist high. The ring of light expanded horizontally with its leading edge much brighter than its trail. It passed painlessly right through both of us. Then a succession of concentric circles of light followed the first, each of them maintaining the same level as the salted water within the bowl. In only a moment the entire room was filled with them, these ever-increasing in size brilliant white circles of light. One by one, they seemed to be generated within the confines of the bowl and just as quickly as they formed, they moved away from it. They slipped individually through us, as if we weren't even there, and then continued unhindered and unaffected through the walls behind us.

It was extraordinary. It truly was just like something out of *Harry Potter* or *The Lord of the Rings* but we were in Diana's kitchen and not at the movies! This was really happening. It wasn't some kind of CGI effect. Both our heads and our shoulders had been thrown backwards, a natural response to the gust of the unexpected and powerful explosion. Even our hair had been blown backwards. Then just as quickly we both fell forwards and found ourselves leaning inward toward the bowl. We were unintentionally made to peer directly into it by the vacuum created by the implosion of the blast. We were now looking inward at exactly where the flash detonation had occurred and the circles of light had originated from.

There before us on the surface of the water was a pattern made of orange light. It extended to the edge of the bowl, to the circumference, and covered the entire area within the bowl. A perfect, delicate, lace etching of interconnected petals made entirely of light hovered just above the water within the perimeter. We could see through the intricate weave of the gorgeous, glowing matrix, down to the water and the crystals below. I couldn't help but think of a hot branding iron and the vibrant tangerine embers of a campfire that has reached maturity. Then slowly as we watched motionless, we saw it dissolve in front of our eyes like a child's sparkler when it fizzles out and leaves a shadow of itself for a moment. As if on cue, as the orange interconnected matrix faded away, the lighting in the room returned to normal.

Diana and I stared at each other, knowing we'd just experienced something very special, again. All at once we both asked each other, "Did you see the pattern over the water?" Then because we both had seen something, before we described it to each other, we decided we should sit down separately and individually sketch it. When we compared our drawings they were identical but neither of us knew what the shape might mean.

The next morning, we were off to the expo for our second day but not before an essential stop at the ATM machine. There'd been so many beautiful things to buy the day before that we, well maybe just I, needed more cash. As we waited in line, I couldn't help notice that the three people in front of us had the same black t-shirts. They must be working at a booth at the expo. When they turned around, boldly printed on the front of their t-shirts was the exact design Diana and I had seen over the bowl of crystals the night before!

We pointed at their chests and laughed hilariously. Then, right there on the sidewalk, in front of the bank and opposite the entrance of the Expo, we told them about our experience the night before and questioned them about the pattern on their shirts. It was called The Flower of Life apparently, and they believed it was the template on which all life was formed. The interconnected pattern symbolized the connection between everything that exists. They said it was a symbol of ancient sacred geometry and defied normal laws of time and space.

After listening to a few speakers in the morning, we left the main Expo site to go to our angel workshop with Kira Raa. Although I knew I wanted to be open-minded, after all maybe this kind of thing would end up happening to me, I wasn't sure I wouldn't feel that she was a fake. I hoped not.

Unexpectedly, or not so unexpectedly, and perhaps according to some divine plan outside of my control, I was introduced personally to Kira Raa before the workshop had even started. Tons of people were there to see her who actively followed her work, but I ended up talking with her one-to-one. Although it was rather strange how it had happened, I thought I might as well make the most of it. After all, how often does someone get a chance to talk to an *archangel channeler*? I took this unique opportunity to ask Kira about my recent aura reading as it had involved angels.

I explained to Kira how Martina had told me that I shouldn't allow an angel to be in my aura and that I must tell it to speak to me at arm's reach. Without hesitation, Kira then said, "You have Archangels Gabriel and Uriel with you. You shouldn't push them away." Then I surprised myself when I didn't react at all stunned by her comment. I'm sure before the Expo and what happened the night before cleaning our crystals I would have. Here was another person confirming and even accurately naming one of the archangels (Gabriel) who I'd thought I might have seen and had been talking to me at Sally's. It was then that I decided that I must stop denying it. Then Kira said something I didn't understand. She said that Martina was in a different dimension than me, and that I need not worry, "I could handle the angelic contact."

In the beginning of the workshop, Kira Raa, who had been declared clinically dead in 1989 from cancer, and her husband, Sri Ravi Kaa, spoke of our existence in the density of the third dimension, the fourth dimension or astral realm and stepping into our extended self in the fifth dimension where angels and ascended masters reside. This was the first time I'd heard this reference to dimensions. I was intrigued and simultaneously flattered as I realized that she had been complimenting me when she'd said I was in a different dimension than the aura reader, Martina.

After their introduction, Kira started to channel her archangel and I was unable to deny what I heard. I was glued to her every word and breath. I was fascinated by what I felt emanating from her. It was more authentic than I could have ever imagined. Diana and I, and one of her good friends (also named Diana), spent the entire workshop enthralled by Kira's presence.

After the Expo, I had another fabulous evening at Diana's, comparing notes and sharing stories. The following day was spent running a few errands, generally playing around and being childish together. Much to our amusement, when I started to pack up to fly home the next day, I realized the weight of my "box of rocks" was going to make my luggage over the baggage limit. I ended up donating almost a third of my larger crystals I'd just purchased to Diana's lovely home.

Chapter Fourteen

Seeing is believing

My San Francisco trip couldn't have come at a better time. Feeling excited, re-energized and spiritually validated I returned home, to England.

Although I hadn't known back then that we draw people to us who match our energetic level and who are interested in what we are focused on, soon I was to meet even more who would act as stepping stones for my spiritual development.

The flood gates weren't just open now, they'd been swept away by the profound experiences of my mom, the angel and the other spirits who'd been in contact with me. At this point, everyone I encountered was secretly or overtly interested in the after-life, including angels, spirit guides and the astral plane (where spirits of the recently deceased and ghosts, I'd discovered, were said to hang out). Without any effort, I was coming in to contact with spiritually like-minded people. Before I knew it, without any solicitation, both new and old acquaintances were asking spiritual advice and sharing their untold, exceptional experiences with me.

My time with Theresa

Later that summer, after my first Expo experience with Diana, I met a lady through my work named Theresa. She came to me originally for EFT, Emotional Freedom Techniques which is commonly called *tapping*. My first book *It's Your Choice: Uncover Your Brilliance using The Iceberg Process* is all about this technique and my amazing discovery, that with your choice of repetitive language you reveal your mind's unconscious focus including aspects of unresolved or traumatic experiences.

I'd learned that Theresa was keenly interested in spiritual things. So once we'd finished our professional relationship, I decided to introduce her to Sally.

After a few weeks of attending our Tuesday night group, Theresa expressed how fascinated she was by the spiritual information I was receiving some evenings during my meditations. She wanted me to help her develop this ability for herself or at least help her talk with her guides more easily.

Coincidentally, around this same time, Sally began inviting extreme novices to join her group. Almost every other week it seemed for awhile there'd be a new person sitting in the shed who wanted to learn how to meditate. Although I'd joined Sally's group in a similar way, it began to feel a bit disruptive and counterproductive, especially when they only came once.

Each time a newbie arrived, Sally had to explain the whole process to them in front of us. After courtesy introductions and a bit of small talk, she'd explain why we all came together every Tuesday and the flow of the evening. Then she'd patiently teach the new person how to pronounce the Sanskrit words to our favorite chant Gate Gate, before she warned them that I might channel at any time during the meditation. This usually prompted further discussion and a few odd or scared looks directed my way. It may have even been the reason some of them never came back a second time. Lastly, Sally would calmly discuss why she performed what she called, "the dedication to the candle." Only after all this was done, would we start our meditation.

I tried not to let it bother me, remembering when I'd been brand new and how generous and kind Sally and the group had been. Anyway, everything was fine once we were meditating, except for one thing. I didn't have enough confidence to voice channel in front of someone I didn't know. Sally without her knowledge had created another a barrier for me. I began to realize that I wasn't learning anything new directly from Sally any more. The tables were turning. Maybe I really did need to find a new group and mentor. I wondered if Sally wasn't doing this on purpose to move me along my path.

That was when Theresa and I decided to meditate together outside of the group. We started meeting up on Tuesday afternoons, usually at my home, just prior to going to Sally's. We didn't want to hurt her feelings, or take away from the wonderful gift she was giving us each week, for a small donation to a charity. We just wanted more time to meditate, so we kept our meetings to ourselves. Unfortunately, Sally still saw me as a raw beginner and I didn't think she'd approve of me dabbling outside of class, even though I'd been meditating now with her weekly for about a year.

By Theresa and me meditating before going to Sally's, we were able to make the most of the night. Even if there were new people who needed the full run down or some extra instruction that took away from our meditation time, we'd still both succeed in reaching a deeper level as we were already primed before we'd arrived.

We seemed to be accelerating from the extra meditation time and we bounced off each others' separate progress and interest. Theresa and I became very close, very quickly, perhaps unnaturally close according to my husband. Almost daily, we'd share the best of whatever we'd read with each other. We were doubling our understanding, and excitement and intensity was building. We became more and more knowledgeable, both due to our investigations and our meditation experiences together. Our outside work was now becoming obvious in the Tuesday group. Dissention began and conflicts started to arise as we expressed stronger opinions or spoke of something we'd read that others didn't agree with.

White Owl

Theresa was now in contact each day with one exclusive guide without even having to meditate, I on the other hand, only felt connected with my guides while I was sitting in meditation with someone else. Respecting Sally's wishes and cautions, I still hadn't meditated alone.

Soon, during one of the times when Theresa and I were meditating together, a new guide introduced himself to me. Strangely he said his name was, "White

One," then, "Wise One," followed immediately by, "White Owl." He kept changing his mind or had various names that he went by. The few times when he spoke to me, he listed each of his names in succession, including finally, "White Arrow." Just as Ramses had unexpectedly revealed himself when I'd reached a semi-rigid meditative state that first time, so had White Owl come to me one day while meditating at my home.

In total, by this time, I'd heard from Ramses, Sean (an Irish lad I haven't told you about), something or someone I refused to call God and now this White Owl. There were four very distinct entities or spirits giving me channeled information, although I'd only succeeded in voice channeling a handful of times since it all began eight months ago. The other occasions when I'd heard their indicative repetitious introductory words, I'd defaulted to writing their communications down in my journal rather than trying to speak.

For one reason or another, I'd resigned myself to using my pen almost exclusively. I hadn't figured out yet how to encourage their voice to come through me. I knew I'd need to stop worrying about what other people thought of me before it would happen. I had to find a way to get over my nerves somehow.

Don't get me wrong, I tried to speak for them a couple of times and even succeeded with Theresa when we were by ourselves – but it was difficult and infrequent. My whole body shook and I had great trouble getting the first words out even the few times I succeeded at it. It seemed almost impossible to let them speak through me in the beginning. My mouth felt like it was almost glued or stapled shut.

I think I was scared that I would blow it and concerned what words would actually come out of my mouth. I also worried, for some reason, what my voice would sound like and how I'd look doing it. With all these reservations, it kept evading me.

White Owl was an American Indian as you might expect. Just as I'd denied hearing from God in my meditation or that I had an angel as one of my guides, I tried to deny White Owl's existence even more. Everything I'd been reading, lately, joked about how many people thought that they had an American Indian as their spirit guide. It was one of the biggest spiritual jokes – ever, amongst *true* spiritual seekers it seemed.

I didn't want to be at the receiving end of any jokes as you might imagine. What I was going through was challenging enough. Then I remembered my "box of rocks" and recalled how Joseph at the Expo had given me those two butt-ugly American Indian Mochi Balls. For a short time, I had done my utmost to dismiss this new Indian guide, White Owl, as pure creative imagination. But when he kept coming to me, I figured that Joseph may have been right. I found the Mochi Balls and although I couldn't bring myself to hold them when I meditated, I added them to a small bowl containing other stones that I loved. At least I had these two unattractive things that looked like petrified turds in full view.

The little girl in our Reiki class and Sean, the guide

The next month, I taught beginning Reiki to Theresa, Lynn (the same Lynn who came to our meditation group), a lady named Pamela and a guy named Frank. This was second or perhaps my third Reiki training course I'd conducted since qualifying as a master with Sally, and while a few strange things had happened in each of my classes, this one took the cake.

On the second day of the course, after everyone had their fourth and final attunement (or Reiki initiation), while we were busy practicing the healing technique everyone stopped what they were doing all at once. They all stared in the same direction, looking at something I couldn't see. Almost in unison, they declared that they saw a little girl standing in our room. I felt something and sensed it was a young girl but I didn't see anyone. They were all really delighted by being able to see her – except for Frank. He was freaked out by it. They all described her in the exact same way, right down to the color of her clothes and hair. They all could see her completely, even Frank, although I couldn't.

The following Tuesday, Sean, one of the guides I'd had for a while by then, kept saying to me, *"To be sure, to be sure, to be sure."* The meditation had been very powerful that night and I'd reached the deepest level I'd ever reached so far. I really thought that I was going to go into trance (meaning that I might become unconscious and unaware of what was happening to me). My right hand felt huge. I felt electricity jerking my body around and my right leg loudly and uncontrollably stomped a few times. Then I saw flashing lights in front of my eyes and again I thought I was on the verge of going into a full trance.

The energy that was running through me was amazing but felt erratic. I kept saying in my head that I felt I was ready, and that Sean could come in and use my voice box. The electric jolts happened again, and I tried three more attempts at speaking. Intense energy ran down my spine, causing me to convulse and stamp my right foot, like a horse pounding the ground. Everything I was feeling was very dramatic. I was stunned at how powerfully I had stomped my foot. This felt different than before. It was more jerky and severe than when Ramses had come. It didn't feel comfortable and felt very much out of my control and unexpected.

Sean kept telling me to say, *"To be sure, to be sure, to be sure."* and I kept negotiating. I didn't want to. I thought saying it would be too embarrassing. He kept repeating the same thing for what seemed like fifteen minutes in my head. I heard nothing else except for a few other random comments from him saying, *"If you can't even say that, how can you say more?"* I kept trying to test if he or I could speak his three words, through my mouth, but my lips seemed stuck. I kept saying the "t" sound but couldn't get out *"to be sure"* until we were out of meditation.

The flashing lights in front of my eyes had been fantastic. They had caused my eyes to move back and forth while my hand had felt as if it were growing in size. That night, Theresa took a chance and suggested to Sally that we all hold hands before going back into meditation, for me to try again. Theresa and I had figured out when we'd been meditating together outside of the group, that by holding hands it helped to raise your energy. Then Sean spoke to me again, but still not through me. He had a message for me to give to Sally. He said I should tell her, *"Pass the baton, so the real work can start."*

Afterwards, Sally told everyone that she'd seen green eyes appear over my closed eyelids. Someone else's eyes had been open, looking at her, while mine were tightly shut behind them. Sally said I'd been, "overshadowed." She explained that this occurs when another person's energy, a spirit or an entity, overlays yours. When this happens, you end up wearing their image, like some kind of semi-transparent mask.

Mia Dolan's reading, apporting and telekinesis

A few weeks later, after the little girl had showed up during my Reiki course, Theresa decided to buy us tickets to see a medium. We were going to see Mia Dolan in Herne Bay at the King's Centre, along with four or five hundred other people. I'd never heard of Mia Dolan but Theresa told me that Mia was an amazingly accurate medium from Sheerness, only about a forty-five minute drive from Canterbury. She'd read her book recently and thought we'd really enjoy seeing her.

During the drive over, Theresa explained the format of these sorts of gatherings to me. She'd gone to quite a few of them over the years. Mia would be on stage and would offer readings to a few people in the audience to demonstrate her skills. Theresa was really excited and thought she had a good chance of being called upon. I didn't really care about having a reading by Mia. I just wanted to listen to everything she had to say and was confident that I'd learn something from her.

Mia's introduction was very interesting. She explained that she couldn't call on the specific spirit of someone's deceased relative, just because they wanted her to. The spirit had to want to talk through her to them instead. The motivation had to come from the spirit, before Mia could talk with it.

I realized as I watched her, that for the first time ever, I was seeing someone's aura. It was very soft and fuzzy but I definitely saw a sparkly pinky-purple and silver glow around her body. It was funny because just as I noticed the colored cloud around Mia, she began to read some of the auras of the audience while she explained how she would decide who she'd do readings for that evening. She mentioned that pink meant stress to her, while soft auras were sensitive people and silver indicated that they were psychic. Purple she said, "meant they had healing abilities," but then she said, "everyone did."

She seemed to look penetratingly into the eyes of many, as she gazed slowly around the auditorium. Then to no one in particular she declared, "Don't mistake a visit as a haunting." She talked about telepathy and how sleep paralysis wasn't a paranormal thing but that it occurred when the body was not awake but the mind was. I felt, for a moment, that all of what she said was just for me. She then discussed something called *apporting*, which she explained as the process by which an item disappears from one room and reappears in another. I'd heard this word for the first time, only last week, when Nick mentioned the word at Sally's.

As Mia said, "apporting," that night, I realized that maybe that was what had happened at my clinic the night before. I was preparing for my next client, who was coming for a massage, and as I turned to go to the cupboard where I kept the face hole protectors (a hygienic piece of soft paper that is placed over the area where the client lays their face), I saw one was already laying on top of my massage couch, but I hadn't taken one out of the storage cupboard yet. I'd only acknowledged to myself that I needed to get one out.

Suddenly, I was brought back from my thoughts about the night before when I felt something which forced me to look up. Mia Dolan's eyes then caught mine, making me feel somehow naked and exposed. She'd been looking around the room for her first victim, the person she would give her first reading to, saying that their aura would call her to them.

She made her initial selections and what I heard her say about the first two people was amazing. Their unprepared responses to her confirmed the trueness of what she'd said. However, what was even more interesting was that out of an audience of more than four hundred people, all of who desperately craved and longed for her undivided attention, the third person she picked was me! Theresa looked at me with both pleasure and a bit of annoyance. Her chances of being read were probably now quite slim.

The first things Mia Dolan said to me were, "You're psychic! I see a book. Do it! You have a powerful Indian artifact. Be careful." She went on to say, "I see you in front of others, speaking to people, many places." She smiled then and appeared to be speaking privately to me rather than to her audience, "We should talk." When she regained the thread of information she was picking up, she continued with, "I see Indian stuff...Red Indian...You have one. Even though I usually scoff at Red Indians or monks as guides as just stuff people say when they are fabricating, you actually have one." She then repeated, "I see you in front of lots of people," and then insisted that I'd written something already. "You've started a book and you should do it. Not a booklet but a proper book. You'll have some inroads."

She saw me teaching others and maybe having healing or spiritual centers. She knew about my recent lease negotiations for my clinic room and then changed tack. She said, "I see flowers on a grave," which of course could have referred to the loss of my mother, Arthur, or even Matthew's Uncle John. Mia then commented about my aura, saying it was blue. "You're a great communicator, and there's silver indicating that you are psychic and intuitive, and pink," which I recalled meant that I was stressed. She ended by telling me again that she saw me teaching and reiterated, "Don't let someone muscle in on your work," referring to my writing.

At the break, I went to the bathroom to wash my hands and fill my water bottle. As I held the plastic bottle under the faucet, it turned off by itself just as the water

107

level was about to reach the top. I smiled to myself and sort of disregarded it as a simple coincidence. Then when I approached the hand-dryer, it came on without me touching it, although it wasn't one of the automatic types. Before I went back to the auditorium, I glanced at myself in the mirror and considered if I had enough time to comb my hair and put a little hairspray on it. I decided that I didn't and quickly turned to leave. As I walked towards the restroom door, my foot kicked something. When I looked down, I was stunned for a few seconds and tried to make sense of what I saw. I'd kicked my tiny hairspray bottle that had been in my closed and zipped purse! Was this what Mia and Nick meant by apporting? Was there a spirit helping me in the bathroom or was I doing some of this with my own mind?

The wine glass

More and more, and perhaps in some mysterious sequential pattern only known to my deceased mom or some spiritual gurus, my senses and beliefs were systematically being transformed by continued and unexpected first-hand experiences. Changes to my beliefs, and apparent limited understanding of my reality appeared now to be unstoppable. I'd discovered through this whole process that most of my beliefs were primarily formed out of fear and a desire to stay safe, rather than being about what was possible in this life. I had no real faith in the unseen before my mom had died. The discrepancy between this lack and what was occurring to me was sinking in. It was forcing me to further question what I'd denied for far too long.

Thinking now that God may have talked to me personally (although I still wasn't totally sure about that one) and about the amazing reading from Mia Dolan that week, my doubts were being chipped away slowly but surely.

Back then, I was what some people refer to as a "recovering Catholic" and it can take a lot to end that kind of steadfast faith rejection. Maybe that's why the heavens asked my mother to get involved? I don't know, but I'd always been too uncomfortable and too scared to even consider any paranormal or supernatural possibilities. So, what I saw in my kitchen, right there in front me, was really challenging. Was this paranormal or was this something spiritual? I didn't know what the heck was going on.

Again, like most of the things which had happened since mom's death, I felt unprepared for this. Even today, I don't fully appreciate the mechanics that were involved in what I saw but that didn't stop it from happening or stop me from doing my best to explain it away.

I instinctively knew not to move or even blink. Although, I'd almost been startled into action, a wiser part of me kept still and told me to wait. Just observing things now was much easier for me. Maybe it was because of the candle gazing meditations at Sally's? Regardless, I'd really changed since my initial surreal connection with my dying mom. A year ago it would have been very out of character for me to just be idle, on purpose.

That morning in my kitchen I must have looked somewhat like a wide-eyed, doomed deer. You know the kind I mean. A fawn that's been hypnotized by the headlights of a fast approaching car which will probably end its life any second. Purposefully frozen, I stood mesmerized and unable to look away. I knew that another of my worldly beliefs would be changed – forever.

Tension was building within me. While you might think that doing nothing would have been easy, it took tremendous concentration to keep me from intervening. What I saw happening wasn't anything to fear. But I had to force myself to stay rigid and only watch it magically unfold before me. I felt shocked and enthralled, all at once. I remember the only movement which I couldn't stop totally was that of my rising and falling chest. I didn't want even my breathing to disturb what was happening. I held my breath for a time and then attempted to breathe more slowly and shallowly as I continued to watch.

While I believed that I was doing all I could not to move, perhaps I couldn't have anyway, if I'd tried. I was confused and excited. I knew changing anything carried a risk and I didn't want to my involvement to stop this incredible thing from happening.

It seemed like an hour had passed in only seconds. I knew I had to stay focused and simply allow it to happen. I heard in my head, "Don't take your eyes away from that glass." In loud silence, if there is such a thing, I continued to watch, paralyzed. Then the glass moved again. It jerked awkwardly but began to progress closer and closer to my outstretched fingers. Propelled by some invisible power, slowly rocking it from side to side, and then backwards and forwards, it came towards my hand, not smoothly, nor elegantly but stubbornly.

The glass was maybe six inches away from me and definitely moving on its own! But then I did what I promised myself I wouldn't. I lowered my gaze for the tiniest of moments, just long enough for doubt to creep in. I considered then if the glass could be rocking or sliding for some easily explainable reason rather than something paranormal. Shit! My logical mind had taken over and the litany of questions began.

Had I spilled water on the tile counter top? Was this the start of an earthquake? The only other time I'd seen a glass shimmy like this was when I'd been waiting to fly back to Seattle after a business meeting in San Francisco. I'd been in my hotel room when I experienced a frightening, but as I was told by the locals, "a very safe and *tiny* tremor." They were common in the bay area and came from the San Andreas Fault. Maybe I'd bumped the glass slightly while arranging the dirty dishes?

I'd just been thinking that this particular long-stemmed wine glass was next to be washed when I saw its base begin to rock. My hand, although near it, hadn't moved towards it yet. That's when I saw it move towards me by itself. I hadn't even touched it. I wasn't close enough. All I had done was think about reaching for it when it first started to wiggle. It shuddered there in front of me, looking a bit like a low budget, clay animation film. Time seemed distorted and all the tiny deliberate transitions it made were visible to me.

At first, I thought it was going to fall over and spill the remaining Pinot Grigio it held. As it continued to wobble, I forced myself to ignore my desire to clumsily save another of my Bohemian crystal wineglasses. Surprisingly, even with all its odd trembling, it stayed upright and now it looked to be picking up speed. It's quivering appeared to have reason. It was becoming more clear to me that my initial idea of an earthquake, or that I'd knocked it had been wrong. It was definitely traveling now. It wasn't falling over.

The delicately cut crystal was vibrating coherently and I recognized its intention. The movements were no longer erratic or abrupt. Then, as if it were floating on a cushion of air, like one of those amazing turbine propeller boats used in the Everglades, my lovely glass (found just off the Old Town Square in Prague) glided miraculously over uneven tiles and grouted crevices right to me.

Astonished, I now held it in my hand and wondered if I'd really seen what I'd just seen. I couldn't accept it – not at first anyway. I also, intellectually, seriously doubted a ghost was involved. Nobody liked doing dishes that much!

For a few moments, I wondered if I'd had a minor hallucination or if there really had been a small earthquake. I'd heard about people being able to move things with their minds but this was the stuff of a highly trained and focused intellect. This was the stuff of people like Uri Geller, surely not me. I knew the term telekinesis but that was all I knew. I'd never witnessed it in person or ever watched it on TV or YouTube. And I surely hadn't attempted anything like it myself. I absolutely did not think that I had this kind of capability. But maybe I did? I had so many other new capabilities since my mom had left this earth. Who knows? After all, there'd been many things moving and showing up unexpectedly since my mom had passed away including the hairspray bottle most recently and the hangers and bobbie pins before that.

But I reminded myself again, that I'd heard it took a superior strength of concentration, by an exceptional being to do these sorts of things. That helped me put things into perspective, at least for a couple of nano-seconds anyway. This wasn't something that just happened, or was it? Especially, not to me…the one Matthew had nicknamed Fluffy, long ago.

My rational and analytical left brain kept searching to find a plausible solution to this. That must be how doubt can create overwhelming denial and destroy many wonderful experiences from ever being recognized. Thinking, "After all, maybe I imagined the whole thing," could easily discredit this. After I'd quickly ruled out the earthquake idea, my brain told me I shouldn't get caught up in a delusion. I slipped deeper into dissent and my child-like anything-is-possible right brain was almost about to lose the battle.

There had to be many much more sensible excuses for something that was less than reasonable. Maybe it was my eyesight? Maybe I shouldn't have had any wine the night before? I felt good that morning, quite clear headed actually. But I couldn't stop myself from searching out other options than what had really happened.

Maybe I'd had a tiny epileptic attack, the least serious kind possible? Not a grand mal seizure but the kind that caused you to just lose a second or two in a conversation. That way there'd be no drooling or convulsing involved. Here we go. Now this could be the answer to the unanswerable. I began to investigate this more fully, as time seemed to obey my request to stand still.

That's when my mind quickly recalled Natalie, a girl friend I had when I was in my early twenties. Natalie was memorable for many reasons. She was beautiful and interesting. She was also an aerospace engineer. Working for Boeing, she was one lone woman among many hundreds of men in her secret, military, high clearance department which they referred to as a 'black box'. As long as she wanted an aerospace, rocket or electrical engineer she could have as many dates as she could imagine!

We'd gone out one night for Mexican food and a few margaritas when she suddenly revealed that she had a major health problem. This was during the 1980's, long before the drink driving laws were tightened up, and I suspect it was the tequila talking. She hadn't even told her boyfriend what she shared with me that night.

Natalie had a rare and mild form of epilepsy. I listened with fascination as she told me how she'd learned to deal with it over the years. Although I'd never noticed, she explained that as we'd been munching our cheesy jalapeno nachos, at the El Torito just minutes from her Southcenter office, she'd had many little seizures. As she lifted her salted glass to take another swallow of her top-shelf margarita, she seemed to be almost boasting. We'd been talking non-stop, in my opinion, and I hadn't been aware that she'd ever seized. She was pleased with her performance.

Natalie was so practiced at picking up the thread of interrupted conversations by using the available clues that no one could tell. I almost didn't believe her. Then she explained that she always missed a bit of whatever was going on around her. It had been that way for so long that she was comfortable with it and didn't know the difference. It was just how it was. She loved that no one ever noticed anymore. Apparently, none of her work colleagues knew except for her boss. She thought it was prudent to tell him just in case she ever screwed up at work. I later found out that she'd been involved in designing the air to ground heads up display system for the bizarre looking Stealth fighter.

Natalie usually lost only tiny bits of information when little electrical blips went off in her head every few minutes but sometimes it was more. If you were talking with her, she might lose a word or even a short sentence and depending on when the gap or pause occurred (as she liked to refer to it), it could present her with a little creative challenge or quite a big one. If she had trouble filling in the blanks, she'd just act as if she'd been distracted.

Still anxiously searching for a viable cause for the wine glass to have delivered itself to my hand, I continued reminiscing.

I recalled a movie I'd seen a few years back starring John Travolta. I love his films. In this one, he played a man who was capable of causing things to levitate. He found he was able to spin forks with his mind after he'd been hit by lightning. It wasn't about being magnetized as you might think. The jolt had amplified his supernatural powers, affecting his entire nervous system, including his brain. He read every book in his local library in just a few weeks. He also didn't need to sleep any longer and could learn a new language to fluency in only a few hours. The movie ended up as a tear-jerker. His character's phenomenal abilities were being caused by an incurable brain tumor, and he was a widower who dies shortly after falling in love again and finding a new mother for his children.

I quickly decided to put the tumor possibility out of my mind. It was too scary to consider and too destructive. It just couldn't be the reason for my increasing psychic and intuitive powers. It was far better to believe that this was some para-normal phenomenon than a deadly disease. Terminal illness wasn't an option I was willing to consider.

Rather than finding more horrible possibilities for something pretty fabulous, I decided to document the-glass-movement-thing in my personal journal. This was definitely a better decision than thinking that I might be on my last days or needed an operation immediately! I'd had numerous clients who'd had brain tumors over the past ten years. I wasn't interested in experiencing surgery up my nose to remove some golf ball sized growth responsible for both my real inspiration and my delusions.

The feather

Only a couple of weeks after the wine glass had moved by itself (or because of me), something else happened which I, again, tried to deny but couldn't. Just like when I had doubted my mother's attentions from beyond the grave and then she provided proof of her existence with the bobbie pins, I was *given* something that I could see and touch which would validate White Owl's contact.

One morning after breakfast, I went upstairs to change into my clothes. There on the floor at my feet, just inside the bedroom, was a huge feather. It wasn't a straight long feather like those that you commonly find from a pigeon or seagull's tail or a tiny one that might have come out of your pillow. It was unlike any feather I'd ever seen before. It was white tipped and the palest grey-white you can imag-ine. It was too big and perfect to have come from any pillow or goose-down duvet.

Uncrushed and unblemished, with most of its delicate veins still connected, the feather was almost the size of my entire cupped hand. It just appeared from out of nowhere like so many things had done lately. When I found it on the floor of my bedroom, I was startled but delighted. Oddly, I was concerned that it might disap-pear like Matthew's father had done when I'd looked at him full on. But there it

112

was. Right there in full view and it didn't seem to be going away so I ran quickly down to the kitchen to get my camera. After taking a picture of it, right where it sat, I went and got Matthew so he could take a look at it in situ.

It was winter time and our windows were all locked shut. So, it couldn't have come in through an open window. Again it was too big and perfect to have squirmed its way out of our bedding and our cat had never been in our bedroom, so he hadn't brought it in. Rapidly I ruled out every possible explanation I could think of as to how that feather had ended up on our bedroom floor before I yelled for Matthew to come upstairs.

Pointing out the feather on the floor, I asked him what kind he thought it was and how on earth did he think it got there. Much to my delight and surprise, Matthew said, "Oh yes, that. I saw it float down from above me earlier today. I watched it appear and then slowly drop down and land at my feet." Oh my God! I was right! It hadn't come out of one of our pillows or been somehow brought in by the cat. Matthew had seen it materialize and delicately cascade to where it sat now on the carpet. I then confessed to Matthew that I'd had another spirit talking to me who called himself White Owl.

Confirmations of my experiences just kept on coming. This was fabulous. I picked up the feather, put it on my dresser and called Theresa to tell her what had happened. I knew she'd get a kick out of it.

That very next weekend, Matthew and I had invited Sebastian and his wife over for dinner. We'd met them at a friend's party and wanted to get to know them better. Over drinks Sebastian happily announced that he was off to Argentina the following month on one of his expeditions. He was a bird enthusiast. Apparently, he frequently travelled all over the world to stalk and observe birds, including owls! I excused myself and ran upstairs to grab the feather. Moments later, sure enough, Sebastian told us that he had no doubt. It was the feather of a large Tawny Owl. They stand about two feet high and according to Sebastian they would have no desire to nest in my bedroom. With all his experience of owls he couldn't explain why I would have found it there.

Chapter Fifteen

Seeing mom again

Theresa and I had what's called "a falling out" over here in England. Her husband, as well as her daughter, started coming to the Tuesday group soon after we'd gone to see Mia Dolan together. Then, for some reason that I didn't quite understand, she wanted nothing to do with me after that. Maybe she was mad at me or jealous, or maybe she'd learned what she wanted to by meditating with me. I felt really used as well as confused by it all. Whatever happened, she seemed to prefer Sally now more than me and had dropped me like a hot potato. I was really hurt by this.

Although I tried to figure out what had happened to cause the rift between us so we could resolve it, it became clear that Theresa didn't want to and couldn't care less if she ever saw me again. All her promises of being friends until we died were quickly forgotten. I reminded myself that she'd first been a client and perhaps I never should have invited her into my private world, because now I was finding it uncomfortable going to Sally's group.

For a few weeks I struggled with feeling okay enough to go there. I decided I would only go on the days when I felt like it, and I'd stay home if I felt uncomfortable in any way. I promised myself, and Matthew, after I finally told him about what had happened that I would keep going as long as I was enjoying it.

Months ago, after Fiona had first told me about the SAGB (the Spiritual Association of Great Britain) I'd found a few workshops I was interested in. Theresa and I had planned to attend one, by a man named John Tunbridge in London. His course was called "Trance and Related Phenomena" and was a hands-on workshop, based around altered levels of consciousness and trance.

I'd read that Tunbridge did what was called *physical mediumship*. He not only had the voices of his guides or teachers come through him (mainly Arthur Conan Doyle in his case), but he took on their appearances as well! He referred to this as transfiguring and it was rare. It allowed onlookers to witness the channeling visually as well as audibly. Theresa didn't want to go with me now that we weren't friends and decided to get her money back. I'd been nervous about attending this workshop anyway, as you can imagine from the title and description. But now, I was going by myself! Although, it sounded a bit creepy, I'm so pleased I summoned enough courage to go alone.

What John taught me that day finally allowed me to progress into voice channeling. First, he cleared up the confusion I had about what it meant to be aware and fully conscious while channeling versus being unconscious or in a full trance. He said that the majority of people who channeled these days stayed semi-conscious, in what he called a light trance. They were just relaxed or subdued when they worked with a spirit rather than being unconscious or in a deep trance. He explained that when you're in a light trance, "Spirits control the body but don't step into it." I didn't quite get this but without me having to ask he explained further, "They don't step into you by pushing you out of your own body but instead *a mental blending* takes place. The mind of the *spirit worker* blends with you as the medium. However, inviting the spirit in is letting them take over your body."

He talked about how spirit work can be a bit intense and that we had to clear our own baggage and emotional stuff first. Then he said, "Working with spirits can give you such a feeling of unconditional love, but, it takes time to work with spirit, to let go and let it happen." When I heard John say this, I felt a lot better about any delays I'd encountered in my channeling. Perhaps things were happening as and when they should. Then he said, "Everyone works in the way that's right for them now. It's individual and according to where you are going and it has different stages."

Then John confirmed some things I'd felt previously, like when I'd sensed that my hand had grown while meditating. He said that sometimes there is a, "morphy feeling," when you feel larger or different in your physical self. "This happens when your mind blends with theirs."

He discussed how our guardian angel is also our, "doorkeeper or gatekeeper." That's the third time an outsider had given me confirmation of what Archangel Gabriel had told me months ago. Tunbridge explained, "Our guardian angel manages the spirit contact and if it feels jerky, it means that it isn't right." Hum, maybe that's why my foot had stomped the last time I'd encountered the spirit called Sean.

Apparently according to John, the spirit steps behind your spine and comes closer and closer, all the while with the approval of your guardian, until finally, "you've blended mentally and they've stepped into your energy." All this talk about mind blending reminded me again of Star Trek. This time I thought of Spock performing a Vulcan mind-meld on Captain Kirk. Maybe good sci-fi was based on real stuff? I read somewhere (only recently) that Gene Roddenberry, the science fiction author and creator of Star Trek, used to sit and listen to Jane Roberts channel Seth! John Tunbridge also talked about how you can feel it when a spirit touches you but that you can never touch them.

Then the course took a dramatic turn towards some really weird stuff, as if what I'd heard and experienced already hadn't been weird enough! He began to lecture about plasma or ectoplasm coming out of us. Ectoplasm, he said, is the physical matter from the spirit world. This sounded a lot like the green slime seen in Ghostbusters with Bill Murray and Sigourney Weaver. Then John discussed something called "table tilting" and "rapping". Other means of validating spirit contact, often associated with the Victorian times. Then he explained how using a cabinet to concentrate and focus energy along with a 15 watt red light was very helpful when you attempted transfiguration. And there was more which I hadn't wanted to know about which I won't include here!

Probably the most important pearl of wisdom that day was when John spoke of how hard it was to start saying the first few words during light trance channeling.

Bingo! What followed made waiting all those months for his class, and taking a very early two hour train into London – (all by myself) worthwhile. He said we had to push through that difficult moment and advised us to, "Just start speaking by saying 'Good Afternoon' and the other words will come."

He'd obviously known what I'd been struggling with ever since the week before Valentine's Day more than a year ago. I suspect it had happened to him in the same way. He said, "Spirit only give you the first words and keep repeating them until you say them, then you get more." Exactly! That's what I'd figured out on my own. I felt really proud that I'd been right all this time. He continued saying, "Once you speak a few words, you often go deeper and others come."

Part of the course was spent participating in spiritual healing exercises. We also tried the table tilting thing and then each of us had a go at attempting to channel and transfigure, under the glow of the red light in front of the make-shift cabinet (the open door of a coat closet). John had us all sit in chairs which were now arranged in slightly off-set semi circles so everyone could see the face and body of the person that was potentially going to channel, or maybe physically change.

Once we'd all found a seat, he went to the door and locked it, saying, "Sometimes this can be a bit emotional and odd but for the safety of the person performing the physical mediumship the door will remain locked. Please stay in your seats no matter what happens." Oh my God! I was really scared now.

John started it off by channeling, in succession, three or four of the spirits he worked with regularly. It was incredible! Right before my eyes he changed into another person, spoke to us as them, and then a few minutes later he changed again. His looks "transfigured" or "morphed" to match the spirit who had "stepped in" along with their mannerisms and words.

Then each of us, one by one, sat in the red light to try it out. Some people, like me, had no luck, while others not only spoke but they appeared to turn from woman to man or take on a different color of hair. One woman even seemed to grow a transparent dark beard! Others appeared to become taller or had their facial features alter. It was bizarre but hypnotic to watch and experience. Then it was Natalie's turn. I knew her by name because we'd been paired up in one of the earlier exercises. Although nothing came out of Natalie's mouth (no words or ectoplasm, luckily) as we watched her, she too appeared to change, right in front of us. Her eyes looked open, but in fact they were someone else's that were open over her own (I suppose much like the night when Sally saw green eyes overlaying mine).

Natalie, or whoever she had become, began to physically move her head and shoulders in some kind of super slow-motion in order to visibly scan the room. Although her real eyes remained closed the entire time, the other set of eyes appeared to be looking for something or someone. She was looking at each individual's face. She'd started with the people to my far right and continued to pan slowly, after gazing for a few full seconds at each person's face. Then when she got to me, she stopped.

I let out a scream, after really looking at her face. Immediately, I tried to get out of my chair to run for the door but the people around me grabbed me and held me down. They tried to reassure me that I was safe. Maybe they'd attended this sort of workshop before and thought this was normal – but I was petrified!

Although they'd kept me in my chair, against my will, my head was now facing the back of the room. I didn't want to look at Natalie. I sensed she was still stopped in front of me. I could feel *those* penetrating eyes staring at me and still, she said nothing. I felt her eyes (or the spirits I guess) on the back of my head. I started to shake and cry.

I told the people, who were now holding me gently, that Natalie's face had looked like my mom's. The lady next to me touched my shoulders again, this time quite lovingly. I remember thinking it was extremely unusual to be touched with this much love by someone I didn't really know. Then she said firmly, "Look at her. She's come to see you. She's waiting for you." Then more loudly, she commanded me slowly and emphatically, "Look at her!"

Holding the hands of those around me tightly gave me enough courage to turn and face the front, but my eyes were still diverted to my lap. Finally I looked up and there she was. Still covering Natalie's was the entire face of my mother. Even my frightened outburst and attempt to escape hadn't scared her off. She looked directly at me without moving or saying a word. I looked right back at her and straight into those eyes. That's when I felt the most incredible love I'd ever felt in my entire life run through me. I cried again but didn't want to turn away this time as I let my mom's love for me sink in.

I left a message for John Tunbridge a few days after the course. I asked that he call me to talk briefly about what had happened when my mother had appeared in our class. When he called he said, "Your mom had stepped into Natalie's energy trying to show herself to you. It was just a way of getting more evidence to us." Apparently spirits will use the person who is most suitable for this and, "often another medium is used verses the person who is close to the spirit."

Chapter Sixteen

Knocking on Heaven's door

After I saw my mom again, oddly enough (or predictably) I wasn't in such a hurry to voice channel. I didn't want to rush it. Seeing her had shocked me but that wasn't the reason I was willing to wait.

When I saw her face, and felt her unbelievable love, it had an amazing and lasting impact on me. No longer could I deny her many attempts to reach me, and I didn't want to now, either. I finally stopped looking for excuses and logical reasons to explain spiritual experiences. It had been real. I knew now that our connection and love had really survived her physical death.

My mom still existed. She was just somewhere else.

She was still watching over me and participating in my life regardless of whether I chose to acknowledge her or not. I knew that she had really touched me, just as she had when she'd been alive. Fully accepting it, I could begin to benefit even more from her contact and what it had done for me.

Seeing her face again, must have been what I'd needed. It showed me unequivocally that she wasn't really gone. I knew, once and for all, that my mom and our loved ones don't really leave us behind – they live on. And I knew now that everything that had happened to me since my mom had died had been genuine. This acceptance and understanding could only improve me.

With less fear I advanced

Since I'd attended that incredible workshop an inner confidence and strength had been building inside of me. I also recognized the massive transformation that had taken place to get me to that workshop on trance phenomena. I was less fearful than I'd ever been in my entire life!

I was a different person now. I felt I was a more complete person than the woman who'd shared in her mom's last dying breaths only a year and a half before. I was stronger in more ways than I knew and I began to integrate all these extraordinary experiences into my normal way of being.

Having felt her intense love that day, somehow allowed me to erase the last ounce of doubt I'd been holding onto. Showing her face to me, regardless of how difficult or easy it had been for her, had achieved her desired results, finally. I knew she wanted me to know that everything was okay and that I didn't need to be afraid any longer.

The workshop had also helped me to understand what I could expect once I was really ready to voice channel. I felt good about patiently waiting for the right time for it to happen rather than forcing it.

Seeing mom's face over Natalie's had instantly advanced my beliefs. I gained an inner peace from seeing her and an assuredness that when the time was right, Ramses, or another spirit (probably not my mom), would be happy to *step into my energy*. I knew it was only a matter of time and that I was being prepared. I could wait as long as necessary now.

It took another six months before I saw any real progress in my voice channeling, or my written channeling, for that matter. It was more than three years after my mom's dying touch and fourteen months after the channeling had naturally happened on its own that fateful Valentine's Day, a day dedicated to love, that my channeling advanced. Although it took some time, when it eventually came, it was BIG.

I'd still been attending Sally's group almost every week, with the exception of a short break after the falling out with Theresa. Theresa was still going to Sally's, and although she and I weren't friends anymore we were courteous and comfortable when we met up there. The atmosphere had calmed, even though I never quite understood why Theresa had dumped me so swiftly and completely. Tuesday nights at the group were very nice again. I'd even come to realize how genuinely lovely Lynn was and enjoyed seeing her on Tuesdays. I was happy with the routine I had now and meditating on Tuesdays gave me something I really enjoyed doing midweek while Matthew was away. I really looked forward to Tuesdays almost like someone else might look forward to going to the movies.

Then in May, in Sally's garden room, I felt many spiritual presences come to me in succession. One after another, each of them announced themselves with their different signal. I'd learned how to recognize them by how I felt when they were around me.

Then my hand started moving, responding to shuttles of energy going up the inside of my body. I tried to isolate the individual spirits and asked them to come to me one at a time as John Tunbridge had told us to do in the London workshop.

The guided meditation that night first took us to a ledge. However, in my mind, I remember it looking more like the edge of a cliff with a massive drop off. When we reached the ledge (in the visualization) we were told that we would meet up with our guides there. As I approached the cliff's edge, in my mind's eye, there, standing beside me, I saw what I felt and somehow knew was GOD!

I thought, "Oh my," in my head and audibly gasped. Then the apparition started to change and somehow I understood that it wasn't sure how it should present itself to me. The apparition didn't know how it needed to appear for me to accept it for what it was. It must have changed six or seven times before stopping.

Only that week had I realized that I had begun to feel that I believed in *"a GOD"* and now in this meditation, there it, He or She was! As I thought about this, I felt this spirit's energy close to me and I decided to do as we'd been instructed in that pivotal workshop. I welcomed them in my head. Bizarrely, I felt I was speaking to a group rather than an individual. That's why I welcomed *them* instead of saying that he or she could come into my energy, via my gatekeeper Gabriel.

I heard myself ask, still silently in my head, "Was that God there on the ledge?" Then amazingly, after having a little discussion with myself – I heard God!

119

Immediately, I heard myself say, *"Oh my, am I privileged enough to be able to talk to God or even channel God?"* I wondered if channeling God were even possible? I put that thought to one side and said to myself, *"Of course I can talk to God but can I hear God talk back? Is this possible, for me?"* I thought again about whether I could channel God and said to myself, *"Hearing Him would be enough!"* I felt it was a ludicrous idea for me to think that I would channel God tonight! Then an answer came, which seemed to be in response to my question about whether I could hear God talk, I clearly heard the words, *"Of course you can, when you are ready."*

I felt His signal again, which I recognized as one that I had felt before while meditating with Theresa last autumn and winter at my home. Just the other day, I'd sensed it again when I found myself attempting to talk to God after finally listening to an audio of a lecture by Susan Shumsky. She had spoken at the Expo on how to hear "the still small voice of God within" and although I hadn't been able to hear her talk, I purchased the CD and brought it home with my partial "box of rocks". That had been many months ago and I'd only just listened to it for the first time that week.

I didn't feel ready to channel God, or even have an in-depth conversation with God, right then in Sally's shed. I was comfortable now with angels but not God! I giggled silently inside to myself. Then I asked Gabriel to see who else was waiting to speak with me, thinking that maybe there'd be someone of less importance I'd feel more confident talking with. I can hardly believe that I did this, but I did, and I'd logged it all in my little journal. How stupid I'd been then, not to want to talk with God that night.

Without much warning, the next spirit presented itself immediately. It had obviously been waiting (as John Tunbridge and Katrina, my good friend in Seattle had said spirits would) and this time I felt it instantly inside my brain. So I asked, *"Are you ready to speak?"* and the response that came was, *"Are you?"* This sounded very sarcastic and actually pretty funny. Just before we'd started our meditation that night, I'd been concerned about trying to voice channel because a man that occasionally attended our group (who didn't believe in angels or spirits) had showed up. Why he came to Sally's Tuesday night group sometimes was beyond me. But I guess, you can benefit from meditating in a group – regardless of your beliefs. However, his attendance added another uncomfortable dynamic to the mix and it made me doubt whether I really was ready to try again.

Then I was told, *"You shouldn't worry what others think,"* and abruptly this spirit left me.

I felt an urge to put my hands face down on my thighs and knew White Owl had approached me. As soon as I did this, these words came to me, *"You're still struggling. Why?"* At first I thought he was referring to my life in general, as I'd been worried lately about normal things like finances like so many people. But then I realized his comment probably referred to me not accepting the messages that were being offered to me. I knew from what he was saying that I needed to put some serious thought into answering his question for myself. I wrote in my journal in large letters, "WHY AM I STILL STRUGGLING?"

Suddenly the next being came to me. This time I felt as if I must sit as erect as possible and found myself throwing back my shoulders. I'd had this feeling or signal before, but wasn't sure who it represented. I thought it was an angel, maybe even Archangel Michael. I felt myself grow and stretch upwards, as if I had massive wings extending to the ceiling, fanning out and enveloping me and the others in the group (except the man who was a non-believer). Then I realized that my mind had influenced the spontaneous vision in regards to him and once I put my personal worries about him aside, I felt the wings envelop everyone in our circle.

I asked the spirit (in my head), *"How can you help me not be afraid?"* I picked up my journal and pen from my lap and wrote the answer I received:

See the final destination and not the problem. Not every tiny thing that stubs your toe. You focus on the bit just in front of you and not in the distance. It's the nature of the human experience but you can work with this to your advantage. See the problem as a step stone on a path towards fulfillment. Be on your way and be always on your way. Never give in to the problem, never relent. Keep moving forward and up. It's the only way. It's easier than you know and much easier than everyone admits.

We have so much to tell you, so much to share. ASK, ASK, ASK and never stop asking. It's so vital for you to take in the light and not push it away, as is so often the tendency for you mortals – that's where you are wrong – the mortal idea.

See us and see more. See it all and see us. See a space and see a star [*]. See it, see it, see it and stop looking so narrow.

*Note: I wasn't sure if the word that was presented here was really *"star"*. I saw something like a star sparkling in my head and I couldn't get the actual word quick enough, before the person leading the group that night had started speaking to call us back from our meditation.

Finally, I heard in my head, *"We must go, as we are interrupting the class now. Bless you."*

I'd written in my journal that I'd found the use of the word *"We"* fascinating.

When I turned the radio on while driving home that night from Sally's, the DJ was just putting on a request of "Knocking on Heaven's Door" by Bob Dylan! Again, I was amazed at how synchronicity worked.

I had to stop my car more than three times, to make notes in my journal on the way home. I'd never done this before that night. While I was stopped, I checked first that I could actually read the messages that I'd received earlier in meditation. Then I found myself asking a question about quantum physics (in my head) and I started to hear an answer coming back which I couldn't believe. I seemed to still be very connected somehow, just sitting there in my car. I decided that rather than staying there in the dark, on the single car-width lane, that I really should get home and see if I could ask questions again of Archangel Michael or another being and actually get a message when I was by myself.

Up to this point, I'd been too concerned to meditate totally on my own. It wasn't so much to do with Sally's safety warnings now but because my senses were always further enhanced after I'd meditated. I was often so sensitive afterwards that I was very jumpy for hours. But tonight I felt it was safe for me try it.

When I got home, I immediately went into the lounge and sat down on the settee (where Matthew's dad liked to sit). I said a kind of prayer, including an invitation of protection (as Sally always did). I asked that only the highest level of spiritual contact be possible. Then holding my pen in my hand, all ready, I forgot to ask about quantum physics and instead heard myself ask, *"How does one know they are in the presence of God?"*

Immediately my eyes welled up with tears and I began to cry. I had a sense of release, as if I was being freed of any stress or pent up emotions I'd been carrying. These old feelings were replaced with a sense of calm and healthy level of excitement. Then very quickly I felt an answer starting to approach my mind and I wrote the following words exactly as they came to me:

There's a feeling, a knowing, a resonance, a sound, a pealing, a bang, a blip, a snap, a spark, a feeling, a sensation, a sound, a gurgle, a sunset, a stream of light. There are many signs of God and one only needs to look and be open to them. It's not perceptible to some but it is to so, so, many. They live for it and through it. They know it like they know themselves - better. They see it and smell it and taste it with their eyes and soul. They become radiant. They become fearless. They become all knowing and safe. They are the special ones – those that know, know God. They are privileged with innocence and grace. They see me and know it. No doubt, no trauma, no worry of it not lasting. No time to worry as they just know it will be there for them forever, this feeling of bliss and security and sanity to all, the unknown.

The unknown, what a funny thought, there is no unknown as you can know it all if you choose. Simply make that determination and you have access. Access and all the dreams and secrets are yours. Again ASK and YE SHALL RECEIVE. I wish you'd listen!

It's so simple really but mankind makes it more difficult for they must – they have to – it's part of growth. I believe in you and [I missed some words here]. I digress. I'm sorry. I am not being derogatory to mankind. I love it with all my being. I'm one with all and can be seen in all.

Back to your question, I do have a bit of a sense of humor, as you'd know if you'd look at some of nature. What is God? I don't know how to put it in your mind's eye easy enough. It's all there is and all you'll ever want. It's beauty and grace, it's polished river rocks and more. It's what you love. It's different to all but just the same as well. I can be seen in the autumn leaves

122

and the brook of crystal dancing stars of reflection. I can be seen in the snowflakes and morning dew. I can be felt in the touch of a baby's hand and the caress of a new love. I can be heard on the wings of doves and thunderclaps. I can be felt in the warm sand and blown away just as easily.

I can be what you need and what you seek. I can be alone there for you or in a group to make you feel welcome. What you need, I am. What you fear, I am not. Never fear me. Never fear if you can help it. Be in love and be special. Be mine and be yours. Be one and be it all. You can see me, feel me, when you want. Just look up.

And you, like others, may feel my presence as an energy of constant satisfaction and overpowering electricity, stopping you and causing you to pause to enjoy and reflect in the moment. Energy is there for all and energy is all there is. I'm there and I'm here always. Be with me and be without fear.

I love you and care for you in the way you need most. Be aware this is not always what you would select for yourself. I don't choose – it's all set out to move you along. I just help when need be and when you look for me.

You keep so many lovely things inside that need to be shown to all. Share your light and I will be present.

Then as quickly as it had started, it ended and I said out loud and wrote at the same time, *"Thank you, God."* Then that same amazing tingling which I'd felt earlier in the week rushed through me and I cried again. They were tears of joy and gratitude, and they were tears of unexpected, complete belief. I held my hands together in the prayer position and shockingly admitted it to myself. I then thanked God again for honoring me by speaking to me directly.

When I reread what I had written, I was amazed and wrote after it in my journal, "Something is happening to me and I love it. I will keep doing this writing – it seems more conducive than my few words of channeled voices until I get stronger. I'd like to speak but it's not necessary. I need to rest now…a little TV to settle me and then to bed. Many thanks be to God! P.S. I love His signal that He's present!! It's lovely for me."

I'd also noted in my journal that I hadn't been confident of the word *"rock"* which had been used in the message I'd received. I'd crossed it out at first, but then realized that the *polished river rock* comment must have been accurate because of my love of rocks and crystals.

I'll never feel alone again

Once I realized that I could receive channeled information and even talk with God, all by myself, even though it was mostly through writing at this point, I felt the reins had finally been released. Anything seemed possible, now that my narrow views and worries about protection were gone.

Because of my mom's after-death determination to comfort me and show me that she still existed, or maybe all the while she was intent on convincing me that there really was a loving God, I learned first-hand that we continue *beyond good-bye*. I also learned that even I am more capable than I could have ever imagined. I'm sure that every one of us must have all these same abilities which I discovered only after my mom touched me from beyond. They must be lying dormant within each of us and all that is needed is something to ignite them, something to open them up from inside of us and *wake us up* to our expanded intuition and unlimited perceptions.

In my case, it was my mom who did this for me. She'd reached into me and knowingly or not flipped my switches to their *on* positions. After remarkably sharing in her transition and finally allowing myself to believe in all the evidence and love she'd so persistently provided from *the other-side-of-life*, I was transformed. For some, their catalyst might be walking in the woods, having a baby or dying while drowning and then being brought back to life. While others, like Gordon Smith and Mia Dolan may just be born more spiritually open and aware.

I had no reason to fear death any longer. My mom was still with me after her physical death. I'd personally experienced her touch. I'd seen an angel and I knew now that there exists a benevolent and loving higher being or God. I also learned that if I listened close enough, and without fear, that I could hear Him speak directly to me. I felt more fulfilled and content than I had in a long while, if not in my entire life. It was as if I'd finally found some missing pieces to my personal puzzle.

Not feeling limited or scared any longer, I knew I'd eventually find a way to voice channel again. When the time was right, it would happen. I also knew that these deep connections, the spiritual blending of energy, must carry with it many beautiful lessons. So, although I wasn't sure what these new lessons would be, I had faith (finally!) that they'd be worth the wait. And I have my mom to thank for all this.

Part Two

My research. What I found out…

Last picture of Annie and Betty together
(Annie 40 years old and Betty 77 years old)

Chapter Seventeen

An overview of what the experts say

One of the most surprising things my research has uncovered, is that these exceptional moments of timeless expansion, when the mind feels more alive and alert than ever, are frequently associated with death. Often they are reported when someone has died briefly or shared in another's death (as I did with my mom). These lingering and impressive states of awareness also occur spontaneously during peak moments in one's life – whether stressful or wonderful.

As I mentioned earlier, to understand what really happened between me and my mom and hopefully to find out why I changed so dramatically afterwards, I investigated not only near-death experiences (NDEs) but spiritually transformative experiences (STEs) and something called after-death communications (ADCs). I also looked into various phenomena which surrounds death and dying, euphemistically referred to as end of life phenomena.

Before I share what I learned and how it relates to my own experiences with my mom, and perhaps your personal experiences, I feel I should tell you a little about the confusion that near-death experiences have caused in the medical and scientific communities. If this doesn't interest you, please feel free to skip ahead to the following chapter where I discuss the common characteristics of these amazing experiences, which have shown so many people that their lives will continue after death. This chapter is intended as an overview and is slightly more technical than the rest of the book. Please don't hesitate to turn to Chapter 18 at any point in your reading.

Conflicting opinions about near-death experiences

As near-death experiences regularly occur when someone has been clinically dead, they have caused significant conflict and division among scientists. The mere fact that someone formed a memory while they were technically dead defies current theories. Additionally, reports of NDEs are on the increase as medical advancements offer the capability of further extending and saving lives.

Scientists are all about proof. That's why they use words like *correlates*, *suggests* or even *strongly suggests* when describing their research results. It takes a lot for a real scientist to use the word *proven*. Scientists are rooted in disciplined practices, theory, mathematics and physics. They are known for their efforts in proving or disproving theories through stringent repeatable protocols and are often reluctant to give up previously accepted concepts.

Although I've been convinced by the findings of near-death studies, remember that I had my own first-hand introduction by way of my mom. My moving experiences with her were what shifted my beliefs beyond recognition. They happened long before I'd ever heard about or looked into NDEs to understand what happened between us. Even though I've had my own experiences, as you've read

I tried repeatedly to ignore the evidence – although my heart knew it to be true.

Instead of embracing the findings of valid NDE studies, many scientists have chosen to keep their heads stuck in the sand (in my humble opinion). They'd rather cling to previously accepted theories about life, death and how the mind works than put their heads above the parapet. It can be difficult to stand out and challenge current beliefs, especially if you run the risk of losing funding for your own projects by doing so. NDE researchers have to be courageous.

There will always be those who refuse to acknowledge new ideas until it is impossible to hold onto a differing opinion. Recent near-death research has revealed radical ideas that don't match up to long-held views. Because of this, some scientists just cannot identify with the results – not yet anyway. A leap in understanding is necessary and a new way of thinking has to be adopted. It's just like the old debate of whether the world was flat or the world was round. In essence, these opposing opinions are what science is based on and strong debates will appear again and again, until an old understanding is finally overturned. It can take many decades and generations before a mass shift is accomplished in a particular area of science and medicine.

Over the past ten years, primarily because of my work as a therapist but also due to my experiences after my mom died, I've learned that people's identities are wrapped up with their beliefs (and history). Their lives are framed by their beliefs, as are their expectations. Therefore, whenever you ask someone to give up or alter a belief they hold, regardless of how obvious the evidence or how correct it might be to do so, you have to help them get beyond their resistance. A mini or major identity crisis, of sorts, usually has to take place before a paradigm shift can occur within them. After all, in essence, you are asking them to admit that they were wrong.

Although I believe the latest NDE research successfully *proves* that we continue to exist after death, albeit in a different form, many scientists still dispute this. Some believe they are even being generous to say the research *suggests* it is a possibility. Much of the clash or divergence in opinion seems to be caused by a split (or even a competition) between followers of various principles of physics, as well as biology and neurobiology.

Supporters of the older mechanistic Newtonian principles of physics, disagree with those who accept the relatively more modern ideas of quantum physics. Many of the extraordinary experiences surrounding death and dying can be easily explained with quantum mechanics – if you are able to accept that the mind might extend beyond the physical body.

However, you don't need to be a scientist or have to understand basic quantum physics to believe in life after-death. It's easy to make that leap if, like me or like so many others, you've personally had a spiritually transformative experience, a near-death or near-death-like experience – or you've received after-death communication from a loved one. Your experiences are your proof. You don't need a study to support them. In my final research interview, Elizabeth Fenwick, the co-author of *The Art of Dying* and *Truth in the Light: An Investigation of over 300 Near-Death Experiences,* shared with me how her own skeptical views were finally changed and then so beautifully declared, "My eyes were opened. I could no longer be a blind disbeliever."

So, although the general population of scientists may publicly reject and even ridicule these *very real experiences* and would rather explain away NDE research results, I've been convinced by them, as have the researchers I've spoken with. Some scientists say NDEs are simply hallucinations caused by a lack of oxygen to the brain (anoxia). Others think NDEs may be a reaction to drugs or the brain's response to extreme states of fear or pain. It's even speculated that NDEs may just be the normal symptoms which occur in the brain when approaching death.

Consciousness, the brain and NDEs during cardiac arrests

Although I've discovered that no one actually knows how the mind and brain in fact work, some people are still more comfortable dismissing or even maligning near-death studies.

Our understanding of how the brain functions is in question right now. I've been advised that significant hypotheses about the brain and the mind (your consciousness) have been disproved in recent years. Many long accepted theories have been shown to be inaccurate! Various well-respected neuroscientists have admitted that they really don't know as much as they thought they did about the mind and brain. What exists, are only theories about how consciousness and the brain *might* work.

Scientists either don't know, can't prove, *or perhaps can't agree* on where consciousness comes from. No one knows how we perceive or create our perceptions and unique experiences. There are on-going heated debates on whether consciousness comes from outside of your brain or whether it is generated by it.

The research of patients who have had NDEs during cardiac arrests *strongly suggests* (or proves in my non-scientific opinion) that your brain only acts as a receiver for your conscious experience.

To clarify, a cardiac arrest is not the same thing as a heart attack. A heart attack is what occurs when a clot blocks the flow of blood, while a cardiac arrest is the point at which someone dies (according to current science and medicine). In the case of a cardiac arrest, the heart has stopped beating and unless something is done very quickly, the person will die in a matter of seconds.

Dr. Peter Fenwick, an eminent neuropsychiatrist, expert on epilepsy, disorders of the brain and near-death experiences, explained that when someone has a cardiac arrest that there is no heart beat, no breathing and no brain function. Within eight to seventeen seconds of the heart stopping, the brain stops working and we are thought to be truly dead. Unless we are brought back to life through medical intervention at that point – that's it for us. Conventional science has considered this state to be the end. However, the studies of cardiac arrested patients who had NDEs repeatedly show that it is at this point of complete clinical physical death and even minutes after, but before resuscitation, that these near-death experiences are thought to have taken place.

Fenwick stated, "The evidence for this comes from those people who have NDEs and leave their bodies, going up to the ceiling and looking back at the cardiac resuscitation being carried out. They sometimes seem to be able to describe accurately what they say they have seen, and what was later confirmed as occurring. Some researchers have placed cards near the ceiling of the room in the hope that patients would be able to describe what they see on the cards when they are 'out of their body'."

These accurate reports of the resuscitation process were startling news, because as Fenwick explained, "When brain function ceases in cardiac arrest it is impossible either to have an experience or to remember what happened during the period of unconsciousness. As the senses are not functioning, they should not be able to gather information at this time. The evidence that there is at present suggests that they might be able to, but this needs to be made stronger before we can be certain." However, this fascinating research suggests that these profound temporary-death experiences, of extreme vividness and clarity, may happen during this supposed unconscious time. This means that the established theories must be questioned and revised.

The brain as a receiver

Rather like your television or your car radio, your brain appears to take in signals from outside of itself, from the mind. Evidence is mounting that the brain is acting as some sort of receiver of information, rather than the creator of it. It is thought that consciousness may truly reside outside of our physical brain and body (at least in part) and could potentially be unending, continuing into the cosmos and intermingling with other signals from everything and everyone else. This intermingling is called entanglement in quantum physics.

If you are interested in finding out more about these ideas, I recommend reading *Consciousness Beyond Life* by Dr. Pim van Lommel (the Dutch cardiologist known for conducting the largest prospective cardiac arrest NDE study at the time of this publication). This book explains his research findings and the basic quantum physics concepts of non-local information and entanglement in regards to NDEs. I also highly recommend Dr. Peter Fenwick and his wife Elizabeth Fenwick's book *The Art of Dying*. It offers a fascinating and substantial contribution to understanding what happens when someone dies. Additionally, you may wish to read Rupert Sheldrake's book *Morphic Resonance: The Nature of Formative Causation*. Sheldrake is one of the world's most innovative biologists and his "extended mind" and "morphic field" theories are compelling.

Subjective Experiences: NDE, death and dying phenomena and after-death communication (ADC)

Near-death experiences and many other experiences that occur around death are extremely subjective, personal and impactful. As they are so personal, they are more difficult to objectively measure scientifically.

In general, NDEs are characterized by a feeling of total comfort, love, compassion and unity. They frequently include a sensation of dazzling (but non-painful) light, and the feeling of being in the presence of a benevolent, loving and all-knowing being. Near-death or near-death-like experiences are said to be beyond words or ineffable, which means that they are indescribable in our own human language. In the next chapter, I explain the common characteristics of near-death experiences and the common after-effects in greater detail.

Experts in the field of death and dying phenomena have also shown that there are many other amazing experiences which occur to the family members and caregivers of those who are preparing to die. I found that NDEs are only part of the story and magic that surrounds death.

Although many of these experiences are not often talked about, except maybe between close family members, there are many documented and even predictable things which happen before, during and after someone has died. Both the person who dies, and frequently those who are close to them, have mystical or spiritual experiences.

Interestingly, the dying refer to their upcoming death in what Dr. Peter Fenwick and Elizabeth Fenwick call "journeying language". They often tell their relatives, medical staff or hospice workers that someone (usually a deceased relative) has come for them and that they will be moving on, traveling or going on their way. They don't say they are dying, but instead say that they are going someplace - the place the Fenwick's refer to as, "Elsewhere."

The person whose physical life is coming to an end and those who witness their death, or are emotionally connected to them, often experience similarly peculiar things. The Fenwick's say these occurrences are part of the process of dying. Special events surrounding the death process extend to nurses, doctors, medics, hospice aids, by-standers, chaplains, family members, pets and even electrical or mechanical items, such as lamps or clocks and other physical things.

It seems that the death of anyone always leaves a wake but also has foreseeable and obvious precursors. When someone dies, they unavoidably (or purposely) impact those they have a strong emotional attachment to as they transition to the after-life or next dimension. I discuss death and dying phenomena in greater detail in Chapter 18.

After-death communications (ADC) or what I've chosen to call after-death contact (because I felt my mother's after-death touch long before I heard her voice) are apparently quite common. I've discovered many people experience after-death communications, in the disruptive wake of death of their loved ones. After-death communications are especially common if you've lost a child or spouse.

You'll find the various forms of after-death communication explained more fully in the next chapter. However, in brief, let me just say that your deceased loved ones are apparently able to employ any number of notification methods to show you that they are still around you and they have continued to exist beyond this physical reality.

After-death communications are also referred to as post-mortem experiences, although I prefer to think of them less clinically and more optimistically. To me, they are ways in which your loved ones keep in touch with you. If you are open to their contact, after-death communications act as confirmation that your loved ones are still active in your life. My mom's after-death communications confirmed for me that love outlasts physical death.

Those who have *left* you, often come back to comfort you, advise and even guide you. You might hear their voice call your name, or hear a snippet of music or the ringing of bells. Sometimes people receive a telephone call only to find that there is no one on the other end of the line. Or you might see part or all of a person. The vision may be semi-transparent or look like the person is still alive (just as Matthew's father appeared to us). You may smell a fragrance or experience a taste related to the deceased. Other times you may just *know* that someone is there with you or feel a recognizable touch, as I did when my mother stroked my hair and gave me a hug.

Some comments the experts made about what happened to me

Even though I wasn't close to dying myself, as it turned out, sharing in my mother's death had the same effect on me. I responded to our experience just like someone who had died and been brought back to life after having a NDE.

My life was turned upside down for many years as a consequence of my mother's unexpected actions. Although, I suspect that if I'd had faith in something greater than myself, that this upheaval or the intensity of it may not have been necessary.

So, even though I didn't have exactly what the researchers consider to be a complete near-death experience, and I may or may not have had what Raymond Moody and others now refer to as a *shared near-death experience* (when a bystander "sees the light" along with the dying), I have had almost all the after-effects that accompany these exceptional events. Additionally, my scenario matches those who have had what is called a mystical or transcendental experience. My investigation shows that no matter what I chose to call what I experienced – it was significant.

Although throughout my investigation there appeared to be little clinical research into the after-effects of people who hadn't died briefly, but instead experienced a death of someone else empathically, or were touched by their loved ones after-death, P.M.H. Atwater addresses these same after-effects in her book

Near-Death Experiences: The Rest of the Story. Atwater asserts, "that near-death states," of which my initial experience, she says, falls into, "are not any type of anomaly, but, rather, are part of the larger genre of transformations of consciousness." Atwater, Yolaine Stout of ACISTE, and all those I interviewed, repeatedly stated that they understand these experiences can happen under a huge variety of circumstances and initiate significant changes within the individuals. These touches of death, either yours or someone else's, provide an unknowable force and impetus.

Atwater has taken a slightly different angle than some of the other researchers of near-death experiences and the after-effects. Neurologist and psychiatrist, Dr. Bruce Greyson explained that there are different perspectives and interests, "Psychiatrists work with individual people, so we're looking at the NDE from the standpoint of the individual experience, whereas other people, for example, Kenneth Ring, who has done so much in this area as a social psychologist, looks at what the NDE means for humanity or for society. Does this play a role in the evolution of our species? It's a slightly different question. He's looking at: *Is our species advancing?* And I'm looking at: *Does the individual change?*"

Even if it may not be right for me to call my experience a *valid* near-death experience, it was some sort of transcendental event and I'm aware that the label isn't really what matters. It's the subsequent after-effects and the chaotic aftermath which I experienced, that even scientists use to justify the authenticity of these subjective death-state experiences.

Although some have focused their research on NDEs which occurred during cardiac arrests, in my opinion this does not discount or invalidate other experiences. Studying cardiac arrest NDEs simply helps to quantify, more objectively, an event which is very subjective by its nature. By concentrating on the available information that is objective in these studies, and therefore less questionable and easier to verify, the validity of all these amazing experiences is promoted in my view. The cardiac arrest NDE is by no means the only *real NDE* – but it helps to *prove* the others are possible – because you shouldn't have a memory when you are supposed to be brain dead! Studying NDEs during cardiac arrests, therefore, in my view, is supportive of these enhanced states of consciousness regardless of when they occur and they also aid advancements in medicine.

A little about the after-effects of NDEs and STEs

The after-effects of these extreme states of awareness (NDEs, STEs and even some ADCs), as well as the actual experiences, are considered by researchers to illustrate that the experiences are profound and also real.

When I spoke with Dr. Penny Sartori and explained how surprised I was that the study of near-death experiences was not just about the one-off event but also about what happens afterwards, she stated, "Yes, that's a huge part of it, really. Because a lot of people sort of dismiss near-death experiences, if you like, and just say they are abreactions of the dying or hallucinations, etc. but you've got to look at it and see the full range of complexities. There are these after-effects, which do in many cases really profoundly affect the person who's had the experience. We haven't got a full explanation as to why all of these experiences occur and why such after-effects. However, they are life changing and it's not the same as when people come close to death but don't have a near-death experience. Obviously their life is changed as well but not to the degree of people who have near-death experiences. So you do have these things [which occur]. People do become a lot more psychic. They have changes in their electrical fields, they become more tolerant of others, more compassionate, more loving, and their whole value system changes. So it's really quite a profound thing that happens and it's interesting that you say this has happened to you having had this communication with your mum as she was passing."

The after-effects are used to validate and measure the intensity or depth of the initial experience in most studies. The deeper the experience, the greater or pronounced the after-effects.

Researchers now know that there are many events which may act to bring about a near-death-like experience, or those experiences more akin to mine that masquerade as relatively innocent events but cause a cascade of changes within you as a consequence. They do not have to involve a brush with death.

These events that activate a personal and spiritual overhaul fall into the category of Spiritually Transformative Experiences (STEs). Yolaine Stout, the founder of ACISTE (American Center for the Integration of Spiritually Transformative Experiences) and previous president of IANDS (International Association for Near-Death Studies), says her organization's main charter is to provide support to those who have had these life altering experiences. She explained that ACISTE's mission is, "to help people who are dealing with the aftermath of it [a STE], partly because a lot of relationships get severed. We want to create a community where people can share in a non-judgmental or invalidating environment, as well as train professionals who may be working with experiencers." ACISTE provides information on, not only, the common after-effects but also provides advice on how to integrate them into daily life.

There are many causes of these exceptional experiences called STEs. While near-death experiences are also considered spiritually transformative experiences, STEs may be caused by other means than death. STEs often identically parallel a near-death or actual temporary-death experience, either in the *event* characteristics or the unavoidable after-effects. Barbara Harris Whitfield, a former researcher with Dr. Bruce Greyson, near-death experiencer, thanologist (thanology being the study of death and dying) and the author of *Spiritual Awakenings: Insights of the Near Death Experience and Other Doorways to Our Soul*, told me that they found fourteen or fifteen different triggers of near-death or near-death-like states of altered consciousness – and the number is rising. These may include (but are not limited to) experiences of near-death, actual-death, fear-death, childbirth, walking in nature, meditating, bottoming out from overwhelming loss, helping someone else die, deep prayer, and detoxing from alcohol or drugs and more.

Although often these incidents of expanded consciousness clearly fall under the label of near-death (NDE) or near-death-like experiences (NDLE), sometimes the lack of *clinically dying,* if even only for a few seconds, has caused undue doubt about authenticity. This can cause confusion for the experiencer and a feeling of separation. But when you look at the ensuing after-effects, they are consistent and confirming even if the conditions which caused the experiences were not.

This split between the assessment of whether someone had actually died or not, when something extraordinary happened, is the primary reason Yolaine Stout created ACISTE. Its intention is to address and include all individuals who have had these very significant happenings, even if they don't fit the classic near-death model. Stout commented, "We don't want to place a limit on them or exclude any spiritual experience that is transformative in nature."

A thorough review and history of near-death experiences is beyond the scope of this book. In no way do I wish to mislead anyone into thinking that I am providing a comprehensive review of the wonderful work done by others. I am not an expert or researcher into NDEs (yet!). I'm just someone with a sincere desire to understand what generated my own transformation. There have been massive contributions and groundbreaking findings by many professionals who have made this their lives work. I'm so very thankful to them for helping me clarify my own experiences.

Chapter Eighteen

What happens when someone dies, common experiences

In these final two chapters I share with you what the researchers have found in their many studies, spanning close to four decades. I've included a list of the common characteristics or elements of near-death experiences, near-death-like experiences, and other spiritually transformative experiences, as well as the situations in which these extraordinary experiences occur and the after-effects. You'll also find an explanation of the variety of loving after-death communications in some detail, as these played an important part in my own experiences with my mom.

I've provided some fascinating information about the many amazing, synchronistic and wonderful things researchers and caregivers know happen around the time of someone's death (referred to as end of life experiences or death and dying phenomena). I briefly discuss the cardiac arrest NDE studies' findings along with the landmark NDE experienced by Pam Reynolds during something called "operation standstill" which shook the medical world. Additionally, I mention some of the theories behind what might be causing these heavenly experiences and what these experiences might mean about life and death. Things are not as black and white as you might think.

I hope that by reading these final summarizing chapters that you find the confirmation you may be seeking to understand your own personal experiences. In the final chapter, I'll share my idea of the possibility of a *"seventh sense"*.

What happens when someone has a near-death experience or near-death-like experience?

Studies and reports show that when people die (briefly or temporarily) and have a near-death experience, they encounter or perceive many of the same things as other experiencers. Most of the researchers I've spoken with think that the near-death experience is what actually happens when you die. It's just that when someone dies briefly and experiences a NDE that they can come back to talk about this part of the dying or transitioning process.

Although some people experience their NDE more deeply or profoundly than others, it is clear that these events usually trigger numerous changes within those that have them. 80% of the experiencers say that their lives were never the same afterwards.

Consistent features appear throughout near-death experiences, temporary-death experiences (NDEs experienced during cardiac arrests) and spiritually transformative experiences (STEs). Additionally, these same elements (or aspects) are also observed in shared near-death experiences and the rare group near-death experience, as written about by Dr. Raymond Moody and other researchers such as P.M.H. Atwater. These shared episodes happen when someone or a group of people (who are physically or emotionally close to the primary near-death experiencer) witness a portion of the dying person's other-worldly experience.

Dr. Greyson, in his many years of research, discovered that there are four main categories of the aspects of a near-death experience. These are: 1) changes in thinking processes, including faster, clearer thinking; 2) changes in the emotional state, i.e. overwhelming feelings of peace, love and well-being, as well as possibly feeling as if you are one with the Universe; 3) paranormal and psychic activities, feelings of leaving your body and having extra-sensory perceptions including the ability to communicate via telepathy and; 4) a transcendental component, feeling that you've entered an unearthly or other-worldly environment.

Experiencers regularly sense that they have separated from and floated above their bodies (referred to as out-of-body experiences or OBEs). They leave their physical, often painful or useless bodies behind and discover (now pain-free) that they can see what the medics or doctors are doing to their bodies below. Experiencers next may then find themselves bathed in a brilliant non-blinding light. Sometimes they pass through a tunnel before reaching *the light*. Other times they are in the light immediately or after spending a brief period of time in darkness. Either way, almost all who have near-death experiences (NDEs) or temporary or actual death experiences (ADEs or TDEs, in the case of those who have their experiences during cardiac arrests) see or sense what they know to be an all loving, non-judgmental and compassionate being, who is often within the light. Sometimes they don't actually see a being with their eyes, but feel instead that the light itself is filled with love and compassion.

Often, for children, the being appears as an angel while with adults they usually sense or see the being depicted as either Jesus, God, Buddha or another religious figure, dependent on their upbringing. Deceased relatives, great friends or pets are also there to welcome them and bring them great comfort.

Sometimes experiencers have a full panoramic life-review, and although it may only last a few seconds or minutes (in our physical sense of time), it includes every action and thought the person ever had in their entire life. They are shown how their actions affected others: they feel or sense the results of their behavior – seeing where they may have gone wrong (in their opinion). Amazingly, experiencers of these reviews say that the being (who is with them) is loving and non-judgmental. Whoever it is, just allows them to see how their actions have impacted others for themselves. Life-reviews do not occur in all NDEs and seem to be provided only when they are necessary to help someone get their life back on track.

In many NDEs or similar STEs, the experiencers are finally told, "It's not your time," and that they must go back. Sometimes, however, the person is given the choice to go back to continue their life or not. Additionally, it is often reported that, without words, the experiencers understand that if they cross beyond a certain point, or boundary, that they will not be able to return into their bodies.

Interesting to note, is that even a person who has been blind from birth and therefore has never been able to see, is able to see during these enhanced episodes of consciousness.

However, not all NDEs are wonderful. A small percentage of cases have been reported that were unpleasant or even frightening. However, even if the experience was not enjoyable or comforting, the overall result of the experience is almost always viewed as being very positive. Often, these difficult experiences are seen as extremely valuable because of the radical transformation they stimulate afterwards. These *bad,* or even horrifying, experiences propel the experiencers to attempt even greater, dramatic, positive changes in their lives. One of the interesting stories told by Barbara Harris Whitfield, from when she was researching with Dr. Bruce Greyson, is that of a mob gangster who could no longer harm others after his NDE. He now works with young offenders helping them to correct their ways.

Although these experiences are profoundly felt by the individuals who are privileged to have them and they usually contain strong elements of light, love, compassion and oneness, it's the tell-tale after-effects which signify a *true* experience, including the various transcendental experiences not involving death or what happened to me.

In what situation can a spiritually transformative experience (STE) occur (including a NDE)?

Spiritually transformative experiences (STEs) are various and go by many names. Often they share the common features of the NDE. However, even if they don't, the experience acts as the catalyst for spiritual transformation.

According to Yolaine Stout, STEs include: near-death experiences (NDEs), near-death-like experiences (NDLEs), out-of-body experiences (OBEs), visions, spiritual emergencies, awakenings, kundalini experiences, enlightenment, exceptional human experiences (EHEs), pre-birth memories, past-life experiences, nearing death awareness events (NDAs), after-death communications (ADCs), empathic or shared near-death experiences (SDE) and peak experiences, among others.

The ACISTE website refers to STEs as being numinous, noetic, transcendent, transpersonal, mystical, anomalous, religious, paranormal, parapsychological or ecstatic experiences. Perhaps we could call these STEs pivotal moments which act to enlighten us.

While some experiences are actually sought through meditation, yoga, drugs, religious practices, dance, drumming, sensory deprivation or prayer, they often occur spontaneously and without expectation. Just as in the case of near-death situations, personal trauma, illness and states of extreme stress or crisis, STEs usually just happen. They also may occur as a result of intense emotions which may accompany childbirth, deep relaxation, ecstasy, grief or sexual activity. Spiritually transformative experiences can take place during dreams as well.

Why do we have them?

There are actually two questions I'd like you to consider when asking why NDEs or STEs occur. The first question might be – why do we have them, at all? There are many theories about this, including the affects of drugs, anoxia (a lack of oxygen to the brain), the sparking neural networks as the brain dies and more. However most of these *"dying brain"* or brain shutting down theories may have been effectively disproved by the cardiac arrest NDE studies.

So the answer to why they happen is still only based on theories and no one really knows for sure. However, researchers in the field of near-death or temporary-death experiences believe their studies suggest that the brain acts as a receiver and reducer, limiting your experience rather than being the creator of it. Therefore, perhaps the reason these enhanced states of consciousness occur in these moments of death, or death-like instances, is because the brain is either struggling to work or not working at all. Only then, apparently, do the scientists think that you are able to see what might actually be your true, more expansive self and larger reality. It's a beautiful thought and a big concept to consider.

P.M.H. Atwater told me, very animatedly and emphatically, that she believes the reason we have these experiences is because of, "where they take us." She went on to explain that it is, "what happens to us because of them, specifically how we change," that is critical. She feels it is, "a biological imperative that people undergo transformations of this depth," and "that it is tied in with the evolution of the human species." When I first heard her say this, I thought it might be a bit over dramatic. However, since reading an article in the American Scientist magazine a few months ago, in which the author speculated that the human brain had reached its evolutionary maximum capacity for intelligence, I think Atwater is right.

Dr. Pim van Lommel, the head cardiologist on the Dutch cardiac NDE arrest study said, "Our results show that medical factors cannot account for the occurrence of NDE. All patients had a cardiac arrest, and were clinically dead with unconsciousness resulting from insufficient blood supply to the brain. In those circumstances, the EEG (a measure of brain electrical activity) becomes flat within 10-20 seconds, and if CPR is not started within 5-10 minutes, irreparable damage is done to the brain and the patient will die. According to the theory that NDE is caused by anoxia, all patients in our study should have had a NDE, but only 18% reported having a NDE...There is also a theory that NDE is caused psychologically, by the fear of death. But only a very small percentage of our patients said they had been afraid seconds before their cardiac arrest – it happened too suddenly for them to realize what was occurring. More patients than the frightened ones reported NDEs."

Additionally, Dr. Penny Sartori told me that drugs are highly unlikely to be the cause of NDEs. She found that certain drugs actually inhibit these experiences. "Quite a high percentage, about 70-80%, of the group had pain-killing drugs, such as morphine or midazolam, yet less than 1% of that group actually reported a near-death experience." Sartori and other medically trained researchers, and generally even the patients, can tell the difference between confusional hallucinations and the extremely lucid memories of a near-death experience.

The second part of my question, why do we have them, might be – why do some people have them and others don't under the exact same conditions? The answer again is quite clearly – no one knows! P.M.H. Atwater told me the experience I shared at the time of my mom's death, "had nothing to do with your mom. It was life at large. You were ready for the next step. Very unexpectedly, forcefully, you were literally pushed into it." She went on to say, "Most real genuine cases are unexpected." Atwater believed that somehow I was ready (or prepared) for my experience or it wouldn't have happened. She said to me, "That moment in time came, when this was possible."

Although I did not have a classic NDE myself, Dr. Fenwick, Barbara Harris Whitfield, and most others I spoke with, told me my mom reached out to me or waited for me before leaving. Dr. Fenwick explained, "What we've found is they [these events] are driven by the dying, not by the person who receives the message. The person who receives the message is in a close emotional relationship with the dying. The dying are in a close relationship with the person, although the person may not be with the dying, although they usually are."

When I asked David Lorimer, program director of the Scientific and Medical Network, former teacher of philosophy at Winchester College and the author of twelve books, including *Whole in One: The Near-Death Experience and the Ethic of Interconnectedness* and *Thinking Beyond the Brain,* for his opinion on why I had my experience (which somehow triggered my transformation) and why certain people have NDEs, while a larger percentage do not, he said, "Well, we can't know for sure but there's a phrase that does spring to mind from Guy Claxton when he said, 'You can't guarantee grace or enlightenment but you can make yourself enlightenment prone.' It's the grace and free will equation in Christian theology [in question here]. The theologians say that you can't attain these things entirely from the bottom up but they also must have a top down transcendent force from above or within, if you like."

Yolaine Stout of ACISTE, who had a near-death experience before she became involved in NDE research, commented, "I've always been interested in knowing if some people might be more apt to have these experiences than others. We know that people who meditate often have spiritual experiences. But it also seems that people who are healers or work very closely with people, touching them or feeling their energy may be more receptive to spiritual experiences. Also, deep emotions of care, love and compassion at the time of someone's death seem to be triggering events. We've read, for example, that hospice workers will begin to see visions along with their dying patients. It would make an interesting research project. Your experience is additional confirmation."

Looking specifically at why some people have NDEs, Barbara Harris Whitfield said, "I think that they happen to everybody when they die and then they are not NDEs but DEs [death experiences]. Only 30-40% of those who come close to death talk about having a NDE and we can't figure out what is happening to the other 60%; whether they just don't remember it, or whether they never let go. You see a really important part of actually having *an experience*, triggered by a multitude of different things is letting go and some people won't let go."

Barbara explained that in one of the studies she worked on with Dr. Greyson and Kenneth Ring, the results showed a higher percentage of near-death experiences by those who had been victims of unpredictable violence as children. Although, van Lommel stresses that this study was done retrospectively, Barbara thought the results suggested that these adults may have had previous out-of-body perceptions, perhaps because of a need to dissociate as kids. They were therefore almost primed, or again, if I use the words of Claxton, more *prone* to have a NDE or spiritual experience. My Reiki training (after giving up my telecommunications career to become a therapist) may have had something to do with me being, as Atwater's said, "ready to be pushed."

While the reasons why one person has a NDE or another similar spiritually transformative experience (STE), continue to remain unanswered as I write this book, Dr. van Lommel emphasized to me that these heightened conscious experiences seem to have an element of unpredictability. He said that they don't yet know why one person has them and another does not. However, he has found (in his study) that if you had one previously, you were more likely to have another. Nevertheless, van Lommel said, "They cannot be forced," with the exception of one drug which has been found to cause a similar reaction in some people.

As P.M.H. Atwater said, "These 'breakthrough' events or 'threshold events' are moments of intense energy which act as initiations with the key always being intensity…when it hits a certain level, what we experience is miraculous. So although they come to you unexpectedly, through NDEs or other types of natural experiences, they push you over the edge." She stated, or almost warned me that, "Always, there are more." So, although these experiences cannot be predicted, perhaps you are innocently being prepared for them. Then when something of an intense nature occurs, it causes you to open a "portal," as Atwater put it.

Common elements of a NDE, NDLE or STE

I learned from these notable doctors and researchers that when someone has a near-death experience, or another event triggering a near-death-like or spiritually transformative experience, there are a few fundamental aspects which typically occur. Although these particular elements are common and consistently reported by the experiencers, they are by no means ordinary. The term *common* only refers to the regularity in which they are presented. These experiences are extremely special, personal and frequently distinctively other-worldly. They also often involve a suspension of time and space.

As NDEs or STEs are extremely subjective events, much of the scientific analysis has come from personal descriptions of them. This is, in my opinion, one of the reasons why the cardiac arrest studies have been so vitally important. They have helped to remove doubt that an experience is legitimate, because having *any memory* during a cardiac arrest should not be possible, let alone an extremely dramatic and remarkable recollection of a NDE.

Even though these fascinating experiences are subjective, rather than objective, dedicated medical staff, scientists and researchers have collected and compared enough subjective data surrounding them to quantify the commonalities and similarities *objectively*. A few widely accepted measurement tools have been created to compare experiences and track the consequences of them. The most frequently used means for calculating, or comparing, the aspects and *depth* of an experience used by researchers around the world are Dr. Bruce Greyson's 32 point "near-death experience scale" also known as "The Greyson NDE Scale" and Dr. Kenneth Ring's five-stage continuum, the "Weighted Core Experience Index". These look at the number and magnitude of the *regular* elements and are used to determine the intensity of the experience.

What are the after-effects of these events?

I found out that there are a whole host of consequences of experiencing these mind expanding moments or episodes. The after-effects loosely fall into the categories of attitudinal changes, physiological changes and psychic (or psychological) changes.

It doesn't seem to make much difference what sort of experience you have or what you choose to call it, your life may never be the same afterwards. Most events force you to change, in response to them, because your previous beliefs and senses are irreparably altered. These unexpected experiences, which shift you momentarily from one dimension into the next, create havoc (both positive and negative) and from what I can tell – you change, whether you want to or not.

Depending on the depth or intensity of your catalyzing event (or events, like in my case), you may experience some or all of these common, yet unusual and unexpected, erratic and often disruptive after-effects. Just as in a near-death or equivalent experience, you may not necessarily have *all* the typical after-effects. You may encounter only some of them. That said, some of the after-effects are more common than others and almost everyone will experience them. Most people, almost without exception, will no longer fear death after their experiences. A few of the other after-effects are reported less frequently and seem to occur to those whose event was more intense or more deeply felt.

As I've stated, from the beginning of this book, I knew something had happened between me and my mom but I hadn't investigated what exactly took place between us until this year. That's when the after-effects caught my attention, and seeing them just felt right. Although, my initial experience to the uninitiated may not appear to fit the standard NDE model, I have had almost every one of the after-effects. My initial and subsequent experiences with my *dead* mom certainly qualify as spiritually transformative.

For me the after-effects, or results of my experience, unfolded seemingly one-by-one. When I was ready or able to acknowledge more, another would take place until I couldn't ignore their influence any longer – even though *I only shared in my mom's death and hadn't died myself.* Listening to myself now, I realize how silly it must sound when I say, "I only shared in my mom's death." Sharing in someone else's death is such an extraordinary thing, especially if you consider how it may usher in these surprising after-effects. I can see clearly now why Yolaine Stout started her charitable organization. She realized that there's a tre-mendous need for a greater understanding of the many changes which occur as a consequence of these experiences.

Although we may never know how the uniqueness of each person's experience, as well as the intensity of each feature of it, may contribute to how and when their senses open up, we know now that it's almost decreed or bound to happen. In some people, especially those that *"see the light"* (in a near-death or similar STE) some shifts in their belief systems happen immediately – while other *expected* and *normal* after-effects may only take place over time (like many of mine did) or not at all.

Below is a list of the after-effects which I experienced. Again, these are com-mon and even predictable if you've had a NDE or near-death-like experience. But as I reluctantly found out, you may experience these after-effects if you've somehow shared in someone else's death or are the recipient of significant or major after-death communications. Again, the severity or excessive nature of the after-effects I suspect go hand-in-hand with the intensity of your experience. My after-effects are not listed in any particular order but encompass the physiological (physical) changes, psychological changes and resultant changes in my beliefs and values (attitudes).

My After-Effects:
- Heightened intuition
- Heightened sensitivities to sound, light, smells, tastes and noises (the five senses)
- Developed food intolerances and chemical or environmental sensitivities – even allergies
- Heightened intelligence (at least I think so!)
- Increased psychic abilities including: telepathy, telekinesis (psychokine-sis), clair-cognizance (knowing things, similar to clairvoyance), clairaudi-ence (hearing guidance, including from God), clairvoyance (seeing things) and channeling

- Experiencing metaphysical or paranormal activity around me (e.g. apporting, shoulder tapping, angel sighting, etc.)
- After-death communications including *physical* contact with the deceased and other forms
- Increased activity and productivity
- Increased inspiration, or moments and periods of genius. Inspired thoughts and ideas pop up much more frequently
- Possible changes in brain structure (according to Atwater)
- Altered thought processing with a shift from sequential thinking to clustered thinking, faster and clearer thinking, as well as deeper more philosophical thinking
- Increased occurrences of synchronicity (feeling in the flow and connected)
- Bursts of energy and having more energy in general
- Changes in my perception of time
- Increased need for light (some have the opposite)
- A desire or requirement to only be around authentic, honest, loving people
- An unwillingness to put up with relationships that don't work or are abusive
- Moments and times when I feel connected to all, feeling in sync with the Universe
- A feeling of not being alone anymore
- A shift from materialism to a desire for less and a more natural life, closer to nature
- Changes in beliefs, especially no longer fearing death, knowing (not just believing) that there is an afterlife, knowing (not just believing) that there is a God or other benevolent higher power
- Became spiritual, when I had been agnostic or almost atheist (after previously rejecting faith)
- Came to believe that life has a purpose and now have faith that everything happens for my own good and because of my actions
- Experienced change in many of my values and what is important to me
- Increased compassion and love for others
- Increased self-love and self-understanding
- Learned to set healthy boundaries, no longer allow others to take advantage or abuse me
- Look younger
- Lowered blood pressure
- Lowered body temperature

While many of the above after-effects may sound wonderful, as you've heard in my story they can be very frightening and confusing if you don't know how to deal with them.

Below is a list of the common after-effects which are often more difficult to adjust to and deal with. Thankfully, perhaps because I didn't have a NDE myself but instead had an empathic death experience or a deathbed coincidence followed by after-death communications, I only experienced four of the following distressing after-effects (the first two, the second and third to the last).

Other Common After-Effects:
- Feeling that you may be going crazy
- Relationship problems including breakups (50% of those who have a NDE end in divorce)
- Lack of motivation
- A total disregard for earthly physical needs
- Disorganization and unfocused direction, especially in attaining material necessities
- Seeking the thrill of the NDE again through a suicide attempt
- Depression
- Getting fearful or stuck in the psychic and paranormal experience stage of the transformation and not progressing to take on the lessons these after-effects have to offer
- Never fully integrating your experience into your new life
- What ACISTE say about the after-effects:

ACISTE describe a spiritually transformative experience on their website (www.aciste.org) in this way, "An experience is spiritually transformative when it causes people to perceive themselves and the world profoundly differently: by expanding the individuals' identity, augmenting their sensitivities, and thereby altering their values, priorities and appreciation of the purpose of life. This may be triggered by surviving clinical death, or by otherwise sensing an enlarged reality."

Yolaine Stout suggests said that the changes or after-effects of a STE (which include NDEs and the other interesting experiences I had) are transformative because they not only tend to be enduring, but involve almost every major aspect of a person's life. The changes, generally, are not sudden but evolve over many years of integrating and reflecting upon the meaning, messages and values derived from the experience. Some of the changes can bring with them difficult challenges.

The after-effects listed on the ACISTE website are:
- Strengthened spiritual or religious views
- Improved behavior and attitude towards others
- Changes in values
- Greater empathy and compassion for others
- A greater sense of well-being
- A more positive outlook on life
- A greater desire to learn

- Increased creativity
- Increased psychic awareness
- Greater sense of purpose
- Loss of the fear of death

The common challenges listed are:
- Processing a radical shift in reality
- Accepting the return and "homesickness"
- Issues related to sharing the experience
- Dealing with invalidation
- Ineffability (language ineffective for expressing what was experienced)
- Integrating new spiritual values with earthly expectations
- Changes towards careers and money
- Changes in religious views
- Changes in societal, political views
- Changes in attitudes toward death
- Changes in attitudes toward healing
- Problems dealing with psychic abilities, which may include: intuitive, auditory or visual knowledge of what is or what is to come, mediumship, telepathy, seeing auras, ability to communicate with animals and automatic writing
- Increased sensitivity to electricity, chemicals, smells, sounds, etc.
- A yearning to find and live one's purpose

If you have experienced a NDE or STE, I encourage you to visit and view The International Association for Near-Death Studies (IANDS) and the American Centre for the Integration of Spiritually Transformative Experiences (ACISTE) websites listed in my references.

The integration process and the overall result of the event on the person

Although I didn't have the luxurious benefit of knowing what I know now when I went through my many changes, perhaps knowing what was to come, or expected to happen, would not have helped me anyway. It might have just scared me even more.

I've discovered that the time it took me to come out of my blur following my mom's link up and after-death contact was apparently, again – typical and even average. Shocking isn't it? I came out of hiding after seven years, just on schedule. I even found that some of the researchers, (notably P.M.H. Atwater) who have been investigating near-death states or STEs for many years, have written about this integration process. The integration period is the time it takes someone to accept and incorporate their experience fully, including the various aspects of their memory of the event and the many changes that occur in their life due to the after-effects along, with the inevitable altered beliefs.

Brilliantly, I found that *integration* often takes approximately seven years! Now I know why I waited that long to talk about my experiences. According to the experts, many of the experiencers took a minimum of seven to ten years to integrate their NDE or other spiritually transformative experience. Sadly though, Atwater told me, "Some don't make it." Some people are unable to integrate. Although, it's reported that experiencers often go through many bouts of depression, when P.M.H. said, "Some don't make it," she was referring to those who "shut down" emotionally, or develop negative behaviors, or in some cases actually commit suicide.

Dr. Pim van Lommel expressed that the ease and degree to which I expressed my experiences with him showed that I had integrated them. He referred to Atwater's research and commented about the average time to integrate, but he also said that for some people it can take twenty years. While still others, never completely integrate their experiences, finding the process too difficult.

The research by Dr. van Lommel is held in high regard, not only for the size and thoroughness of his study of NDE during cardiac arrest, but also because he stayed in contact with the surviving patients. He followed up each of those who survived, both after two years and again after eight years. He interviewed all his patients who'd had a cardiac arrest during his study, even those who had not reported experiencing a NDE which he calls a TDE or temporary-death experience. The data van Lommel collected confirmed that the after-effects, or the lack of them, could really be used to validate whether or not someone had a NDE (TDE). Dr. van Lommel's surveys directly support Atwater's findings of the minimum and average time it takes to integrate these life-altering events.

While I'm sure the details of each person's integration period and process would be fascinating and unique, like my own, what van Lommel reviewed was more objective. He wasn't looking at the interesting stories they told but more the categories of change. He reviewed changes in social attitudes (ability to show emotions, acceptance of others, and whether they felt they were more loving and empathic, etc.), religious attitudes (sense of life purpose, meaning of life and interests in spirituality), attitudes toward death (whether they had a fear of death and believed in life after death now), and a miscellaneous category he called, "Other," which included things like understanding oneself and the appreciation of the ordinary things in life.

As would be expected, some individuals took more time than others to come to an understanding and acceptance of their experiences, including the changes that manifested in their lives. Successful *integration* seems highly dependent on whether or not you are able to share your experiences with others and how supportively they respond to them.

Some people continue to deny their experiences due to drastic conflicts in their beliefs. Others have difficulty integrating NDEs (or STEs) because their peers view their experiences as impossible or ridiculous. In my view, as well as some of the researchers, it's critical that you allow yourself to believe that what you experienced was real before the integration period can truly progress. Denying your experience and the unavoidable after-effects of it can cause confusing and even disastrous complications. I suspect that delaying the integration process or totally ignoring it may be in part why some people sink into deep depression and despair.

P.M.H. Atwater told me that in some cultures people who had NDEs are actually put away as they are thought to be mentally ill or subversive, while others are even tortured.

I suppose looking at it now, this integration process which involves both the initial event and the after-effects in my view is really the focus of this book and the primary reason why I've shared my unique and perhaps very different death story. My personal development and challenges after my mom's repeated contact highlight the hurdles I had to clear to reach the invisible goal of integration.

Although I'm sure not everyone will have to go through the same psychic and paranormal things that happened to me, some may. So, I hope by vicariously watching my progression and my openness and honesty has been helpful or at least interesting. Maybe my experiences, which I don't think have been written about to this degree before, will help someone validate their own confusing yet very real personal experiences. As I've found out, once I stopped being frightened and started to embrace and accept my new gifts things improved tenfold. I now believe that once you rightfully acknowledge and integrate your experiences you will gain something that is immeasurable – a wonderful expansion of your sense of being, your sense of self.

As I began to open up and talk about my experiences, almost everyone I shared them with told me that they'd also had unexplainable things happen to them, but they'd never felt comfortable enough to tell anyone. If you've had experiences like I have, I invite you to contact some of the organizations I have mentioned (IANDS, ACISTE) or the equivalent in your country. While it's very important for your personal growth that you share your experience in a safe environment, you'll also speed up your process of integration and help others feel they are not alone.

While Yolaine Stout and I discussed my after-effects, she shared with me the results of ACISTE's first survey of their members, all of whom have had spiritually transformative experiences (some NDE, NDE-like or another form of STE). Below are the percentages of the members who responded that they had encountered these specific challenges and changes in their life after their STE.

The First ACISTE Survey Results:
- 86.7% Changes in attitude toward death
- 80% Increased love and compassion for others
- 76.7% Increased meditation and spiritual activities
- 55% Changes in religious views and practices

- 53.3% Increase in volunteering and generosity
- 50% Experienced depression
- 46.7% Changes in views of money
- 45% Suffering from homesickness (wanting to "go to the light")
- 41.7% Career changes
- 38.3% Financial difficulties
- 35% Alienation by avoidance from others
- 30% Changes of political and social views
- 16.7% Divorce (A lot of these were childhood experiences. The divorce rate in adults who have had a NDE is 50%)
- 10% Substance abuse
- 6.7% Suicide attempts

Why I've decided to consider the cardiac arrest NDE studies?

Being new to the topic of NDEs, and a bit of a techie in my previous career, I found the studies about patients who had near-death experiences during cardiac arrests tantalizingly interesting. I must say though that every occurrence of a NDE, near-death-like or other spiritually transformative experience (STE) reported is amazing and all are worthy of research. However, these particular studies involving cardiac arrests have provided fascinating support for all of these death-states and transcendental experiences in general. They have elevated, in my opinion, the acceptability of the NDE by the scientific community, which in part still attempt to refute NDEs as purely anecdotal.

It was for these reasons, alone, and no other preference, that I have focused on the cardiac arrests studies in the final chapters of this book. My personal experiences were not during cardiac arrest at all, but rather occurred while fully conscious and in perfect health. My interest therefore in NDEs during cardiac arrest is more about the validation they provide. They display that these things really do happen when someone is clinically dead and aren't just someone's imagination.

There have been many prior authoritative and priceless studies that have provided landmark findings and invaluable evaluation tools over the past three decades alone. I must underscore that by my decision to use the NDE cardiac arrest data in this book, it is not my intention to dismiss any other studies as less important. The knowledge gained by the pioneers and the long-term research conducted around the world into the wide range of genuine NDEs have lead us to this point. These narrower cardiac arrest NDE studies benefitted and came about due to the previous work in this field of study. Additionally, my use of cardiac arrest research is due to the initial email I received from Dr. Bruce Greyson who recommended I speak with Dr. Peter Fenwick and Dr. Penny Sartori, among others. Although, I had not heard of their research, Greyson knew them and knew they were in England where I live now.

The studies and frequency of near-death experience (NDE) during cardiac arrest

The first prospective clinical study to be published that looked exclusively at cardiac arrest patients who had near-death experiences was conducted at the Southampton Hospital in the United Kingdom. Dr. Sam Parnia, a pulmonary and critical-care specialist, now leading expert on near-death experiences and the author of *What Happens When We Die,* and Dr. Peter Fenwick, the world renowned neuropsychiatrist and expert on end of life experiences (ELE) were responsible for this research published in 2001. (A prospective study means that the research data is collected at the time of the incidents rather than retrospectively or after the fact.) Dr. Parnia said this first cardiac arrest study into NDEs was designed to try to establish the cause of these experiences.

Almost simultaneously, other cardiac arrest NDE studies were underway around the world. Then one by one, as their results were published it became evident that our understanding of life and death needed to be re-evaluated. Dr. Pim van Lommel, published his findings also in 2001 like Parnia and Fenwick in the United Kingdom. While in the United States, Janet Schwaninger, a registered nurse (R.N) and Cardiovascular Coordinator at Barnes-Jewish Hospital at the Washington University School of Medicine in St. Louis, Missouri announced her results in 2002. A further cardiac arrest NDE study was published by Dr. Bruce Greyson's in 2003, which was conducted at the University of Virginia Hospital. Then a second British prospective study, which spanned five years, was published in 2006 by Penny Sartori. Dr. Sartori who worked under the supervision of Dr. Peter Fenwick was an experienced Intensive Care nurse at the time of her study but has since been awarded her doctorate for her extensive near-death research.

The largest prospective study of this kind, completed to date, involving cardiac arrests was the study undertaken in the Netherlands by Dr. van Lommel. This study included 344 patients of fourteen hospitals and spanned a ten year period.

Currently Dr. Sam Parnia, together with Dr. Peter Fenwick, are in the process of a further prospective cardiac arrest study involving teams across twenty-five hospitals throughout Europe, Canada and the United States. The physicians involved in this study, which goes by the name "AWARE" (AWAreness during REsuscitation) will use the latest technologies available to study the brain and consciousness during the cardiac arrest and attempt to validate claims of out of body experiences (OBE).

To complicate matters, the UK and Dutch medical professionals and scientists involved in these studies have used slightly different acronyms to describe a near-death experience. Dr. Pim van Lommel refers to a NDE occurring during cardiac arrest as a temporary-death experience or TDE, while Dr. Parnia, Sartori and Dr. Fenwick use the term actual-death experience or ADE. Each of these teams have elected to use a more accurate, descriptive title, because the patients, for all intents and purposes, have clinically died (albeit somewhat briefly) during their cardiac arrests – according to current medical views.

Dr. van Lommel's study was somewhat unique to the others for a few clinical reasons he mentions in his book. However, the main reason I feel his study was different and very important in regards to my investigation, was the prospective longitudinal aspect it had. He clearly from the start planned to evaluate the long-term changes and after-effects encountered over time by the patients. Dr. van Lommel, following in the footsteps of Dr. Greyson's groundbreaking work in the United States, made reviewing the after-effects of the NDE (or TDE, as he prefers) a major part of his study. That's why it took ten years before it was published.

Dr. van Lommel's conclusions confirm Greyson's earlier findings. It displayed again that there are common after-effects of a *true* or *bona fide* NDE. Additionally, van Lommel's cardiac arrest study and those of the UK and USA, convincingly suggest that consciousness actually continues beyond the death of the physical body and that the brain must somehow be acting as a sort of receiver of consciousness.

In each of these prospective cardiac arrest NDE studies and specifically in the Dutch study, personal histories were taken. These included information about such things as the individuals religious or spiritual beliefs and values, for example, did they believe in God or an after-life? And had they had a NDE before? Etc. Thorough medical statistics were (of course) also logged. These included information about any drugs that were used, oxygen and blood levels, and even the length of time the patient was unconscious (*clinically dead*) after their cardiac arrest before being successfully resuscitated, among other things.

In all these prospective studies, along with capturing real-time medical data to hopefully determine what might be the cause of these special experiences, the researchers interviewed the patients who regained consciousness as soon as was reasonably possible. Almost immediately, they recorded the details of any perceptions and memories reported, when technically *there should have been no memories at all* according to today's known science. They then evaluated these experiences according to The Greyson NDE Scale and often Ring's Weighted Core Experience Index as well.

Dr. Fenwick highlighted that according to generally accepted neuroscience theories, brain activity and specifically the creation and storage of memories should not be possible during a cardiac arrest when the monitors show that brain function has ceased.

Although both the UK and Dutch prospective studies represented excellent clinical attempts to objectively evaluate the subjective experience of temporary but actual death, they also helped to further progress the understanding and effectiveness of resuscitation methods to help sustain lives in the future.

The findings

Researchers found that during cardiac arrest approximately 11-23% experienced what qualified as a NDE using The Greyson NDE Scale. Extraordinarily, only a percentage of those who *died* in cardiac arrests reported these heightened states of consciousness rather than everyone. As I mentioned at the beginning of Chapter 17, these findings have caused tremendous upheaval in medical and scientific groups for a number of reasons. Let me explain.

If you follow the school of thought of Dr. Susan Blackmore, a professor in psychology at the University of Plymouth, who has stated in the past that NDE-like memories are only the normal response and experience of the brain's neural networks shutting down as the brain ceases to function and who derogatorily called NDEs folklore, or if you, like some, support another of the *dying brain* hypotheses, believing that NDEs occur due to a lack of oxygen supply to the brain which takes place within seconds after the heart stops in a cardiac arrest, then everyone who had a cardiac arrest would have reported a NDE (or TDE, ADE)!

If these *dying brain* theories are true, then like any NDE researcher worth their weight you must ask yourself what has happened to the other 82-88.8% of the cardiac arrest patients? Why haven't they had a NDE? Why didn't they all report these memories when the conditions were the same for each of them?

Blackmore has also vehemently suggested that these symptoms of a dying brain, which others believe to be the true memories of the near-death experience, must be occurring just before one becomes unconscious during a cardiac arrest or just after resuscitation while semi-conscious. She feels the near-death experience is occurring not while someone is totally unconscious but rather during the semi-conscious portion of their cardiac arrest event and believes that the exact timing of them has not been adequately quantified. Blackmore hypothesizes that NDEs are normal brain responses that may happen on either side of unconsciousness, on the borders or edges of it.

However, these *dying brain* hypotheses no longer seem to hold up. They are too simplistic to address some tremendously exciting findings. Even Blackmore's plausible border explanation for NDEs has been successfully challenged now. It's become more clear that something we just can't explain, at least today, is going on. The cardiac arrest NDE studies and the unique case of a lady named Pam Reynolds has specifically validated the realness of NDEs for me as being something spiritual and not just the result of a dying brain. They strongly suggest to the distinguished NDE researchers that the mind continues after bodily death.

Dr. Michael Sabom, a cardiologist published the rare and astonishing story of Pam Reynolds deep NDE in his book *Light and Death*. The unchallengeable evidence in his report has rocked psychological, medical and neurological views of how the brain and consciousness work, perhaps for good.

The case of Pam Reynolds' NDE

Pam Reynolds did not have her NDE during a cardiac arrest. She had it in a peculiar situation which has made it one of the most interesting and reported NDE cases thus far. Pam had suffered a severe aneurysm in her brain, in a very difficult area to reach and operate on. It was right down at the base of her brain stem. Pam's chances of survival were extremely poor, however, Dr. Robert F. Spetzler, of the Barrow Neurological Institute in Phoenix, agreed to attempt to repair some of the damage caused by the bleed which was obstructing the information flow to and from her brain, and the rest of Pam's body.

Before the operation started, Pam was anesthetized, meaning that she wouldn't feel any pain, she wouldn't have any dreams and that she would have no memory of the operation at all. Her body was then chilled and all the blood was drained from her head. Dr. Spetzler called this process, "operation stand still." Special clicking devices were inserted into Pam's ears which were used to test the function of the hemispheres of her brain throughout the surgery. Once there was no longer any blood in her brain, Pam's head was opened with a surgical saw which had been under a cloth to keep it sanitized. Spetzler then operated for approximately an hour. Pam was clinically dead during the entire time. Every known vital sign and clinical measurement of life and death were being monitored. She had multiple EEG (electro encephalogram) machines checking surface and deeper brain function as well. These showed no brain function, just as expected during her state of "standstill".

Pam was both unconscious from the anesthesia and technically dead for an hour – not for the five or eight minutes which it might take to resuscitate a cardiac arrest patient, but for an entire hour. It was only after her bloodless head had been cut open and the brain surgery had actually begun that Pam had her NDE! Her memory of it and her recollection of the surgery, which she shouldn't have known anything about, shocked the medical staff including her neurosurgeon, Dr. Spetzler.

She accurately described the surgical saw which had been used to cut through her skull when she was fully unconscious. She said it had looked like an electric toothbrush, even though her eyes had also been taped shut and draped. Only the top of her head had been exposed during the operation. Remember, Pam had no blood circulating to her brain at all.

She was able to describe things in the room, the sounds of the saw and she had heard the clicking sound from the devices placed in her ears. These amazing details provided verifiable evidence that Pam had in fact experienced and recorded memories during a state of unconsciousness when she was unquestionably brain dead.

Pam's near-death experience matched those of other deep experiencers, including feelings of being "in the light", talking with spiritual light beings and being in the presence of a deceased relative (her uncle, in her case), who eventually pushed her back into her dead body.

Dr. Spetzler, her neurosurgeon, could not explain how Pam could have experienced and recalled what she did during her operation, particularly in the state she was in. What she said she heard and *observed* (after leaving her body and finding herself looking down upon it being operated on) was correct.

Pam's true story illustrates that these experiences are real and that they are just beyond what we know scientifically today, about life and death and how the mind works. Her rare and exceptional near-death experience has helped many rule out *dying brain* challenges used principally to counter the findings and suggestions of NDE studies. Pam Reynolds' NDE occurred during a confirmable heavily monitored state of unconsciousness. It did not happen during the times of entering or exiting unconsciousness, in the borderline states when Blackmore speculates NDEs may be occurring.

This case cannot be dismissed as a hallucination either. Additionally, Pam's NDE could not have been caused by drugs or lowering oxygen levels in her blood – there was no blood supply to Pam's brain and therefore no oxygen reaching it. Even a bewildered hallucination should not be experienced or recorded during the state Pam was in.

Death and Dying Phenomena - Common experiences which occur when someone actually dies

As I pointed out briefly in Chapter 17, there are many things that can happen to you when someone else dies. I've learned from the researchers that there are lots of expected yet startling things that occur to those who are in the process of dying and those who are around them. These experiences are called end of life experiences (ELE) or death and dying phenomena and are another intriguing area of study.

While NDE researchers concentrate on those that have died briefly and come back to life to tell about it, others focus their attention on what happens when someone finishes their life here. Some of the experts I spoke with are collecting and analyzing information on both categories, including Dr. Peter Fenwick.

Although according to Dr. Fenwick, experiencing my mother's dying symptoms is considered quite uncommon, particularly because I was fully conscious and awake, being contacted in some way when a loved one dies is actually very common. There are reports of people, who are in another state or even half way around the world like me, who sensed something at the time their loved one passed away or just after. It can be as simple as a feeling of dread, seeing a fleeting image of them pass by, which is called a *deathbed apparition*, or just a knowing that a particular person has died. But sometimes it's much more extreme, as I'll share with you.

In my case, I received *notification* of my mother's impending death through acute coughing and gagging, a very uncommon result of her linking in with me. Because it started almost half an hour before her death, I was extremely lucky and was able to say goodbye to her over the phone. When I expressed my story to Dr. Pim van Lommel and told him how much I regretted that I hadn't been able to be with my mother as she died, he said, "Oh, but you were with her."

I asked Dr. Fenwick why it was that I felt her physical symptoms as if they were mine. I wondered if it had something to do with my abilities as a healer. I also wanted to understand who instigated the link up – was it me? Fenwick was adamant that it wasn't about me at all, although it appeared that I had to be open enough to even sense her contact in the first place. In his notable opinion, derived from many years of research into this sort of phenomena and near-death experiences, he believes when these things occur that it is always the dying person who is responsible. They are the ones who reach out to you and not the other way around. It wasn't really about her allowing me to sense her physical feelings as she prepared to die, but rather it was about her interest in reaching me before she did. Fenwick explained that his research showed that it was the dying who attempted to contact those who they were emotionally close to at the exact time of their death or just after.

It had nothing to do with proximity or distance, I was told. It was about love and connection. Apparently, when someone enters the dying process, no amount of miles, time-zones or physical barriers have any meaning any longer. As Dr. Peter Fenwick explained, as the brain begins to die, "consciousness loosens and in some way a number of changes occur in the way it presents itself. One of these is that there are non-local effects. Non-local can be understood in terms of distant effects, but non-local also means that there is an alteration of time and space. So you then have a quantum physics explanation." The mind of the physically dying person (not the brain) then is no longer bound by any constraints of time and space which seem to limit us while we're in physical form.

I can't help but be reminded of Albert Einstein's famous formula $E=mc^2$ (energy equals mass multiplied by the square of the speed of light) which to the layman means that Einstein realized that matter and energy are just different forms of the very same thing. Matter can be turned into energy and energy into matter. Energy cannot be destroyed, it merely transforms or changes form. I learned that energy can take four primary forms. It can appear as a solid (physical matter), a liquid, a gas, or as plasma. And combined with energy, it can change back and forth between these various four states. Barbara Whitfield said, "As people die, their physical energy becomes weaker and transforms to their spiritual energy. Quantum physics tells us this is true in the laws of thermodynamics which in part says that energy doesn't dissipate – it transforms."

Dr. van Lommel said that during this time of death (even if temporarily as in a NDE), the consciousness of the dying can enter the realm ruled by quantum mechanics. That's when non-local information becomes accessible to them. In my case, the mind of my mother chose to reach out to me for her own reasons. Dr. Rupert Sheldrake, who developed the "extended mind theory", told David Lorimer of the Scientific and Medical Network, "Our minds reach out to touch what we're looking at," or therefore whatever we are thinking about.

When someone embarks on the beginning of their physical death, or the dying process, particular things are observed by relatives, caregivers, hospice workers and medical staff. Whether the dying are cognizant, lucid or impaired mentally or physically, they begin to receive and talk to visitors who usually they can only see. These spirit visitors are often dead spouses or other close relatives, friends or angels who have come to prepare them and accompany them on their *journey*. The dying also normally put their affairs in order, including trying to reconcile any unfinished business. This is seen occurring even when the death is unexpected.

After the visitations have happened, death is not far behind. Although, the dying person can apparently negotiate with their escorts to delay their death, it seems they can't postpone it for very long, perhaps a few hours or a few days only. There are reports of hearing the dying speaking to someone who they see in their room and requesting that the visitor come back later because they wish to wait for a particular person to arrive. Maybe my mom resorted to this kind of delaying tactic while I was getting my client out of my house.

So the dying, it seems, can postpone their journey to a point and then they must go. A particularly interesting story in *The Art of Dying* by the Fenwicks, told of a dying person who'd been overheard talking about "those people". No one else could be seen in the room and then "those people" (the invisible visitors) were said to be now waiting behind a bush in the grounds just outside the hospital. They were willing to wait out there, at first, but then as the time of *death* approached "those people", who only the dying could see, entered the hospital room and eventually were said to be seated next to the dying, right on top of their bed.

Although I didn't see my mom the day she died but instead felt her dying symptoms as she reached out to me across the heavens, I now know how important I was to her and that she obviously wanted me to be with her as she died. I have also learned from my research that my experience was rather rare. It's much more common to be contacted just after someone has died or perhaps at the exact time of their death. It's kind of unusual to be contacted before death and rarely does it happen when someone is totally awake. There have been very few reports of such extreme physical reactions while someone has been dying at a distance. Additionally, notification is more easily received when someone is sleeping, in which case the acknowledgement of death takes the form of a dream. It's definitely much less common to be fully awake like I was, but it's not unheard of. However, I did get the distinct impression from most of the researchers who I interviewed that my experience was quite fascinating, even for them who have heard so many. Dr. van Lommel even commented on my mother's determined activity and persistence.

During their waking day, people have reported being notified via their senses of a death. Often though, it's only later that they learn that a close friend or family member had died at the exact time when they'd experienced something odd or unexpectedly felt sad or upset. Occasionally people who are fully awake will hear the voice of their loved one call their name. All of these forms of contact, recognitions or other occurrences which occur at the approximate or exact time of a death Dr Fenwick said are referred to as, *"deathbed coincidences,"* because of the timing of them. Deathbed coincidences will be discussed later in this section.

Sometimes people will even see an apparition or vision of their loved one and hear them speak to them or have a conversation. This is referred to as a *"deathbed vision"*, a *"deathbed apparition"* or a *"deathbed crisis"*. Usually this type of contact occurs when someone is asleep. Dr. Fenwick told me that if I'd been asleep when my mom had died, I would have probably just seen her in a dream. More than likely, she would have told me that she was okay and then I would have learned the next day that she had actually died that previous night. At the time of writing this book, Dr. Greyson's department of Perceptual Studies at the University of Virginia is actively researching occurrences of *deathbed* phenomena.

People who are near the person who is dying, those who are actually in the room with them, often see or sense things at the exact time of death. There are many reports of seeing something like a smoke or mist rising out of the body through the crown of the head or out of the mouth or nose. Sometimes it's a transparent image of the person which then transforms into a cloudy form. Other times, people have seen a glow or light around or leaving the body. It's as if the soul is exiting on its journey to its next destination and witnesses are privileged to see it go.

As I mentioned earlier, Dr. Fenwick and his wife, Elizabeth, found that the dying use "journeying language", as if they are going on a trip or traveling someplace. They do not say they are dying and it seems to be clear to all those concerned that the dying person feels they are just moving on and continuing. In most cases, as they reach this final point, they have become calm, even if they'd been agitated or fearful before. They often reach an acceptance and understand that there's nothing to fear and regularly slipping in and out of the dimension we live in and enter the other dimension the Fenwick's call "Elsewhere".

Additionally, when someone dies even if they've been unconscious or suffering from a form of dementia, in the days or moments just before their death they often regain lucid consciousness. They speak or otherwise acknowledge their relatives who are in the room and may even say that they're going soon. They are also heard speaking or negotiating with those invisible *"take-away escorts"* or *"visitors"*.

Other phenomena that happens at the exact time of someone's death, also referred to as *deathbed coincidences,* include things like, electric disruptions, e.g. lights flickering, going out or dimming, clocks stopping, previously broken mechanical or electrical items miraculously functioning, chimes or bells being heard and many other symbolic or momentous happenings. Even animals are witnessed behaving oddly as they sense the approach or actual time of death.

Although my own experience when my mom reached me before she died can technically be considered a *deathbed coincidence,* Dr. Peter Fenwick described my experience with my mother as a, *"deathbed coincidence with direct linking."* He and Elizabeth both commented on how insufficient these accepted terms may seem to me for something so extraordinary and touching. The magnitude and realness of my experience could not be denied, it wasn't *only* a coincidence of timing!

Dr. Fenwick, referring to my mother's energy while she was dying, said that it "probably radiates throughout the universe however the resonance was with you. That's probably the important thing." Both David Lorimer and Dr. Fenwick spoke of the fact that Dr. Carl Jung's favorite oak tree was struck by lightning at the time of his death and this set precedence for *deathbed coincidences.*

Sharing in someone else's death experience or NDE and touching *"the other-side-of-life"*

Although I scored 21 points out of a possible 24 using Dr. Fenwick's *deathbed coincidence* questionnaire and this high score indicates that my experience was truly authentic, I prefer to think I had something greater than a *coincidence.* I believe that although I missed the light, that so many speak of, I too experienced or touched what I now call, *"the other-side-of-life."* Some may call this, "crossing the veil," or "passing over." Regardless of what you want to call it, my mother assisted me in stepping through or perhaps just sticking my toe into this other dimension – not normally inhabited by what we currently refer to as the living.

I feel this must be the case, purely because of the after-effects that now have become commonplace for me. My mom must have taken me with her to *the other-side-of-life.* There's no other explanation that I can think of for the changes that occurred within me that match those of someone who had a deep near-death experience.

If I must use a label for what my mom and I shared together, seven years ago on January 2nd, I choose to call it an *empathic shared-death experience.* I felt her dying as if it were mine. Although it was a shared-death experience or deathbed coincidence, it certainly wasn't a shared near-death experience as my mom had been ready to go and had declined to be resuscitated.

Shared near-death experiences, as I understand them, typically happen when a person who is in the same room joins in on a loved one's NDE. But it's not always that way. They may be somewhere else, yet still emotionally close and connected, when they participate or share in someone else's near-death experience. Those that share in another's near-death experience, passing over into what probably waits for all of us when we physically die, are often in good health and fully awake. They may take part in some or most of the other's near-death experience and are not necessarily related to them. There are reports of the participant also seeing the light, seeing the deceased relatives or angel escorts, sensing the presence or seeing a loving, spiritual being, and even feeling the oneness and wholeness of the beautiful experience.

About after-death communications (ADC) also known as post-mortem communications

Like a NDE, or other transcendental spiritual experience, hearing from or feeling your loved one's presence after they have died is often not discussed with others openly. Dr. Pim van Lommel says discussing things that occurred after-death is considered taboo in many societies. After-death contact or these after-death communications (ADC) when received by someone other than a professional medium are usually kept under wraps.

Over and over again, when people finally decide to share experiences of after-death communication, they frequently are laughed at and the contact is dismissed or thought to be grief-induced or pure fantasy. Some cultures are more open to them than others, but the few times I told of my mom's repeated after-death contact, what I saw in the individuals' eyes showed me that they thought that I had either made it up or was a bit mad.

After experiencing their own significant after-death communication which saved their child's life, Bill and Judy Guggenheim started investigating. Since 1988, they have been conducting intensive research into after-death communications. In their book *Hello from Heaven*, first published in 1996, they include a collection of more than 350 true-life examples, explain the different forms which after-death communications may take and discuss their frequency. They feel, as I do, that these accounts offer genuine evidence of life after death.

As it ends up, almost all of the experiences I had involving my mother as she died and after (and some of those I had with other deceased individuals), fall into this category of after-death communications (ADC). Even my experience during my mom's last minutes of life, when I had difficulty breathing, could be considered an *after-death communication,* as well as a *deathbed coincidence with direct linking* or *shared empathic death experience.*

In *Consciousness Beyond Life: The Science of the Near-Death Experience*, Dr. van Lommel distinguishes between peri-mortem and post-mortem experiences. Peri-mortem experiences occur when you sense the moment or sometimes even the manner of death, often at a distance, while post-mortem communications refer to encounters with the consciousness of a person after their physical death. These are all still considered forms of after-death communication (ADC) by the Guggenheims.

Thankfully, I was recommended to read *Hello from Heaven* by both Yolaine Stout and Dr. Pim van Lommel because, much to my surprise, the Guggenheims described every form of after-death communication or contact that I have experienced, including seeing only the legs of my father-in-law. I was delighted as I read the table of contents listing the many categories they discussed in their book. There were sentient ADCs or sensing a presence, hearing a voice (auditory ADCs), feeling a touch (tactile ADCs), smelling a fragrance (olfactory ADCs), partial and full appearances of deceased loved ones (referred to as visual ADCs, also known as "apparitions"), visions or premonitions, encounters just before you fall asleep (called twilight ADCs, occurring while you are in the hypnagogic stage of sleep) and ADCs experienced while you are dreaming or in the REM state (sleep-state ADCs), as well as others.

Probably the most significant thing I took away from the Guggenheim's research was the confirmation of the rarity of my experiences. These included what they highlighted in their chapters on after-death communication of physical phenomena (i.e. spirits moving things or causing items to appear spontaneously), as well as evidential ADCs, in which information provided by the dead is able to be verified. These evidential after-death communications offer proof that your spouse, child or mother still exist and are there for you. All of these types of after-death communication my mom used to reach me.

Although after-death communication, on the whole, happens quite frequently especially to those who have lost a child or spouse, the types of contact I encountered were considered either uncommon or quite rare. Being touched by someone, a tactile ADC may be experienced by feeling a light tap, a soft caress or sensing an arm around your shoulder, a kiss or even a full embrace. Although many of my experiences did not feel like light touches but were firm and persistent, these tactile ADCs were found to only take place between those who were very close. The Guggenheims considered these very intimate occurrences and reported that they were relatively less common when experienced while you were fully awake.

In *The Art of Dying* The Fenwick's state that being touched by the deceased is the least common after-death contact they encountered. It occurred in only 2.7% of the cases of bereavement they researched.

Surprisingly, seeing a person who is deceased (either completely or fully) even if it is startling and significant to the person who sees them, is quite common. These sightings make up 14% of the after-death communications talked about in the Guggenheim's research. However, sensing the oncoming death of my mother, by feeling her physical symptoms while I was fully awake, Bill and Judy Guggenheim said was rare, as did Dr. Peter and Elizabeth Fenwick. Reading this meant a lot to me, as it shows the depth of my mom's love for me. As well, all of her contacts were significant and not just fleeting or events which would leave you wondering. Only four such cases of feeling the symptoms of the dying while totally awake are mentioned in *The Art of Dying* and are referred to as, "the strangest deathbed occurrences of all."

Another very interesting thing to note, is that occasionally loved ones may appear many years after their death to assist or guide you. This must have been why Matthew's father finally came to us.

At this point, I wish to point out the value of what the Guggenheim's referred to as "ADCs with a witness" or "shared ADCs". These are said to occur when two or more people experience the same after-death communication. They are therefore immediately confirmed as authentic. These experiences, which Matthew and

I had when we smelled smoke in our room, and my Reiki students experienced when they saw the little girl, are wonderful when they occur and unquestionable because of the other witnesses.

I was pleased to read that Bill and Judy Guggenheim agreed with my new-found understanding, that after-death communications are, for the main, very positive, uplifting events which speed up spiritual growth. Their research showed that the content of various after-death communications, including the movement or appearance of items, like the hangers in my hall, the bobbie pins, the owl feather and even perhaps the wine glass moving, were only signs of after-death existence and that it is the receiver (me in this case) who may find them fearful. Once I became used to these after-death communications and the rather paranormal or metaphysical activities happening around me, I certainly progressed spiritually and I have never felt in danger of them since.

As I read *Hello from Heaven, The Art of Dying* and some of the other books by these fabulous researchers, I had to acknowledge the great efforts and lengths to which my mom had gone to get it across to me that she continued to exist after her death. I had been bear-hugged in the middle of the day in my field, I'd seen her face overshadow someone else's, she'd firmly stroked my hair many times, left me *gifts* and helped me feel her unending love. What more could I have asked for from her?

Chapter Nineteen

"The Seventh Sense" and what's next?

I suppose it's only poetic and fitting that I've only now seen the significance of my mom's childhood experience of seeing an angel hovering over her sick-bed. It was brought to light while working on these last chapters during my final research interview with Elizabeth Fenwick.

After hearing of some of the many dramatic ways in which my mother tried to reach me – before, during and after her death, Elizabeth asked if my mother was, "a sensitive or more." I told her that although it had never been discussed while she was alive, I suppose she must have been. Then I shared with Elizabeth my theory which I call, *"the Seventh Sense,"* or *"Death Sense."*

I believe now, that long before I was awakened by sharing in my mom's transition and receiving her after-death communications that perhaps she was already operating at a different level than the average person. Elizabeth and her husband, Dr. Peter Fenwick, wrote that when someone dies or is in the process of dying that they can enter, "the area restricted to only those of the dying." I'm sure this is the same *area* that Dr. van Lommel said allows our consciousness to access and exchange non-local, quantum information, irrespective of distance.

Maybe this is not just the realm of those who have died or are just about to die, but maybe it's the realm of those who have been touched significantly in some other way by death? Perhaps it's possible for another person's "threshold" experience, an experience which has the ability to push you over the edge and change your world forever, as P.M.H. Atwater and William James have said, can come into play in your life.

Maybe as we approach these spiritually transformative events, we are almost willing them to happen through the experiences of our lives to date. And through singular or repeated exposure to others who have themselves had close calls or brushes with death and experienced *the other-side-of-life.* Maybe my mom had her own near-death experience when the angel told her it wasn't her time and her altered perceptions and enhanced abilities rubbed off on me because of the time we spent together on our own?

My developing theory of *"the Seventh Sense"* or *"Death Sense"* is this: I think that once you have been exposed to death yourself, or touched by someone who is touching *the other-side-of-life,* the non-physical dimensions beyond the physical body that your *"Death Sense", "death-state senses"*, or my favorite description of all – your *"Seventh Sense"* is opened within you.

This is a sense, or set of senses perhaps, that go beyond the five known physical world, three-dimensional senses of sight, sound, smell, touch and taste. It goes beyond even what is commonly referred to as the Sixth Sense by psychics or mediums. Dr. David Lorimer compared my *"Seventh Sense"* theory, when I shared it with him, to the idea of "meta-senses" or inner senses and said, "As we have other bodies than the physical, we have greater senses."

The *Seventh Sense* is more than the Sixth Sense. It's more than just pronounced intuition, enhanced psychic abilities or clairvoyance. It's as if being touched by something, so utterly gripping and other-worldly, acts like a booster chair or amplifier for your spiritual self and growth in general. It's an expansion of your abilities both seen and unseen. It enhances you in all ways. Once this opening of the *Seventh Sense* has occurred, you can't shut it down or turn it off. It's in *the on mode* from then on, although you can choose to ignore it or deny it I suppose. But that would probably eventually unbalance you or drive you crazy if you did.

In my opinion, it's not really about psychic or paranormal experiences at all. This *Seventh Sense* is about being open to receiving or processing more information than you could before, either in your brain or outside of it. It's like taking the governor off the throttle of a high-performance car or the training wheels off a bicycle. (It could even be called the "quantum sense".) You become more open to everything and more able to use the information. You become more inspired and more inspiring to others. You have more meaning to your life. You are more creative and purposeful, that is if you embrace your *Seventh Sense*. Like Elizabeth Fenwick commented, experiencing things is all about receptivity. That's what the *Seventh Sense* is all about.

Once bitten by this bug, or once you've touched *the other-side-of-life,* either by yourself or through someone else's assistance, you not only can never be as you were before but your new abilities seem to be infectious or contagious to others. Those around you will inadvertently begin to experience changes, both within them or around them. Perhaps this is another reason why relationships often break up after one person has had a NDE or STE. Being around someone who is open to their Seventh Sense gnaws at them, beckoning them to change as well.

Barbara Harris Whitfield told me that when she joined the research team working with Dr. Bruce Greyson she apparently acted as a conduit for the others. They experienced more than they had ever before psychically whenever Barbara was around.

This S*eventh Sense* theory also applies to those who may have sat with the dying and significantly shared somehow in their passing or near-death experience. It might pertain to certain hospice workers, nurses, ambulance care assistants, medics, and of course family members (like me) who experienced something extraordinary which they cannot explain. I'm sure it doesn't happen to everyone, but if you are ready, something may occur within you that opens you up and moves you closer to your full potential here on earth.

When I discussed this theory with Dr. Penny Sartori, she remembered a moment when she was attending a dying patient the night before he died. "We just connected and as I looked into his eyes, our eyes locked and it was as if everything just stopped around us. It made me think 'is death such a bad thing that we have to subject our patients to such horrible suffering, simply because we're a death denying society?'" That's when it happened for her, in my opinion. Like me and my mom, I think they bridged together and Penny touched *the other-side-of-life* without being consciously aware of it.

From that point on she told me, "I was driven." She became depressed and began reading about death. That's when she came across near-death experiences and recalled as a student nurse that, "this lady had told me about her near-death experience and at the time I didn't think it was anything other than a hallucination. I listened to what she said and I never took it any further. I just thought in my mind, yeah, you know, it's sort of wishful thinking. But it was only then when I started really engaging with near-death experiences that I realized that they are by far much more than what we realized. And it completely captivated me – and it completely changed my life." Penny's moment of connection with the dying man provided the impetus for her to start her research into near-death experiences. Interestingly, she told me that although she had acknowledged this experience with the dying man as being the catalyst for her research, she had not realized that she, too, may have had an empathic death experience like me until I pointed it out to her.

My mom must have been very close to death and flipping in and out of this world "restricted to those of the dying", *the other-side-of-life,* when she saw and spoke with the angel over her bed as a child. My husband may have as well, stepped over the dimensional ledge, in either or both of the helicopter crashes he'd survived when he worked as a geochemist on the oil rigs in the 1980's. Twice his helicopter crashed into the sea, killing many on board, and twice he survived. He doesn't recall having anything like a NDE. However, maybe in some way, he accompanied the journey of one of the others who died. And perhaps like my experience, it may have caused him to be more sensitive.

After all, Matthew had seen a ghost, at the house of the creator of the real Chitty Chitty Bang Bang car, long before I'd ever met him. Maybe he was part of my preparation for my mom's death and helped to sensitize me, along with my Reiki training, to get me ready.

While discussing my idea of the *Seventh Sense* with Dr. Pim van Lommel, he said William James calls this susceptibility as the "receiving capacity". This is what van Lommel says allows someone to, "be able to recall non-local information that is not received by your senses and not received by your body." Van Lommel calls the heightened ability that happens after a NDE, "enhanced intuitive sensibility." I'm not sure that either of these fully encompasses what I am referring to with my idea of the *Seventh Sense* or *death sense*.

Remember Dr. Peter Fenwick said that when someone dies, even temporarily, "consciousness loosens". Barbara Harris Whitfield, who was a respiratory therapist as well as a NDE researcher, referred to this "loosening" with an analogy of the brain being a reducing valve used to regulate our view of reality, "The Bigger Reality," as she calls it. Like a high-pressure regulator, which is necessary to safely dispense oxygen directly into a patient's nose from a bottle of compressed oxygen, or air from a scuba tank to a diver, the brain appears to limit our perception of our true, more grandiose reality.

Talking to all these wonderful people has made me wish I could ask my mom whether I had a close call with death earlier in my life, before I encountered death with her.

Only very recently, as we sat eating a beautiful roast dinner with some friends, the hosts asked me what my latest book was about. Remarkably, when I told them, they preceded to tell Matthew and me that they'd both had near-death experiences but didn't normally talk about them. I was shocked. What were the chances of this? How common are these occurrences? Both of the hosts had experienced NDEs! Not just one of them, but both of them. They'd both, on separate occasions, left their bodies and entered *the light*. The man had even had two NDEs – he'd died and come back to life twice!

I mentioned how it seemed lately that everyone I was meeting or working with was telling me of their *odd* experiences once they heard the topic of this book. As I munched on my piece of fabulous pork crackling, I was suddenly reminded of Matthew's helicopter crashes and it all clicked into place for me. All of us at the table had experienced death in one way or another. Matthew must have the *Seventh Sense* too!

Piecing it all together…and what's next?

Although I feel I understand (well enough but not fully I suppose) *what* happened between me and my mom and the many after-effects of these encounters with her, I still find it baffling and staggering that it happened at all.

After consistently reading and being told by expert after expert that my experiences were *normal*, I still haven't stopped wondering – why?

Yolaine Stout agreed that while I could call what first occurred with my mom an empathic death experience or shared-death experience, it definitely qualified as what I lightheartedly referred to as a STE'er to Yolaine on the telephone. She then said, "I like Bill Guggenheim's definition, his terminology. You had an after-death communication and of course they're like gifts…gifts that you have been receiving as a result or in preparation because you are being prepared first." Perhaps that's the true answer as to why all this happened. Maybe there's still more yet to come? It excites me as I wonder what my mom's love and dying touches might bring my way in the next seven years.

Whatever is coming into my life, I know that I've learned some very important lessons through these experiences which will help me greatly when it arrives. I trust my senses now, all of them, and know that all of what I experienced was real. Most importantly though, I no longer worry about what other people think of my experiences. They are mine and they are very special to me. I don't need anyone's recognition to believe in them.

While I'd love to understand all the technical ins and outs of why and how everything happened, all the learned researchers, professors, physicists and doctors around the world haven't been able to do that for themselves. Even if they're very close to cracking this, they can only theorize right now. So I feel lucky and happy to have my own experiential first-hand knowledge.

I remember so vividly what David Lorimer said when we spoke. He told me he could only provide a sort of provisional view to some of my questions because as he put it, "The questions you've asked are the great philosophical questions of the universe."

My understanding of my experiences and my life has vastly improved since I began this journey, first alone and now with the help of so many wonderful experts. Some I spoke with had gone through their own near-death or equally profound experiences and the often difficult integration period which follows. A few of them had even shared in the passing of someone they love, and like me had sensed it in some way from a distance. Others were total skeptics, with no direct personal knowledge, before their research convinced them to believe otherwise. Elizabeth Fenwick who openly admitted that she had always been very skeptical before her husband began investigating end of life phenomena said it's almost impossible not to be convinced by the many stories described by perfectly sane and honest people.

Regardless of their personal beliefs, backgrounds or first-hand experiences, the dedication and contributions of these researchers should be heralded. Not just for the scientific and medical advancements their work may have provided (or is a springboard for) but for honoring and positively impacting thousands of people's lives by really hearing their intimate stories which might not have been shared otherwise. In these sincere acts of openly and actively listening, they unknowingly helped each of those they interviewed. Although in my case, it was me who interviewed them, just like the others I benefited immensely by their expertise, acknowledgment and validation of my fantastic experiences.

I'm confident that someday soon these wonderful people, the researchers of near-death experiences and death and dying phenomena, who I've had the sincere privilege to interview, or the likes of people like Stuart Hameroff or Sir Roger Penrose whom Dr. Fenwick told me, "believe it's the microtubules of the brain which act as quantum computers which suggests that consciousness is non-local..." will be credited with *proving* to the world that consciousness does exist outside the brain and continues to exist after physical death.

Dr. Pim van Lommel told me that we can no longer ignore the evidence that is arising out of these studies. We must change our perspective. He too believes, as do many others now, that the brain does not create consciousness but acts as a receiver for it. Dr. Penny Sartori, who was also involved in the UK marketing of the Warner Bros film *Hereafter,* summed it up by telling me that the results of her study caused her to believe that, "the brain mediates your experience." It acts as a filter, screening out your experience rather than creating it. Her view, based on research but not yet proven, is that when the brain is actually disabled and unable to function, as it is when you are clinically dead, is when you are allowed to see your full reality.

Whether you're inclined to believe, as I do now, or not, I know from my personal experiences that there's much more *beyond goodbye* for each of us. I can no longer believe otherwise. There's no need for me to worry anymore about whether I get put in the ground or cremated after-death. It won't matter, as I'll be off on my next adventure…perhaps with my mom.

Even without concrete medical or scientific explanations or confirmation, I know my mom's personality has lived on. Long after her body had died and her ashes had been dropped into the Puget Sound, she continued to be there for me. Her many loving attempts to comfort me, with her touch, leaving me her bobbie pins and even showing her face to me once more, proved that she wasn't really gone. She successfully erased any valid reasons for me to fear death.

My mom is still around me now, although I sense her presence less and less these days. I know that if I really need her, she'll be there for me – just as she was when she was alive. She was a good mother and I wish I'd appreciated her back then as much as I do now. But I know she hears me and she knows how much I love her and that I always will. While what I've shared with you have been my very personal experiences, I'm sure there will come a time when it is commonly accepted that there is this *other-side of life,* where my mom and your deceased loved ones reside – waiting for us to join them.

About the Author

Annie Cap is the seventh child of seven siblings who experienced an unexpected spiritual transformation after her mother somehow linked in with her as she was dying. Although Annie now lives full-time in the south of England with her husband and their rescue cat, she grew up in Oregon and Washington in the United States, where her brothers, sisters and father still reside.

Before becoming a therapist, breakthrough coach and author, Annie held prominent positions as a high-tech telecommunications professional for almost twenty years. It was this career which eventually brought her to London and Europe. Annie now calls England her home and has dual citizenship. She's lived in Kent for more than ten years now and works and practices in Canterbury, Petham, London and worldwide over the telephone and Skype.

Her first book, *It's Your Choice: Uncover Your Brilliance using The Iceberg Process* (Paragon Publishing, ISBN 978-1-907611-20-9) was released October 2010 and immediately drew worldwide attention as it announced her amazing finding that her clients' repetitive choice of language reveals their unresolved issues and subconscious mind's preoccupation. Annie created *The Iceberg Process* to encourage rapid change for her clients.

Annie loves people, international travel, anything spiritual, snow skiing and nature. One of her most memorable moments was scuba diving with giant manta rays in Australia. She's also into meditation, gardening and growing things, painting and taking photographs as well as entertaining close friends. She was honored with a one-woman exhibition of her paintings of butterflies and angels (inspired by the angel sighting in this book) at The Marlowe in Canterbury and exhibits in a few galleries and venues near her home.

www.anniecap.com
www.beyondgoodbye.com

Share your stories

Have you had an empathic or shared death experience with your mother, like me? Or experienced convincing after-death communications or deathbed coincidences with a loved one? I'm especially interested in hearing about experiences that helped you confirm that your loved ones were still around you and any stories of shared death experiences at a distance like the one I had with my mom. Please email your stories to me at: annie@anniecap.com.

Author Contact Details:
Websites: www.anniecap.com   www.beyondgoodbye.com
Email: annie@anniecap.com

Resources

Recommended Reading and Helpful Websites

Atwater, P.M.H., *Near-Death Experiences, The Rest of the Story: What They Teach Us About Living and Dying and Our True Purpose,* Hampton Roads Publishing Company, Inc., 2011

Atwater, P.M.H., *Coming Back to Life: The After-Effects of the Near-Death Experience,* Transpersonal Publishing, 2008

Atwater, P.M.H., *Beyond the Light,* Transpersonal Publishing, 2009, HarperCollins Publishers, 1995

Cap, Annie, *It's Your Choice: Uncover Your Brilliance using The Iceberg Process,* Paragon Publishing, 2010

Dolan, Mia and Chissick, Rosalyn, *MIA's World: An Extraordinary Gift, an Unforgettable Journey,* Arrow Books, 2005

Fenwick, Peter, M.D., and Fenwick, Elizabeth, *The Art of Dying: A Journey to Elsewhere,* Continuum, 2008

Fenwick, Peter, M.D., and Fenwick, Elizabeth, *Truth in the Light: An Investigation of over 300 Near-Death Experiences,* Headline, 1996

Garfield, Leah Maggie and Grant, Jack, *Angels and Companions in Spirit,* Celestial Arts, Ten Speed Press, 1995

Greyson, Bruce, M.D., *The Handbook of Near-Death Experiences: Thirty Years of Investigation,* Praeger, 2009

Guggenheim, Bill and Guggenheim, Judy, *Hello from Heaven: After-Death Communication confirms that life and love are eternal,* Watkins Publishing, 2010

Harris Whitfield, Barbara, *The Natural Soul,* Muse House Press, 2010

Harris Whitfield, Barbara, *Spiritual Awakenings: Insights of the Near Death Experience and Other Doorways to Our Soul,* Health Communications, Incorporated, 1995

Harris, Barbara and Bascom, Lionel C., *Full Circle: The Near Death Experience and Beyond,* Simon & Schuster Adult Publishing Group, 1990

Kübler-Ross, Elisabeth, M.D., *On Death and Dying,* Tavistock, 1970

Lorimer, David, *Radical Prince: The Practical Vision of the Prince of Wales,* Floris Books, 2004

Lorimer, David, *Thinking Beyond the Brain: A Wider Science of Consciousness,* Floris Books, 2001

Lorimer, David, *Whole in One: The Near-Death Experience and the Ethic of Interconnectedness,* Penguin Group (USA) Incorporated, 1991

MacLaine, Shirley, *Out on a Limb,* Hay House, Bantam Books, 1983

Moody, Raymond, M.D. and Perry, Paul, Glimpses of Eternity: *Sharing a Loved One's Passage from This Life to the Next,* Ideals Publications, 2010

Moody, Raymond Moody, M.D., Life After Life, Bantam Books, 1973

Morse, Melvin, M.D., and Perry, Paul, *Transformed by the Light,* HarperOne, 2001

Morse, Melvin, M.D., and Perry, Paul, *Closer to the Light*, Villard Books, 1990

O'Brien, Stephen, *The Power of your Spirit: Develop your Natural Psychic Abilities*, Voices, 2003

Parnia, Sam, M.D., *What Happens When We Die: A Groundbreaking Study into the Nature of Life and Death*, Hay House, 2007

Roberts, Jane with Butts, Robert F., *Seth Speaks: The Eternal Validity of the Soul*, Amber-Allen Publishing, 1993

Roberts, Jane and Butts, Robert F., *The Seth Material*, Amber-Allen Publishing., New World Library, 1993

Roman, Sanaya and Packer, Duane, *Spiritual Growth: Being your Higher Self*, H.J. Kramer, Inc., 1993

Roman, Sanaya, *Opening to Channel: How to Connect with Your Guide*, H.J. Kramer, Inc., 1992

Sabom, Michael, M.D. *Light and Death*, Zondervan Publishing House, 1998

Sartori, Penny, Ph.D., *The Near-Death Experiences of Hospitalized Intensive Care Patients: A Five Year Clinical Study*, Mellon Press, 2008

Smith, Gordon, *Through My Eyes*, Hay House, Inc., 2007

Stevenson, Sandy, *The Awakener: The Time is Now*, Gateway Books, 1997

van Lommel, Pim, M.D., *Consciousness Beyond Life: The Science of the Near-Death Experience*, HarperCollins Publishers, 2007

Virtue, Doreen, Ph.D. and Lynnette Brown, *Angel Numbers*, Hay House, Inc., 2005

Virtue, Doreen, Ph.D, *Archangels & Ascended Masters*, Hay House, Inc., 2004

Walsh, Neale Donald, *Conversations With God: An Uncommon Dialogue (Book 1)*, Hodden & Stoughton, 1997

Weiss, Brian L., M.D., *Many Lives, Many Masters: The True Story of a Prominent Psychiatrist, His Young Patient, and the Past-Life Therapy That Changed Both Their Lives*, Simon & Schuster Adult Publishing Group, 1988

Sheldrake, Rupert, *Morphic Resonance: The Nature of Formative Causation*, Inner Traditions/Bear & Company, 2009

Websites of Useful Organizations

www.aciste.org   ACISTE, American Center for the Integration of Spiritually Transformative Experiences

www.al-anon.alateen.org Free help for those affected by someone else's problem drinking (United States)

www.al-anonuk.org.uk Free help for people affected by someone else's problem drinking (United Kingdom and Ireland)

www.iands.org IANDS, International Association of Near-Death Studies (United States)

www.nderf.org Near-Death Experience Research Foundation

www.scimed.org The Scientific and Medical Network

Specific Websites of the Researchers and Experts Referenced in this Book

www.pmhatwater.com P.M.H. Atwater

www.miadolan.com Mia Dolan

www.davidlorimer.net David Lorimer

www.sriandkira.com Kira Raa

www.drpennysartori.com Dr. Penny Sartori

www.drpennysartori.wordpress.com Dr. Penny Sartori's blog

www.gordonsmithmedium.com Gordon Smith

www.josephsmithmassage.com Joseph Smith

www.pimvanlommel.nl Dr. Pim van Lommel

www.horizon.org Dr. Peter Fenwick

www.sheldrake.org Dr. Rupert Sheldrake

Additional Websites

www.jknight.com JZ Knight

www.lazaris.com Jack Pursell

www.orindaben.com Sanaya Roman

www.sethcenter.com Jane Roberts (now deceased) and the Seth collection

Index